LINCOLN CHRISTIAN COLLEGE A

W9-BQY-134

From Cloister To Commons

Concepts and Models
for Service-Learning
in **Religious Studies**

Richard Devine, Joseph A. Favazza, and F. Michael McLain, volume editors

Edward Zlotkowski, series editor

A PUBLICATION OF THE

AMERICAN ASSOCIATION
FOR HIGHER EDUCATION

Published in cooperation with the Wabash Center
for Teaching and Learning in Theology and Religion

Acknowledgments

This volume is published in cooperation with the Wabash Center for Teaching and Learning in Theology and Religion at Wabash College, Raymond Brady Williams, director.

From Cloister to Commons: Concepts and Models for Service-Learning in Religious Studies
(AAHE's Series on Service-Learning in the Disciplines)
Richard Devine, Joseph A. Favazza, and F. Michael McLain, *volume editors*
Edward Zlotkowski, *series editor*

About This Publication

This volume is part of AAHE's Series on Service-Learning in the Disciplines. Additional copies of this publication or others in the series from other disciplines can be ordered from:

AMERICAN ASSOCIATION FOR HIGHER EDUCATION
One Dupont Circle, Suite 360
Washington, DC 20036
ph 202/293-6440, fax 202/293-0073
www.aahe.org

ISBN 1-56377-054-7
ISBN (set) 1-56377-005-9

Contents

Appendix

Foreword

by Raymond Brady Williams

Director, Wabash Center for Teaching and Learning in Theology and Religion, Wabash College

We at the Wabash Center for Teaching and Learning in Theology and Religion are pleased to be associated with this project on service-learning in religion. The authors' reflections illustrate the creativity, engagement, and power of what Parker Palmer calls "good talk about good teaching." They explore issues of learning and transformation that, although at the heart of our work as teachers, are too often not expressed, examined, or tested in discussion with others. We are pleased that this volume joins those from other disciplines in the AAHE series. Scholars in religion are often absent or silent during discussions about teaching and learning, which is unfortunate. We have much to learn from the experience of those in other disciplines, and this book enriches mutual reflection with what has been learned from best practices in other disciplines. Equally important, these teaching scholars in religion bring insights from best practices and philosophical and theological reflection from service-learning components of religion courses.

Peter Antoci and Sandra Smith Speck note in their chapter that "the notion that higher education provides a vital public service is neither radical nor novel," and they indicate that scholars in religion and theology should build on "this heritage of addressing the public good." Charles Strain traces the evolution of what "service" means in the history of higher education in the United States. The mission statements of most colleges and universities contain a remnant of a dedication to the common good. The founders claimed that they were establishing Wabash College to nurture the public good on the American frontier, directly through the transformation of individual students and indirectly through the education of preachers, teachers, doctors, and lawyers. All good teaching is local. These authors describe their best practices (and admit to their shortcomings) in service-learning, and place them in the rich context of the institutional missions of schools where we teach, the teachers' commitments expressed in course syllabi, and the students' goals for their own learning and lives.

The book invites readers into a deep reflection on basic issues of teaching and learning and provides sufficient resources to enable teachers to determine whether service-learning components will enhance their students' learning and, if so, how they can undertake aspects of engaged, experiential, and service-learning in their courses. That's a lot for one book to do, but this one delivers on its promise.

About This Series

by Edward Zlotkowski

The following volume, *From Cloister to Commons: Concepts and Models for Service-Learning in Religious Studies,* represents the 19th in a series of monographs on service-learning and the academic disciplines. Ever since the early 1990s, educators interested in reconnecting higher education not only with neighboring communities but also with the American tradition of education for service have recognized the critical importance of winning faculty support for this work. Faculty, however, tend to define themselves and their responsibilities largely in terms of the academic disciplines/interdisciplinary areas in which they have been trained. Hence, the logic of the present series.

The idea for this series first surfaced late in 1994 at a meeting convened by Campus Compact to explore the feasibility of developing a national network of service-learning educators. At that meeting, it quickly became clear that some of those assembled saw the primary value of such a network in its ability to provide concrete resources to faculty working in or wishing to explore service-learning. One such resource would be a series of texts on service-learning in a variety of academic disciplines. As this idea began to gain momentum, AAHE, with the encouragement of then vice-president Lou Albert, stepped in to provide critical assistance. Thanks to its reputation for innovative work, AAHE not only was able to obtain the funding needed to support the first six volumes (of 18 initially planned) up through actual publication, it was also able to assist in attracting many of the teacher-scholars who participated as writers and editors.

The Rationale Behind the Series

A few words should be said at this point about the makeup of both the general series and the individual volumes. To some, a discipline such as religious studies may seem a natural choice of academic areas with which to link service-learning, since it is largely concerned with questions of meaning and value. "Natural fit," however, was not the determinant factor in deciding which disciplines/interdisciplinary areas those 18 volumes should include. Far more important were considerations related to the overall range of disciplines represented. Since experience has shown that there is probably no disciplinary area — from architecture to zoology — where service-learning cannot be fruitfully employed to strengthen students' abilities to become active learners as well as responsible community members, a primary goal of the initial volumes was to demonstrate this fact. Religious Studies is the first volume to be added to that initial series, and regardless of its "fit," it owes its development primarily to the vision and tenacity of its editors. It was they who were determined to demonstrate that, in the discipline of religious studies, service-learning can be a powerful, indeed transformative, educational force.

Like its predecessors, the present volume has been designed to include its own appropriate theoretical, pedagogical, and bibliographical material. Also like them, it is not meant to provide an extended introduction to service-learning *as a generic concept.* For material of this nature, the reader is referred to such texts as Kendall's *Combining Service and Learning: A Resource Book for Community and Public Service* (NSEE, 1990) and Jacoby's *Service-Learning in Higher Education* (Jossey-Bass, 1996).

In conclusion, I would like to thank Raymond Williams, director of the Wabash Center for Teaching and Learning in Theology and Religion, for his steadfast support of this project. Working with him, and with the volume editors, has been a pleasure from start to finish.

April 2002

Introduction

by Richard Devine, Joseph A. Favazza, and F. Michael McLain

This volume originated in a series of presentations at a 1999 national conference[1] on service-learning and religious studies ("A Future of Service") generously supported by the Wabash Center for Teaching and Learning in Theology and Religion. It may seem especially appropriate to link the study of religion and service-learning, since the practice of many religions includes an admonition to serve, bolstered by a theological rationale for doing so. However, as the following essays make clear, things are not that simple. The study of religion in colleges and universities has become extremely broad and detailed and the method of study increasingly historical and phenomenological. Even in institutions whose mission statements would suggest otherwise, the theological defense of religious claims is suspect among many who teach in the discipline. The academic study of religion is very often taken to be incompatible with a sympathetic reading of religion, not to mention its propagation. Of course, this generalization does not hold for all institutions and all faculties. But it is one that everyone who reads this volume will recognize, and it sets the stage for much of the theoretical work on service-learning we have included.

What is service-learning? For the purposes of this volume, we accept the widely used definition provided by Hatcher and Bringle, one linking it to both the course and the discipline in which it is used:

> *Service-learning is a type of experiential education in which students participate in service to the community and reflect on their involvement in such a way as to gain further understanding of course content and of the discipline and its relation to social needs and an enhanced sense of civic responsibility. (Hatcher and Bringle 1997: 153)*

Service-learning is a type of experiential learning. Eyler and Giles (1999) may be correct in claiming that a similar form of learning takes place in a variety of experiential learning opportunities found on many campuses —

We wish to thank all those who helped bring this project to completion. In particular, we wish to acknowledge the support of Raymond Williams and Lucinda A. Huffaker at the Wabash Center for Teaching and Learning in Theology and Religion; Edward Zlotkowski, Bry Pollack, and their colleagues at the American Association for Higher Education; and Brooke Foster for her superb editorial assistance. Resources for the preparation and publication of the volume were contributed by the Wabash Center, the Rhodes College Department of Religious Studies, and funds associated with the R.A. Webb Chair of Religious Studies at Rhodes College.

internships, field-based education, and campus outreach programs, as well as designated service-learning classes. However, such an observation does little to address the inquirer who asks what service-learning is from a course and disciplinary perspective, and how the multiple meanings assigned to it in the current literature are to be compared and assessed from a religious studies standpoint. Our contributors examine the theory and practice of service-learning with an eye to salient features of the discipline that bear on the use of this pedagogy, for a thoughtful approach to service-learning should take account of, and raise questions about, the disciplinary and institutional context in which it is practiced. Although each reader's professional context will be different, the essays suggest that comparable analysis is appropriate in a wide range of circumstances.

Service-learning more narrowly considered is viewed by all of the authors represented here as a legitimate and potent pedagogy that can enhance learning outcomes for students when properly linked to course objectives. This claim has been well documented in the literature by Eyler and Giles, among others. The reader unacquainted with service-learning may wish to turn first to Tom McGowan's essay (beginning on p. 83) to see how theory suggests service can be used to achieve course objectives. The course narratives that follow his essay represent many subdisciplines in a broad field and do not necessarily conform strictly to McGowan's theoretical maxims. However, our editorial strategy has been to propose a core understanding of the concept and its practice while asking the reader to note the variety of ways in which service is employed.

Service-learning, we stress again, is more than simply a useful pedagogy for achieving course objectives. Like any pedagogy, it raises fundamental questions about the nature of our discipline, the aims of education, and whose interests are served by our educational system. Furthermore, it brings into focus the relationship of our colleges and universities to other groups that seek to shape our communities and nation. These fundamental matters occupy the essays in the first two parts of this volume.

In Part I, our contributors look at service-learning from the point of view of the discipline of religious studies and theology, and the mission of the institution in which service-learning finds a home. Part II explores the various ways in which the players — students, teachers, the college or university, community partners, and their clients — are affected by the practice of service-learning. Service-learning offers a fresh, many-sided perspective on all such groups and their relationships, frequently raising more questions than we can hope to answer. In the view of our authors, these are questions well worth asking. Finally, in Part III, McGowan's "best practices" essay is followed by course chapters in which each author shares his or her triumphs, failures, and anxieties in the use of service-learning to teach one of the subdisciplines in the field. The diversity of courses represented is matched by the diversity of ways in which service-learning pedagogy is used to achieve the aims envisioned for the course.

Part I: Service-Learning and the Discipline of Religious Studies

The essays by Fred Glennon (see p. 9) and Charles Strain (see p. 25) assess service-learning with an ear to the contentious discussion about the nature of the discipline and the mission of the university. The title of Glennon's essay, "Service-Learning and the Dilemma of Religious Studies: Descriptive or Normative?" captures well the concerns he addresses. He examines the use of service-learning as a pedagogy in the midst of a religious studies identity crisis. His survey of the literature exposes the dysfunctional family the teachers of the discipline have become. The rebellious children have rejected the authoritative parental voice of theology in favor of their neighborhood peers — the scientific, objective Enlightenment boomers. Their influential buddies have persuaded theology's offspring that the parents are more concerned with indoctrination than accurate description, eager to convey their values and clone their beliefs. If religious studies is to leave home and achieve maturity, goes the modern story, it must adopt the neutral stance of observation, codifying the parents' beliefs and practices while holding them at arm's length.

The older, theological children, few in number but dutiful to the end, remember the good times with their parents and try to understand them by reflecting on shared experience. They want to move on too, but in a way that sorts through the family album for fresh insights and understanding. They have their own children to raise, after all, and they suspect that scientific neutrality is not a rich enough mixture to draw from in shaping the children's moral and spiritual development. Understanding one's parents from the outside may expose the warts and wrinkles they wish to hide, but it could also overlook that parental wisdom children find it so difficult to acknowledge.

After carefully surveying this disciplinary melodrama, Glennon muses over the proposed adoption of a new family member, service-learning. If the prospective adoptee could claim neutrality in the family debate, a mere tool for objectively viewing the parents, the scientific children might be persuaded to sign the papers. But Glennon is skeptical. The child up for adoption has a history, and her values are well known. She is socially responsible, with a vision of the common good and an agenda of personal transformation. An unscientific poll conducted by Glennon of religious studies faculty who

employ service-learning reveals that those who adopt this pedagogy antici-
pate its transformation of students into good community members and
socially responsible citizens. He concludes this provocative essay by com-
mending adoption to those who view religious studies, and education more
generally, as rightly embracing transformational goals for its students. Thus
he predicts, and seems willing to accept, a deepened division within the religious studies family over the question of whether to adopt the pedagogy of
service-learning.

Charles Strain, in "Creating the Engaged University: Service-Learning,
Religious Studies, and Institutional Mission," guides the reader's reflections
on the place of service-learning within the framework of institutional mission. Both a faculty member and an administrator at DePaul, Strain played
a prominent role in that university's recent revision of its mission. For the
first time in its history, DePaul articulated as one of its three institutional
goals the development of educationally related programs and services "that
will have significant social impact and will give concrete expression to the
University's Vincentian Mission."

Strain's recounting of the DePaul family saga suggests how it arrived at
such a place and offers his assessment of that location. Like other essayists
in this volume, he takes his bearings by consulting the map of higher education drawn by Ernest Boyer. Boyer traces the route of those who have come
to inhabit the modern university, and we soon recognize ourselves as members of this party of travelers. At the end of the modern journey, the voyagers
arrive at "a faculty-centered/research-centered model of scholarship."
Strain, who will be viewed by family members as either disgruntled or pre-
cocious, does not suggest that we forsake entirely our new home. He does
urge, however, a recognition that our journey has arrived, paradoxically, at
no place. The modern scholars who adopt, in Thomas Nagel's (1986) felici-
tous phrase, "the view from nowhere," fail to attend to place. As a result, the
institutions they inhabit tend not to be engaged in their surroundings. Like
a family that divides its attention between the scrapbook and planning the
next adventure, there is no time to care for the yard or paint the house.

Paradoxically, if the university would journey further, it first must plant
its feet on the ground and begin to explore its more immediate surroundings. Responding to local needs, it must scatter its rich resources as it walks
a path through pressing social, civic, and ethical terrain. Instead of a distant
horizon, we should look at the children, the schools, and the cities that are
landmarks of any family's particular location. Like the once popular bumper
sticker, Strain believes our institutions would do well to think globally and
act locally.

Strain's narration of the DePaul family history leaves us with two rather
surprising conclusions. For one, there are many paths that lead to service-

learning and community engagement, and the place for such activities fits "not only with the mission of a land-grant or religiously affiliated institution but potentially with the mission of any college or university" (see p. 30). Strain's second conclusion to some degree challenges the bias of the Enlightenment children in our dysfunctional religious studies family. In Strain's experience, religious studies students engaged in service think more clearly about religiously motivated change when their service involvement is not an identifiably religious one. Such service provides an analogue to the forms of ultimate transformation studied by our discipline without requiring commitment to an explicitly religious practice. Strain is thus led to propose that religious studies might well take the lead among disciplines in creating a multitude of practices within the university, including community service, that illuminate one another.

Part II: Service-Learning and Its Communities

Part II of the volume offers three essays that look at the communities engaged by service-learning, each with an eye to particular ways in which theology and religious studies guide such engagement.

Whatever one's view of the nature of our discipline, Keith Morton reminds us, in "Making Meaning: Reflections on Community, Service, and Learning" (p. 41), that undergraduate students engage in the process of making meaning. Scientific offspring may wish to raise their own children in the tradition of objective analysis, eschewing normative discussion of any kind. But this, too, is a way of making meaning. Morton, a cultural historian and storyteller, thinks our culture in general is as dysfunctional — *fragmented* is his term — as the religious studies family. Perhaps he sees the latter as symptomatic of the former. In Morton's view, students sense that fragmentation and are engaged in the task of seeking wholeness in the face of such recognition. Morton proposes a form of family therapy, as it were, to help his students find the wholeness they seek. Indeed, he finds the attraction of community service in its promise of a transformed understanding of the self and the world it inhabits. Morton believes that we can see this process at work in the stories of others. For him, these stories are a kind of therapy for fragmented family members in search of wholeness.

The stories selected and artfully woven together by Morton belong to Jane Addams and Dorothy Day, his own story as shaped by a period in Bangladesh, and those of his students. Morton is persuaded that Addams found it necessary to create Hull House as a way of making herself whole again. Day, like Addams, sought to link love and community. Both saw modern economic values as creating conditions that give rise to charity. Both viewed charity as inimical to persons and community. Against this historical backdrop, Morton's story and those of his students gain added depth in the search for service that moves from a "thin" form of charity to a "thick" experience of process.

Reading "On En/Countering the Other" (p. 55) by Liz Bounds, Bobbi Patterson, and Tina Pippin is an exercise in uncovering constructions of the *other* that flow from family circumstances. Although other essayists make a similar point, this contribution, which shows intimate acquaintance with discussions of representation in anthropology and literary criticism, makes this concern focal. Strong advocates of service-learning, Bounds, Patterson, and Pippin nevertheless are keenly aware of the danger in perpetuating dehumanizing models of service. Like Morton, their answer is family therapy, but in this case we must expose the sources of cultural fragmentation. The self in relation to the *other* is the therapeutic subject, and we find that the *other* to which the self is related has many faces. The *other* is encountered not only in the one served. We find the *other* also in our students, academic institutions, and ourselves.

In probing their experience, the authors invite readers to bring to self-consciousness their own constructions of the *other* and the power relationships entailed by the ways the *other* is viewed. The stakes are high in their estimation. Without such self-awareness, we cannot identify the forms of knowledge our academic institutions resist or the implications that follow from those they welcome. Assuming a liberal democratic and multicultural society prevails, the task of engaging the *other* is central. Where, if not in the academy, will this task be carried out? Service-learning is the pedagogy, perhaps, that shows significant promise in prompting in student, teacher, and institution a reflexive awareness of the *other*. Accepting its challenge, the authors articulate the questions raised by their experience with service-learning in teaching religion.

Peter Antoci and Sandra Smith Speck, in "Service-Learning and Community Partnerships: Curricula of Mutuality" (p. 69), begin by placing service-learning in the context of the university's historic mandate of public service. So engrained is the habit of seeing faculty and research as central to the university's mission that we ignore the historically fundamental issue of the public served. Antoci and Smith Speck's guide in setting the record straight is again Ernest Boyer. Placed in historical context, service-learning's bid to delineate, or at least contribute to, a contemporary discussion of the university's public mission is hardly exceptional. Furthermore, since religious studies transmits and critically engages traditions of reflection on the good, it should occupy a central place in the academy's discussion of its public mission.

Returning to the theme of Strain's essay, Antoci and Smith Speck offer their own reflection on the nature of the engaged university and engaged learning. Their candor will likely roil the members of our dysfunctional family. Whether dispassionate analysts of religious phenomena or proponents of religion's normative claims, faculty enjoy and embrace their title to authority. It is that identity, the authors contend, that all family members should be willing to place in question as they create "curricula of mutuality." As good parents know, one cannot both invite others to share in shaping one's children and maintain control of the outcome. If Antoci and Smith Speck are correct, the outcome is worth the effort.

We append to this section Beth Blissman's (p. 77) related reflections on curricula of mutuality, reflections first delivered as part of a panel on this theme at that 1999 "A Future of Service" conference. Blissman provides an example of the use of disciplinary reflection in forming one university's response to the challenge of mutuality. What is especially interesting is her attempt to expand mutuality beyond the social to include the ecological. In her view, no responsible educational initiative can neglect the fragile ecological context of which we are becoming increasingly aware.

Part III: Course Chapters

The final section of the volume is made up of case studies involving the use of service-learning in subdisciplines of religious studies. Each author introduces a description of his or her course with an explanation of why service-learning was used and a candid account of successes and failures. The studies embody variety in two ways. First, they include the most obvious course utilization of service-learning, namely, an ethics course, but also less obvious courses — Islam, Jewish studies, comparative religion, and Hebrew Bible, for example. We hope this variety will stimulate reflection on how service-learning might be used in virtually any religious studies class.

Second, the way service is employed does not conform to a single definition or set of practices. Some configurations of the service component blur the lines between the customary use of service and other forms of experiential learning. Eyler and Giles, cited earlier, find it impossible and perhaps unwise to offer a purportedly adequate definition of all current service-related pedagogies. We find at best, invoking our metaphor one last time, a family resemblance among the conceptions and practices here represented.

It does not follow, however, that we have no guidance on what makes for good service-learning. The essay by Tom McGowan records the effort of one campus to develop criteria for sound service-learning practice and to evaluate efforts to use it. We invited each case study contributor to Part III to respond, at least implicitly, to McGowan's work, and we invite readers to keep in mind his analysis as they reflect on the way in which the case studies model service-learning practice. As McGowan notes, and our essayists emphasize, service-learning encounters with the *other* can profoundly challenge a student's self-understanding, and no discipline better grasps than does ours the dynamics of such self-awareness or the possibilities for personal and social transformation. Whatever one's view of religion and the study of it, service-learning offers a way of accessing what lies at the heart of the religious experience and the traditions it has shaped. We offer this volume as a guide to reflection on the prospects and promise of using service-learning in theology and religious studies.

Note

1. "A Future of Service: A National Conference on Service-Learning in Theology/Religious Studies" was a preconference to the annual meeting of the American Academy of Religion held November 18, 1999, in Boston.

References

Eyler, Janet, and Dwight E. Giles, Jr. (1999). *Where's the Learning in Service-Learning?* San Francisco. Jossey-Bass.

Hatcher, Julie A., and Robert G. Bringle. (1997). "Bridging the Gap Between Service and Learning." Reflection. *College Teaching* 45: 153-158.

Nagel, Thomas. (1986). *The View From Nowhere.* Oxford: Oxford University Press.

Service-Learning and the Dilemma of Religious Studies: Descriptive or Normative?

by Fred Glennon

The current interest in service-learning in higher education has spilled over into the discipline of religious studies. Many faculty members are using service-learning as a pedagogical tool. This concerns some professors, who wonder whether or not service-learning commits a course or department to a value-laden agenda in its pedagogy. By incorporating service-learning, does a religious studies professor or department run the risk of undermining an academic approach to the study of religion, with its emphasis on tolerance and neutrality (value-laden terms themselves), by connecting students with committed practitioners who advocate particular religious perspectives and values?

The issue is more complex than this. What is also at stake is the understanding of the nature of religion and the discipline of religious studies. Is religion simply a phenomenon of human experience, or does it seek change in society or in individuals? Is the study of religion an objective and descriptive discipline, such that those who study it should approach it in a detached way? Or is the only way to study religion to become involved with it, even to embrace it? If religion makes normative claims on its participants, can the responsible scholar avoid articulating and evaluating those claims?

In addition, this issue raises questions about the relationship between epistemology and pedagogy. Is experience valuable or not in learning about religion? How do we know what we know? Is it purely from objective, disinterested observation? Or does engagement with the subject in some way critically affect our knowing? Does the answer to this question affect how we should teach the subject matter?

There are also questions about service-learning. Even if one values experience in the educational process, it does not necessarily mean one would gravitate toward service-learning. Why do people choose service-learning, with all of the difficulties inherent in the word *service*? Is service-learning simply a good way to help students learn the content of the course, or is it also about moving students outside the narrow confines of self-interest toward a commitment to the common good? Why would a faculty member utilize service-learning? It is a more time-consuming pedagogical approach. Is the reason intrinsic? It is one of the best ways for students to learn. Is this intrinsic motivation sufficient?

This essay addresses these questions about the use of service-learning in religious studies by analyzing what practitioners say on surveys I distributed to professors and departments in undergraduate programs across the country. What that analysis and this essay suggest is that service-learning is not for everyone who teaches religious studies, especially not for those who take an objectivist approach to the discipline. Service-learning can, however, be a valuable pedagogical tool for teachers and students of religion who want to engage religious phenomena experientially and who affirm higher education's role in promoting commitment to the common good. Before getting to that analysis, however, this paper sets the stage by exploring debates within religious studies and among advocates of service-learning about the approach each should take.

Religious Studies: Scientific or Confessional?

Debate exists about the definition and nature of religious studies as an academic discipline, a debate that has implications for the epistemology and pedagogy of those who study and teach it. The roots of the debate extend to the attempt by religious studies to differentiate itself from theology and to establish its own identity within the university as a fixed field of study, along the lines of the humanities and the social sciences yet distinct from them.[1] This desire on the part of the discipline to specify its own niche has created an identity crisis for religious studies, straddling the fence between interpreting data religiously (theology) and interpreting religious data (the human and social sciences) (Smith 1988). At a time of institutional downsizing, this crisis leaves religious studies vulnerable. By separating itself from other fields of study, especially the humanities, religious studies has had a difficult time justifying its existence (Juschka 1997).

To resolve this identity crisis, many in the field of religious studies have adopted the identity and epistemology of the scientist[2] and see religious studies as "scientific," which Donald Wiebe defines as "the attempt only to understand and explain [an] activity rather than to be involved in it" (1998: 95).[3] He suggests that the only way the academic study of religion can be taken seriously as a contributor to human knowledge is through accepting the objective stance of the dispassionate observer that is the norm for scientific knowledge at the university level.[4] Those who adopt this identity fear that any religious orientation on the part of the scholar (some use the terms *impassioned participant* or *confessional practitioner*) could become a disguised form of indoctrination. The attempt will be made to persuade students and others of the truth of particular religious perspectives or values, making normative claims upon them. Wiebe argues that this could have disastrous results for the discipline and the university:

A study of religion directed toward spiritual liberation of the individual or of the human race as a whole, toward the moral welfare of the human race, or toward any ulterior end other than that of knowledge itself, should not find a home in the university; for if allowed in, its sectarian concerns can only contaminate the quest for a scientific knowledge of religions and will eventually undermine the very institution from which it originally sought its legitimation. (1998: 97)

The only way to eliminate this risk is for scholars in religious studies not to invest themselves in the data but to be neutral observers and to use their interpretive skills to reveal the truth about religious phenomena.

While agreeing with Wiebe's concerns about indoctrination, many professors in religious studies find an objective, scientific approach both epistemologically and pedagogically unsatisfactory. They contend that religious studies, as a discipline, is at its most crude when it "uses an ideology of academic neutrality which presumes a cool, objective approach to the phenomena of religions" (Ford 1998: 5). The reason is that they see this approach as a misguided attempt by the scientist to distance the subject from the subjects (professors and students) in the name of objectivity and neutrality.

Parker Palmer argued recently that there is an intricate connection among epistemology, pedagogy, and ethics. The relationship of the knower to the known becomes the basis for the relationship between the actor and the world upon which he or she acts. In an objective, scientific epistemology, what is known is kept at arm's length; thus, teachers and students are disconnected from what they know. Passion and subjectivity are seen as vices, not virtues. Why? Palmer writes, "When a thing ceases to be an object and becomes a vital, interactive part of our lives . . . it might get a grip on us, biasing us toward it, thus threatening the purity of our knowledge once again" (1998: 51). This, of course, is Wiebe's concern.

Such an approach, many contend, does not do justice to the religious phenomena in question. One of the claims in religious studies, especially in introductory textbooks, is that religions provide people with a way of generating meaning and order in their lives.[5] Religions enable individuals and communities to make sense of experiences that are a vital part of their lives. By treating religion as an object and not a subject, the "scientific" approach to the study of religion does not fully grasp the essence of religions and their vitality.

Nor does the scientific approach do justice to the passion many students and teachers of religion have for knowing the subject. In our postmodern world, there are no neutral observers or universal audiences. Both what one believes and the audience one addresses shape what one has to say (and even how one teaches). Many teachers and students of religion seek to bring already acquired knowledge of and experiences with religion into dialogue with their study of religion. Thus, they proceed from a different epistemological starting point. As Parker Palmer writes, "Knowing of any sort is relational, animated by a desire to come into deeper community with what we know" (1998: 54). Subjective knowledge and experiences may indeed become what Dewey called *miseducative;* they may arrest or distort future learning and experience (1997: 25). But they do not have to do so. Our concern should not be to exclude these experiences, as the scientist seeks to do, but to enable them to emerge in the discussion of religion in a way that is inclusive and respectful, and leads to new insight and understanding.

Finally, the scientific approach may not only distort our relationship with what and how we know; according to Palmer, such an epistemology may even be morally deforming, because it sets students at a distance from what they know. As a result, it keeps them from taking responsibility for their knowledge or taking action in response to it (1998). This runs counter to what many who teach religious studies intend. Warren Frisina argues that the purpose of higher education is not only the expansion of knowledge, as Wiebe contends, but also "the enlargement of meaning which is the ultimate object of the educating act" (1997: 30). It is here that the humanities in general, and religious studies in particular, can make significant contributions. Religious studies is one of the places where teachers and students ask, Who are we? What can we know? What shall we become? Our literatures, philosophies, and histories have always provided a critical moral and ethical edge and engendered transformative experiences for students. Thus, contra Wiebe, Frisina contends that what we do should contribute significantly "to the intellectual, moral, and yes (though not in the way it is usually understood), spiritual development of our students" and "directly to the overall health and well-being of the community" (1997: 33). If we lose these contributions, it is difficult to see how we can continue to gain support from a skeptical public that questions the value of religious studies.[6]

Making these contributions may require that we reject both the objectivist, scientific and the apologetic, indoctrinating approaches to the study of religion, as many teachers of religion have sought to do. Brian Malley suggests we need an "engaged religious studies" that pushes us to address real-world problems faced by communities and contributes to deliberations of policymakers who have the responsibility for resolving them (1997). Stephen Webb proposes a "confessional" approach. This approach, he contends, understands and accepts the postmodern reality that one's location affects what one teaches — rather than assuming a higher level of objectivity than is really possible. It does not close out inquiry, as the scientist fears, but generates space within the classroom where people can bring their own perspectives and subject them to public discourse and discussion. As a result, discussions become more engaging and more honest, reflecting faculty and student concern for and interest in the existential questions religions seek to answer (1999). Peter Hodgson argues for a "transformative" pedagogy, one that forms both students and teachers of religion in ways that enable them "to live humanly in the world, and transforms them toward an end or vision of human flourishing" (1999: 69).

One may find other formulations that seek to distinguish the study and teaching of religion from both scientific and indoctrinating approaches. But all these approaches tend to share a common perspective: Religion can be understood and taught "as a live option," a phenomenon that has the potential to change lives (Webb 1999: 149). Rather than fearing that religious phenomena and experiences will taint or bias their knowledge and teaching of it, the "live option" approach embraces those phenomena and experiences, and invite their students to do the same, conceding that all knowing is relational, and that in this truth lies the possibility that we will "have encounters and exchanges that will inevitably alter us" (Palmer 1998: 54).

Service-Learning: Is It Value Neutral?

Similar concerns about how we know, academic rigor, advocacy, and indoctrination exist among practitioners of service-learning. Researchers suggest that some professors resist incorporating service or social values into their classrooms because they fear doing so would move education "from enlightenment to indoctrination" (Delve, Mintz, and Stewart 1990: 2) and get in the way of objectivity (Eyler and Giles 1999: 131).

In response, there has been a growing movement among some advocates to emphasize service-learning's academic side. They feel the only way for service-learning to have academic credibility in higher education is to ensure its connection with the classroom (hence the phrase *academic service-learning*). This is the argument Zlotkowski makes when he suggests that service-learning is not just about social commitment but also about academic rigor, maintaining that service-learning enhances academic effectiveness (1998). Similarly, Jeffrey Howard stresses that academic service-learning is a pedagogical model, not a social responsibility model. Service-learning is not an add-on experience to a course but functions as "a critical learning complement to the academic goals of the course" (1998: 21-22).[7] In this case, learning becomes a blend of experiences that happen inside and outside the classroom. This mandates that the service be relevant to the academic course of study. This is significant because it suggests that some forms of community service make no sense for some courses (for example, serving in a soup kitchen makes sense for a class on social issues but not for an engineering class).

Along this academic vein, Keith Morton makes a distinction between two reasons for combining service and academic content in service-learning courses. Those courses designed specifically to assist students in reflecting on and learning from the service in which they are already engaged he labels *service-centered courses*. Those that have discipline and content objectives that the instructor decides can be more effectively reached by the inclusion of service Morton calls *content-centered courses* (1996). Service-centered courses are inductive and attempt, in David Kolb's phrase, to "transform experience into knowledge" through reflection on the service (1984: 37). Morton suggests that the content-centered courses may include liberal education or values objectives, such as engaging students in a commitment to the common good, but they may not. Most frequently, he suggests, they include service because those who teach them think this is the best pedagogical approach to reach the learning objectives, "to enhance the knowledge and skills determined to be important within an academic discipline" (1996: 278).

Recent studies of service-learning by Eyler and Giles support the conclusion that service-learning can be highly effective. Where course and community service are well integrated, these components meet the academic goals of enhancing student understanding of course content and improving student critical-thinking skills (1999). Eyler and Giles contend this is because service provides the opportunity for students to use and apply the information and knowledge from their courses in real-world contexts, enabling them to gain a greater depth of understanding and improve their problem-solving abilities.

Yet while it is true that service-learning is rightly seeking academic credibility as a pedagogy, most advocates still do not see it as value neutral. At the very least, it represents an approach that tries to encourage participating students to move out of the confines of a narrow self-interest and see that they are citizens who must be committed to the good of others as well. This is what responsible citizenship entails.

Timothy Stanton and associates note that the term *service-learning* first appeared in publications of the Southern Regional Education Board (SREB) in 1969, in which the term is defined as "the accomplishment of tasks that meet genuine human needs in combination with conscious educational growth" (Stanton et al. 1999: 2). The authors suggest that the SREB's concern was "with developing learning opportunities for students that were related to community service, community development, and social change" (1999: 2). Thus, the early service-learning pioneers focused on the interrelationship among education, democracy, and service. Different pioneers attempted to answer one of three questions: (1) What is the purpose of education in a democracy? (2) How does education serve society? (3) What is the relationship between service and social change? While some pioneers focused on social justice or democratic education, most concerned themselves with education's service to society. Evident in all three concerns, however, is that these early advocates did not see service-learning as value neutral.

This same threefold focus exists today in ongoing discussions of the role of service in higher education. Academic goals and values goals are not mutually exclusive but complementary. Rhoads and Howard contend that service-learning "addresses fundamental issues related to the role of higher learning in fostering socially responsible and caring citizens" (1998: 1). Zlotkowski affirms that the development of such values among students is a critical component of any service-learning effort. It represents the *soul* or *spirit* of service-learning (1998: 84-85). Postmodern views of higher education realize that values will be advocated in every classroom. The only question is which values? Howard notes, "Service-learning's goal of advancing students' sense of social responsibility or commitment to the broader good conflicts with the individualistic, self-orientation of the traditional classroom." He also contends that this goal of "advancing students' commitment to the greater good" is what distinguishes service-learning from other forms of experiential learning (1998: 23-24).

A study by Giles and Eyler suggests that service-learning is effective in promoting such values. One of the most consistent findings of service-learning research is an increase in social responsibility among students. "Students are more likely to see themselves as connected to their community, to value service, to endorse systemic approaches to social problems, to believe that communities can solve their problems, and to have greater racial tolerance when involved in service-learning" (1998: 66).

Other advocates emphasize service-learning's contribution to social welfare. Harkavy and Benson assert that the fundamental purpose of knowledge is to improve human welfare and that service-learning does this quite well (1998). Weigert has a similar view: Service-learning both advances knowledge and helps "to remedy the deficiencies in our common life" (1998: 4).

For others, the goal of service-learning is social change (or at least educating students to be agents of social change). Eyler and Giles note that many service-learning practitioners favor such "transformational learning" — education that pushes people to question the assumptions that underlie social arrangements and to see how such assumptions contribute to social problems (1999: 132). They claim that the transformation of students' perspectives about these social arrangements is critical to their becoming aware of the need for social action to address such problems. Mendel-Reyes agrees. She contends that service-learning connects personal and political transformation: "Students transform themselves into citizens and their society into one that welcomes and promotes active citizenship" (1998: 34).

This issue of social change highlights the debate about what form the service in service-learning should take. Morton notes that some view service as a continuum from charity to project management to social change, with the latter being morally superior to the former (see p. 48 for a fuller definition of each). In contrast, he suggests that we look at each form of service as its own paradigm, emerging from a particular worldview and ethos. Thus, each can have legitimacy so long as it is used with integrity (1995).

Others are not so sure. A frequent concern with the charity approach is that such service is inherently paternalistic and reinforces unjust social arrangements. Hence, Jane Kendall and associates note, "A good service-learning program helps participants see their questions in the larger context of issues of social justice and social policy — rather than in the context of charity" (1990: 20). This is one feature of service-learning that distinguishes it from other approaches to community service. A second feature is that it emphasizes reciprocity — "the exchange of both giving and receiving between the 'server' and the person or group 'being served'" (1990: 21-22). In this way, professors who implement service-learning avoid the paternalism inherent in many charity-based community service programs.

While this debate will undoubtedly continue, clearly both positions agree that service-learning makes some normative claims and value commitments. Thus, as a form of experiential learning, it can rarely (if ever) be value neutral. It seeks to educate students for citizenship and for commitment to the broader social good. It teaches about education's responsibility for the welfare of the community and education's role in promoting social change. Indeed, it implicitly critiques higher education as an allegedly value-neutral enterprise.

Service-Learning in Religious Studies: Educational or Transformational?

In light of the discussions above, why would teachers of religion want to use service-learning in their classes? Is it an appropriate pedagogical tool for those interested in the science of religion who seek to bracket out questions of values and norms in the interest of knowledge for knowledge's sake? Can the "objectivist" use service-learning for her or his own purposes in spite of the expressed values orientation of service-learning advocates? Or is service-learning best employed by those who see religion as a phenomenon that has the potential to change lives? Or for those who want to use it to sharpen the critical, ethical, and moral edge religious studies can offer society and to encourage the moral development of students and the well-being of society?

To get at answers to these questions, I conducted a survey among professors of religion who currently use service-learning as a pedagogical tool in their classes. I sent out more than 80 surveys to religious studies departments and colleagues at different colleges and universities across the country. I included participants from the conference "A Future of Service," and I included religious studies departments that were at institutions that had commitments to community service as a part of their institutional mission. (Unfortunately, in the latter instance, many departments responded that no members of their faculty utilized service-learning as a pedagogical tool. I can only speculate as to the reasons for this).[8]

While I make no claims about the empirical validity of the survey process, I did attempt to be geographically and institutionally diverse. Out of the 31 completed surveys I received, 20 percent came from the Southeast, 30 percent from the Northeast, 33 percent from the Midwest, and 17 percent from the West. In addition, I sent surveys to three types of institutions: private church related, private nonchurch related, and public. Of those professors who completed the survey, 67 percent taught in church-related institutions, 10 percent taught in private institutions, and 23 percent in public universities. (The majority of the departments that responded that they did not use service-learning came from the nonchurch and public groups.)

The survey brought important information to light. First, my colleagues in religious studies use service-learning in a wide range of classes. On the survey, I included biblical studies, theology, introduction to religion, ethics, world religions, and ritual studies. But the respondents also use service-learning in classes on peace and justice, women's studies, peacemaking, religion and ecology, religion and conflict, religion in America, African-American religion, death and dying, the Holocaust, and religion and public life.

Second, I learned about the broad range of service opportunities provided in the classes. Following Morton, I classified the service into three categories: direct service, project, and advocacy (1996). Ninety-three (93) percent of the respondents indicated they connect students with direct service, including tutoring, mentoring, work in soup kitchens, day care, nursing homes, hospitals — even home building/rehab. Sixty-eight (68) percent involve students in projects, including community surveys/assessments, interviews, community organizing, and the like. Fifty-four (54) percent engage students in advocacy on political or social issues.

The most important lessons from the survey, for the purposes of this paper, relate to the objectives professors have in using service-learning. I listed six objectives on the survey. The first two — to increase student understanding/knowledge and to enhance student critical thinking — I labeled as educational goals and saw them as value neutral. They were more in keeping with the academic service-learning goals noted in the previous section.

The last four objectives — to change student values, to change student perspectives on social issues, to encourage citizenship, and to promote social change — I considered to be normative. They included some value commitments on the part of the professor (about the course content or the purpose of higher education) or sought to promote some value change in students or their perspectives on social issues. (I also provided opportunity for respondents to note other objectives and to make comments — something I will discuss below.)

The results indicate that professors who use service-learning in religious studies courses clearly have educational goals in mind (93% of respondents sought to enhance student understanding/knowledge, 72% wanted to improve critical thinking). But this is only half the story. Most colleagues also have normative goals. They want to promote change in student values (55%) or student perspectives on social issues (72%), encourage citizenship (66%), and/or promote social change (62%).

Why are these results significant? They suggest that professors in religious studies use service-learning as more than simply a way to get students to increase their knowledge or enhance their critical-thinking skills, although it certainly does both. In addition, professors find in this pedagogy a way to engage students more fully in religion as a subject and to connect their knowledge and their actions with critical social issues. To flesh out the normative goals that professors have for using service-learning, let me analyze some of the comments they made on the survey.

Some professors who use service-learning concurred with Frisina's argument that the study of religion provides a critical moral edge with which students can assess themselves, cultural values, and social structures (see above). Many comments by respondents echoed the notion that service leads students to "critical self-assessment of personal and social presuppositions." Service-learning is a way to "clarify student values," if not to change them, and to "challenge stereotypes" students hold, even if not always successfully. Service-learning in religious studies enables professors to challenge the individualistic mind-set of contemporary society by showing that "religion is communal." It is an avenue for "consciousness raising about diversity." Moreover, by connecting a religious text with current social issues, service-learning enables teachers and students "to critique societal points of view and structures."

The respondents also expressed the belief that higher education is about more than the generation and transmission of knowledge. It includes concern for the moral and spiritual development of students and their role in contributing to the common good. Some respondents chose service-learning as a vehicle to enable their students to live a life of greater integrity, where their beliefs and their actions find coherence and wholeness. One professor, who uses service-learning in Bible and theology classes, wanted to help students make the "connection between Christian values, to be hearers and doers." Another encouraged students "to integrate theological concepts with life." One professor said she wants students to "appreciate the connection between religious beliefs and social action." This occurs best, another wrote, by connecting students with "committed practitioners," as service-learning does. This approach not only transforms students but also pushes those who teach it toward a relational epistemology. Asserted one respondent, "Service-learning transforms the study of religion, allowing the word and the text to be intimately related to the deed."

The focus of such deeds is on the needs of others and on the common good. Parker Palmer suggests that we, as teachers, must honor a vital need in our students "to be introduced to a world larger than their own experiences and egos, a world that expands their personal boundaries and enlarges their sense of community" (1998: 120). Through service-learning, respondents seek to "encourage reflection on social responsibility," "encourage doing for others," and "motivate civic engagement." The "hands-on practical experience" service provides can "change students' lives by . . . strengthening identity and community involvement." The power of service-learning can be seen in its ability to "increase student confidence to be actively involved," while it also enhances their understanding and practice of "reciprocity." Furthermore, such civic engagement is as crucial for poor and working-class students as it is for students who are financially privileged: "It is critical for them to also see themselves as responsible for the ethical and spiritual health of their communities." The hope of many respondents was that "changing values will lead to social change." Indeed, several suggested that this pedagogical approach, this experiential way of knowing, is critical for learning and for the outcomes they seek to engender. I think they also implied that this experiential way of exploring religion is essential to understanding the essence of religion. In the words of one respondent, "Religion is a natural discipline for service-learning."

Some might assume that the type of institution at which one teaches would have a significant impact on one's objectives — that, for example, normative objectives would be more important for church-related institutions, less so for public and private schools. But according to my limited survey, this is not the case. In public universities, 83 percent of respondents sought some normative goals, 85 percent in church-related institutions, and 100 percent in private institutions (see Charles Strain's argument elsewhere in this volume that mission statements are key in promoting faculty use of service-learning).

Even for those few respondents who felt that the purpose of the service was solely educational and not normative — i.e., to provide an experiential base from which to achieve content objectives — I suspect there still was some normative agenda. Otherwise, incorporating service really makes little sense. The word *service* is itself so value laden for many people that its very use raises questions. (One instructor, who does not use service-learning in her courses, asked whether it was possible to do service-learning without inherently being paternalistic.) Would it not be more appropriate to engage students in experiences that do not include a service component if one wanted to avoid any normative implications?

While it is impossible to answer this question definitively from the comments on the surveys, I would suggest that perhaps professors utilize a service component because they intuitively understand the impact such an experience can have on all involved. David Kolb has written that experience has two dimensions: one subjective and personal, the other objective and environmental. These two dimensions interrelate and interpenetrate each other, and once they become related, they both are "essentially changed" (1984: 36). So while many service-learning practitioners may not "intend" to change either their students or the environment, they know such change is inevitable. (Of course, as one respondent noted, service-learning is a risky business. The change that occurs may not always be what one hoped for.)

Finally, aside from epistemological and pedagogical issues — objective and individualistic versus experiential and relational — the survey also raised operational questions. Respondents were asked to assess what most contributed to the success or failure of service-learning in their courses. All agreed that success depends upon the effective integration of the service and the classroom experience. This means that the service should be related to course objectives, readings, and discussions and that students should engage in high-quality reflections on the theoretical implications of their service.

Equally important, however, is support from the community and the institution. Almost all respondents agreed that good, quality placements were essential to the success of service-learning. They also indicated that having departmental and institutional support made their job much easier. Some respondents noted that having service-learning or community service directors on their campus, professional staff whose role it is to secure placements and to work with the community organizations, was key to success. Others suggested that having students who had already successfully participated in a service-learning course work with them as tutors/mentors was crucial.

The main point here is that even if one is epistemologically and pedagogically receptive to service-learning (a matter of the will), one still needs support from one's colleagues, one's institution, and one's community for such an undertaking to be successful (a matter of the way) (again, see Charles Strain's essay).

Conclusion

Should professors in religious studies use service-learning? Parker Palmer contends that the choice of pedagogical technique should flow from the identity and integrity of the teacher. His point is that teachers do not simply teach what they know but who they are. To teach well, we should have some sense of who we are and of the nature of our discipline, and our technique should flow from that sense of identity, from the "heart" of the teacher (1998: 23-25). Another way he frames this issue is that there should be coherence between our epistemology and our pedagogy (and our ethics). If, as a teacher of religion, one feels that a scientific approach to religious studies is the only valid approach and that the purpose of higher education is fundamentally to generate and transmit knowledge, it is difficult to see why or how one would use service-learning. As a pedagogical tool, it does not simply aid the intellectual development of students; it also contributes to their moral development and to the well-being of the community. Moreover, as a form of experiential education, it implies that experience is itself critical in the educational process — a notion that many who adopt an objectivist epistemology deny.

However, if one's approach to the study of religion is relational, if one thinks that experience can contribute significantly to that study, and if one believes that higher education has normative as well as intellectual goals, then service-learning may be an appropriate pedagogy (though not the only one).[9] According to the survey I conducted, service-learning has provided a valuable way for teachers of religion to engage religious phenomena and critical social issues and to enable students to connect their learning with their world. Such engagement may actually require an experiential approach to the discipline, not only for the teacher but also for the student. In this way, religion as a subject can once again become a "live option," a phenomenon with the potential to change lives.

Notes

1. See, for example, Hart 1991 and Ogden 1995 for two perspectives on this debate.

2. Juschka suggests that this is really a "non-identity" (1997). The "non-identity" of the social scientist has also led some to question whether one could even call religious studies a discipline. Tim Fitzgerald argues that it really offers nothing distinct from social scientific approaches to the study of religion (as quoted in Juschka 1997: 8). If this is the case, he argues, then why even have religious studies as a distinct and separate entity on the college campus?

3. Russell McCutcheon defines religious studies as "the effort to define and secure an institutional space by developing an objective science of religion clearly demarcated from the confessional practice of religion" (quoted in Juschka 1997: 9).

4. Wiebe writes, "The sciences . . . espouse a search for objective knowledge of the world and involve a conscious attempt to avoid (or at least minimize) idiosyncrasy and bias in that search" (1998: 96).

5. See, for example, the treatment provided in Ring et al. 1998.

6. In addition to the epistemological and pedagogical concerns noted here, Frisina points to a concern for institutional survival. Many question the value of religious studies in today's higher education context, a context in which religious studies faculty are losing support from both above and below. Academic administrators and deans are shifting resources away from this area, and students are not choosing religious studies as a major. To be sure, this is not a problem for religious studies alone but a problem for all of the humanities. But in such a context, it is especially important that religious studies faculty defend their place in higher education by reclaiming their contributions to the moral well-being of both students and communities. As Frisina has noted, "If we were to remove the ethical and moral challenge that has always been at the heart of what we do, all that would be left is mere fluff, a bit of style and not much more. In the end I do not think that will be sufficient to sustain us before a skeptical public that needs good reasons to continue supporting us" (1997: 30).

7. Although they emphasize the academic aspect, they also emphasize that service-learning represents a pedagogical shift. Howard argues that service-learning actually "raises the pedagogical bar" by placing responsibility on students themselves for creating knowledge and by bringing into the picture educators other than the instructor (1998: 23). Morton suggests that because "they place students' interpretations of experience at the center of teaching, service-learning courses are, in essence, countercultural" (1996: 279).

8. One reason may be that professors in those schools do not appreciate the value of service-learning because they have a scientific approach to the study of religion or are not persuaded that service-learning is an effective educational strategy. A second may be that, although the institutional missions of research universities may encourage effective teaching and community service, such institutions remain at their core research universities. Hence, service-related teaching may not be rewarded, and faculty members may run tenure and promotion risks if they spend too much time on anything other than research and publication.

9. One respondent noted service-learning's affinity with liberatory and critical pedagogies. For a discussion of their use in a religious studies classroom, see Pippin 1998.

References

Delve, Cecilia I., Suzanne D. Mintz, and Greig M. Stewart, eds. (1990). *Community Service as Values Education.* San Francisco: Jossey-Bass.

Dewey, John. (1997). *Experience and Education.* New York: Simon & Schuster.

Eyler, Janet, and Dwight E. Giles, Jr. (1999). *Where's the Learning in Service-Learning?* San Francisco: Jossey-Bass.

Ford, David F. (1998). "Theology and Religious Studies at the Turn of the Millennium: Reconceiving the Field." *Teaching Theology and Religion* 1(1): 4-12.

Frisina, Warren G. (1997). "Religious Studies: Strategies for Survival in the '90s." *CSSR Bulletin* 26(2): 29-34.

Giles, Dwight E., Jr., and Janet Eyler. (1998). "A Service-Learning Research Agenda for the Next Five Years." In *Academic Service-Learning: A Pedagogy of Action and Reflection,* edited by Robert A. Rhoads and Jeffrey P.F. Howard, pp. 65-72. New Directions for Teaching and Learning, no. 73. San Francisco: Jossey-Bass.

Harkavy, Ira, and Lee Benson. (1998). "De-Platonizing and Democratizing Education as the Bases of Service-Learning." In *Academic Service-Learning: A Pedagogy of Action and Reflection,* edited by Robert A. Rhoads and Jeffrey P.F. Howard, pp. 11-20. New Directions for Teaching and Learning, no. 73. San Francisco: Jossey-Bass.

Hart, Ray L. (1991). "Religious Studies and Theological Studies in American Higher Education: A Pilot Study." *Journal of the American Academy of Religion* 59(4): 715-827.

Hodgson, Peter V. (1999). "Liberal Theology and Transformative Pedagogy." *Teaching Theology and Religion* 2(2): 65-76.

Howard, Jeffrey P.F. (1998). "Academic Service-Learning: A Counternormative Pedagogy." In *Academic Service-Learning: A Pedagogy of Action and Reflection,* edited by Robert A. Rhoads and Jeffrey P.F. Howard, pp. 21-29. New Directions for Teaching and Learning, no. 73. San Francisco: Jossey-Bass.

Juschka, Darlene. (1997). "Religious Studies and Identity Politics: Mythology in the Making." *CSSR Bulletin* 26(1): 8-11.

Kendall, Jane C., and Associates, eds. (1990). *Combining Service and Learning: A Resource Book for Community Service. Vol. 1.* Raleigh, NC: National Society for Internships and Experiential Education.

Kolb, David A. (1984). *Experiential Learning: Experience as the Source of Learning and Development.* Englewood Cliffs, NJ: Prentice-Hall.

Malley, Brian E. (1997). "Toward an Engaged Religious Studies." *CSSR Bulletin* 26(1): 11-12.

Mendel-Reyes, Meta. (1998). "A Pedagogy for Citizenship: Service-Learning and Democratic Education." In *Academic Service-Learning: A Pedagogy of Action and Reflection,* edited by Robert A. Rhoads and Jeffrey P.F. Howard, pp. 31-38. New Directions for Teaching and Learning, no. 73. San Francisco: Jossey-Bass.

Morton, Keith. (1995). "The Irony of Service: Charity, Project, and Social Change in Service-Learning." *Michigan Journal of Community Service Learning* 2: 19-32.

———. (1996). "Issues Related to Integrating Service-Learning Into the Curriculum." In *Service-Learning in Higher Education: Concepts and Practices,* edited by Barbara Jacoby and Associates, pp. 276-296. San Francisco: Jossey-Bass.

Ogden, Schubert M. (1995). "Religious Studies and Theological Studies: What Is Involved in the Distinction Between Them?" *CSSR Bulletin* 24(1): 3-4.

Palmer, Parker J. (1998). *The Courage to Teach: Exploring the Inner Landscape of a Teacher's Life.* San Francisco: Jossey-Bass.

Pippin, Tina. (1998). "Liberatory Pedagogies in the Religious Studies Classroom." *Teaching Theology and Religion.* 1(3): 177-182.

Rhoads, Robert A., and Jeffrey P.F. Howard, eds. (1998). *Academic Service-Learning: A Pedagogy of Action and Reflection.* New Directions for Teaching and Learning, no. 73. San Francisco: Jossey-Bass.

Ring, Nancy C., Kathleen S. Nash, Mary N. MacDonald, Fred Glennon, and Jennifer A. Glancy. (1998). *Introduction to the Study of Religion.* Maryknoll, NY: Orbis Books.

Smith, Jonathan Z. (1988). "'Religion' and 'Religious Studies': No Difference At All." *Soundings* 71(2-3): 231-244.

Stanton, Timothy K., Dwight E. Giles, Jr., and Nadinne I. Cruz. (1999). *Service-Learning: A Movement's Pioneers Reflect on Its Origins, Practice, and Future.* San Francisco: Jossey-Bass.

Webb, Stephen H. (1999). "Teaching as Confessing: Redeeming a Theological Trope for Pedagogy." *Teaching Theology and Religion* 2(3): 143-153.

Weigert, Kathleen Maas. (1998). "Academic Service-Learning: Its Meaning and Relevance." In *Academic Service-Learning: A Pedagogy of Action and Reflection,* edited by Robert A. Rhoads and Jeffrey P.F. Howard, pp. 3-10. New Directions for Teaching and Learning, no. 73. San Francisco: Jossey-Bass.

Wiebe, Donald. (1998). "The Politics of Religious Studies." *CSSR Bulletin* 27(4): 95-98.

Zlotkowski, Edward. (1998). "A Service-Learning Approach to Faculty Development." In *Academic Service-Learning: A Pedagogy of Action and Reflection,* edited by Robert A. Rhoads and Jeffrey P.F. Howard, pp. 81-89. New Directions for Teaching and Learning, no. 73. San Francisco: Jossey-Bass.

Creating the Engaged University: Service-Learning, Religious Studies, and Institutional Mission

by Charles R. Strain

Ecology and Mission

Coyote says, "You people should stay put here, learn your place, do good things. Me, I'm traveling on. (Snyder 1996: 121)[1]

Coyote, that old trickster, is a familiar character to scholars in religious studies. Beat poet and Buddhist practitioner Gary Snyder's version of Coyote is steeped in ambiguity. I suggest that we consider Coyote as a metaphor for our ambivalence regarding our own institutions. For better or for worse, most of us, given the limited professional mobility in the humanities, will stay put for large chunks of time in a very few places. We will consider ourselves lucky compared with our colleagues who will wander from one non-tenure-track position to another. But I suspect most of us will nurture the illusion of the fetterless freedom that Snyder's Coyote represents.

The word *mission* in the title of this essay, however, implies that there is also something vital and necessary in traveling on. Coyote challenges those of us who have adopted a monolithic model of professional life based on our graduate school socialization, those of us perplexed and perhaps a bit resentful when our institution — indeed, when higher education itself — starts yanking out the tent stakes and loading up the wagons. Service-learning, I will suggest, is one of those crucibles of change in which these complex, "Coyotean" dynamics play themselves out in many of our colleges and universities. It is also one of the forms of engaged learning where, to use another mobile metaphor from Snyder, we are both "on the path" and "off the trail" (1990: 151-154).

"Stay put?" we may ask. "Learn your place?" If only it were that simple. Close to 40 years after the Supreme Court decision that opened the door to the comparative study of religion in public universities, all too many religious studies faculty members feel all too much like real coyotes, skulking around on the edges of the "real" academy. We hunger for legitimacy, a place around the campfire, not in the shadowlands. Those of us in religious-affiliated institutions share this feeling scarcely less than do our colleagues in

I am grateful to Sister Jane Gerard, CSJ, for assistance in preparing this chapter.

secular universities. The fierce debates about the discipline of religious studies have always struck me as having less to do with academic rigor and more
about hoping to come in from the margins (see Fred Glennon's essay elsewhere in this volume).

In such a context, a discussion of the role of service-learning within the
discipline of religious studies can be particularly problematic. Service-learning, as I have already hinted, is more than pedagogy. Service-learning is not
about staying put; it is about moving on. While some argue forcefully that
service-learning is adaptable to what has come to be considered a "traditional" understanding of the academic enterprise, I will portray and reflect
upon it as part of a profound reconsideration of the meaning and tasks of
education; in short, as part of redefining institutional mission.[2] Viewed in
this way, service-learning calls into question the epistemological certitudes
that peg the academic tent, revealing them in their historicity. It thereby
affects all disciplines. In a time of change, it may be just as well that we have
no cozy place by the campfire to forfeit.

The Transformation of Mission in Higher Education

Staying put implies checking out the territory. Where are we? What is going
on? Mission, on the other hand, implies movement. Where have we been?
Where are we headed? The late Ernest Boyer, former U.S. secretary of education and then head of the Carnegie Foundation for the Advancement of
Teaching, was for many years the most reliable scout in higher education.
Boyer argued that in the post–World War II period, the GI Bill, along with the
social changes that marked the last half of the 20th century, transformed
higher education "from an elite to a mass system." "Ironically, at the very
time America's higher education institutions were becoming more open and
inclusive," Boyer noted, "the culture of the professoriate was becoming more
hierarchical and restrictive" (1990: 11-13).

> Thus in a few decades, priorities in higher education were significantly
> realigned. The emphasis on undergraduate education was being overshad-
> owed by the European university tradition with its emphasis on graduate
> education and research. (1990: 11-13)

The decision of the cold war national security state to harness the
potential of university-based research abetted what some scholars have
called "the academic revolution" (Jenks and Riesman 1968) — a sea change
"that put many comprehensive universities on a uniform path to a faculty-
centered/research-centered model of scholarship and created mission
creep" (Holland 1999: 53). Mission creep is the attempt to emulate a single
model successfully developed by a few, very elite institutions that have the

resources to replicate the European research university. In the hope of attracting noted scholars, external funding, and national prestige, institutions resort to mimicry. From an ecological standpoint, this is the higher education equivalent of unchecked suburban growth with its malls, expressways, and prefab communities invading corn fields, wetlands, and forests. Mission creep undermines generative diversity. It is the opposite of what Buddhists call *mindfulness*. Genuine mindfulness, Snyder insists, pays attention to place, to what will flourish and what will not in this place. It is a "field-sensing of the world" (1980: 107-108, 141).

In the aftermath of the cold war, a skeptical public — including state legislators, corporate leaders, parents of college-bound children, and working adults completing their degrees — has questioned the priorities that mark this historical hybrid of academic aspiration and national security policy. It was, above all, Ernest Boyer who in 1994 pointed the way back to a diversity of models with his call to create "the New American College." Boyer sought a regeneration of the land-grant tradition with its fusion of education and public service and its productive pattern of research applied to local needs (1994: A48). Boyer was, in fact, echoing a long-neglected challenge by Clark Kerr in the late 1960s to create "urban grant" institutions (Kerr 1991: chap. 25). The engaged college in Boyer's definition would be responsive to local needs, "connecting the rich resources of our university to our most pressing social, civic, and ethical problems, to our children, to our schools, . . . and to our cities." In Boyer's capacious vision, engagement was not a one-way relationship:

> *I'm convinced that . . . engagement also means creating a special climate in which the academic and civic cultures communicate more continuously and more creatively with each other, helping to enlarge . . . the universe of human discourse and enriching the quality of life for all of us.*[3]

Coming at the end of the cold war era, Boyer's call precipitated a rethinking of the public purposes of higher education. Leaders in many institutions echoed this call. In spring 1996, to cite but one example, Richard Meister, DePaul University's executive vice president for academic affairs, launched a university-wide discussion by playing upon the title of Boyer's article:

> *I believe that DePaul can be the New American University: a model of a university that serves the "public good." . . . In this university, teaching and learning are primary; scholarship is broadly defined; interdisciplinary work is encouraged; and service to the larger society is part of the mission. . . . Faculty, staff, and students are representative of the larger society. The definition of faculty is also broadened: faculty are both mentors and academic leaders of this university, with the responsibility of learning being shared with staff and students. (Meister 1996: 3)*[4]

Boyer and those who heeded his call successfully dislodged the dominant model of higher education. Staying put now meant moving on.

Service-Learning and Institutional Mission

Institutional missions, when effective, mediate. They distill local history and tradition, linking past to future. They also mediate between public expectations of the academy and the purposes articulated by the faculty and staff who inhabit it. The purpose of this mediation is action. It is to descriptions of institutional mission that proponents of service-learning frequently look for a "legitimizing hook" upon which they can hang their hopes and proposals for institutional support. In public and private, religiously affiliated and secular institutions, the hook is almost always there:

> Founded in 1855 as the nation's first land-grant university, [Michigan State University] served as the prototype for 69 land-grant institutions later established under the Morrill Act of 1862. . . . Central to the university's land-grant mission is service to the state, the nation, and the world. Public service and extension missions are fulfilled by long-standing commitments to international development and education and an extensive lifelong education effort throughout the state. (http://www.msw.edu/dis/pacts/FIB.htm#MSU)

> Oberlin was the first college to grant undergraduate degrees to women. Historically a leader in the education of African Americans, Oberlin's heritage is one of respect for the individual and active concern for the larger society. Recognizing that diversity broadens perspectives, Oberlin recruits culturally, economically, geographically, and racially diverse students of promise, whose interaction fosters effective, concerned participation in the larger society, so characteristic of Oberlin graduates. . . . Oberlin College [aims] . . . to expand [its students'] social awareness, social responsibility, and capacity for moral judgment so as to prepare them for intelligent and useful response to the present and future demands of society. (Course catalogue, 1997-98)

> [Boston] University's learning environment is further enriched by an extraordinary array of direct involvements with the broader artistic, economic, social, intellectual, and educational life of the community. These relationships provide a distinctly practical edge to the University's educational and research programs, while enhancing the life and vitality of one of the world's great cities. (http://www.bu.edu.about)

The mission of Indiana University Purdue University Indianapolis is to serve as a model for collaboration and multi-disciplinary work through partnerships with Indiana University and Purdue University and the community, drawing upon the distinctive strengths of the academic health sciences and the resources of the capital city and state. (http://www.jaguars. iupui.edu/plan/mismay.html)

Boston College draws inspiration for its academic societal mission from its distinctive religious tradition. As a Catholic and Jesuit university, it is rooted in a world view that encounters God in all creation and through all human activity, especially in the search for truth in every discipline, in the desire to learn, and in the call to live justly together. . . . Boston College pursues this distinctive mission . . . by fostering the rigorous intellectual development and the religious, ethical, and personal formation of its undergraduate, graduate, and professional students in order to prepare them for citizenship, service, and leadership in a global society. (http://www.bc.edu/ cwis/mission/mission.html)

Rhodes [College] helps students to . . . cultivate an appropriate set of dispositions and sensibilities. . . . An appropriate set of dispositions and sensibilities includes the attributes of personal integrity and respect for one's own abilities and values; respect for other persons and a concern for their dignity and welfare; a sense of community; an appreciation of cultural diversity. . . . Cultivation of that set of dispositions and sensibilities involves . . . opportunities for participation in service projects that involve working with people from different social and economic backgrounds, in off-campus learning experiences here and abroad. (http://www.rhodes.edu/ default1htmls/mission rev.html)

In the case of Michigan State University and Oberlin College, distinctive historical traditions provide a secular rationale for engagement. An urban location, in the case of Boston University and Indiana University Purdue University Indianapolis, calls for an institutional response. Place is paramount. In the case of Boston College and Rhodes College, religious and moral traditions shape the commitment to service. But note how these institutions also add distinctive notes to these common ways of articulating a commitment to engagement with society. Boston University emphasizes "a distinctly practical edge" to its teaching and research; Oberlin points to a long tradition of socially committed alumni and alumnae. IUPUI emphasizes the strengths of its programs in the health sciences, while Michigan State points to the traditional extension services of a land-grant university. Boston College, as an institution connected with a religious order that has a global mission and reach, emphasizes "leadership in a global society," whereas Rhodes College, as a small liberal arts college with a personalistic emphasis, underlines the importance of cultivating the moral sensibilities of its students. In other words, there is more than a single rationale for service-learning and community engagement, and such activity fits not only with the mission of a land-grant or a religiously affiliated institution but potentially with the mission of any college or university.

At DePaul University, in similar fashion, it is the most particularistic aspect of our tradition — our history as a Vincentian institution — that has served to unify a variety of projects that engage the university with society. Our mission statement focusing on the "central purposes" of the university begins its discussion of service to the community in more or less generic terms:

> In meeting its public service responsibility, the university encourages faculty, staff, and students to apply specialized expertise in ways that contribute to the social, economic, cultural, and ethical quality of life in the metropolitan area and beyond.

But it is in speaking of the "distinguishing marks" of the university that the mission statement catches fire:

> Motivated by the example of St. Vincent, who instilled a love of God by leading his contemporaries in serving urgent human needs, the DePaul community is above all characterized by . . . a sensitivity to and care for the needs of each other and of those served, with a special concern for the deprived members of society. DePaul University emphasizes the development of a full range of human capabilities and appreciation of higher education as a means to engage cultural, social, religious, and ethical values in service to others. (http://www.depaul.edu/mission.html)

In our case, this "Vincentian commitment" is more than a legitimizing hook. It unifies people across a religious/secular border and across ideological dividing lines. It bridges differences in our institution. Given what I understand to be the service-learning movement's rejection of narrow ideological commitments, such a bridge concept is most useful.[5]

The utilitarian impulse to find a "legitimizing hook," however, narrows the relationship between service-learning and institutional mission in unfortunate ways. If we heed Boyer's challenge to create an engaged university, the mission, with its mediating concepts, should not be viewed so much as a hook — not even as a coat rack with lots of hooks — but as a fulcrum and service-learning as one multipronged lever to launch the university in a new, engaged direction.

Levers without a fulcrum do not work. To realize the potential of an institutional mission as a fulcrum, we need to free ourselves of the cynicism that declares all mission statements to be "just rhetoric, just PR." This attitude assumes that faculty in particular are not guided by institutional imperatives, are not socialized into a particular academic culture. But as my discussion of the cold war university implies, we are willy-nilly the expressions of some academic culture with its imperatives, only it may be the culture of our graduate institution. Our institutional mission, at some level of our awareness, is not "just rhetoric." Whether that mission is appropriate to where we are is another matter. A mission, at its best, is the practice of mindfulness about this place at this time in its history with its distinctive potential before it.

Barbara Holland, in an essay appropriately entitled "From Murky to Meaningful: The Role of Mission in Institutional Change," argues a twofold thesis: first, that the shift from bland mission statements to ones with clear distinguishing marks is one prerequisite for institutional change and, second, that a specific commitment to community service has often been a vehicle for recovery of a distinctive institutional history that had been eclipsed by the dominance of a single "faculty-centered/research-centered" model of higher education (Holland 1999: 48-49, 53). In short, Holland suggests that the fulcrum and the lever are created interdependently.

Holland shows how moving past a "murky" to a meaningful mission of engagement begins to affect (1) promotion, tenure, and hiring, (2) organizational structures, (3) curriculum development, (4) faculty and community partnerships, and (5) the university's self-presentation to external audiences. She draws a spectrum running from institutions whose murky mission rhetoric has little or no institutional relevance to institutions whose articulate rhetoric pushes the institution toward "full integration" of service to the community as a defining aspect of its identity. While many institutions will struggle to reach the latter end of the spectrum, I believe that the spot on her spectrum one step below "full integration" is an attainable goal for many institutions. At this stage, mission rhetoric about engagement with the community will have led to (1) reformulation of promotion and tenure guidelines, (2) the creation of new organizational structures such as centers and institutes to support community partnerships, (3) a variety of course offerings, including service-learning, across curricula, (4) the involvement of senior faculty in such curricula, (5) the creation of active partnerships with community leaders, including their presence as adjunct instructors, and (6) a prominent place for such activities in communications to external audiences (Holland 1999: 60; cf. Holland 1997: 30-41).

That is, to be sure, a rather ambitious agenda. Holland, however, suggests an alternative to trying to tackle all of these elements head on.

In institutions seeking to enact a specific commitment to community engagement as a valid component of the institutional mission, successful enactment of the role of community service most often occurs through the vehicle of the curriculum. *Institutions that begin the exploration of community service by considering the implications for faculty roles and rewards rarely change anything, because to discuss roles and rewards in the abstract creates a limited conversation. In contrast, to match the educational enterprise of the institution to the mission is to support an experiential exploration by the faculty of the influence community engagement may have on their scholarship.* (Holland 1999: 64) [emphasis added]

Teaching, Holland believes, offers a "safe context" in which faculty can explore how community engagement may affect their scholarship. The expansion of teaching roles through new forms of curricula provides actual cases upon which to model revisions in the reward structure. New curricular experiences create a demand within cohorts of students for further curricular innovation. Curricular innovation allows faculty to slowly experience the benefits of working with a community partner (Holland 1999: 64-65). What I said before about institutional mission as fulcrum and service-learning as one multipronged lever needs to be modified in light of Holland's argument. Service-learning is, in many ways, the ideal lever for activating an institutional mission of engagement as the fulcrum of institutional change. As this book illustrates in the case of religious studies, service-learning can be adapted to virtually all disciplines. It affects faculty at the level of their daily work. Without initially challenging received models of scholarship, it does immediately transform classroom dynamics, opening up new sources of knowledge in the persons of student-practitioners, community leaders, and the general community that is served.

Admittedly, this is an abstruse point. Let me illustrate it by examining the case of my own university. In summer 1997, DePaul adopted three strategic goals that give specific focus to different aspects of our mission:

Goal I: To provide all full-time students a holistic education that will foster extraordinary learning opportunities through a highly diverse faculty, staff, and student body. . . .

Goal II: To be a nationally and internationally recognized provider of the highest quality professional education for the adult, part-time student. . . .

Goal III: To research, develop, deliver, and transfer innovative, educationally related programs and services that will have significant social impact and will give concrete expression to the University's Vincentian Mission.

For the first time in its history, DePaul formulated its commitment to engagement with the community as an educational goal. In other words, service to the community was seen not as extraneous to its core mission but as a form of teaching and scholarship. At DePaul, several dozen centers and institutes already ostensibly carry out this educational goal. But for the most part, regular faculty have not been actively involved in such activities, except for those heroic few faculty directors who by sheer dint of will have created the community partnerships we have. Merely stating this third educational goal will not bring the work of these centers in from the fuzzy margins of faculty consciousness.

Thus, as part of a strategic planning process, we envisioned "community-based service-learning" as the vital link that would connect Goal III with the more traditional Goals I and II. In our plan and in its subsequent implementation, faculty develop service-learning courses for general education and departmental curricula that basically further either Goal I or Goal II. They adopt a service-learning pedagogy because such an approach furthers the learning outcomes appropriate to Goal I or II. Simultaneously, service-learning brings Goal III into closer proximity to Goals I and II. We encourage centers and institutes with active community partnerships to become "brokers," placing students appropriately in positions with affiliated community organizations. Benefiting from this brokerage, faculty become more familiar with the efforts of the centers. Students reinforce the work of the centers and provide tangible benefits to the community organizations. By creating these multiple connecting links, service-learning makes it possible for us to bring our institutional mission to engage society in from the margins. It goes beyond elevating *service* in all of its aspects to a level of equality with teaching and research; it actively reconceptualizes such service as an aspect of teaching and, subsequently, of research.

Service-Learning and Religious Studies

We religious studies faculty interminably lament our marginality within the university. Some scholars interpret our marginality as symptomatic of American higher education's loss of "soul" (Marsden 1994). Others search for academic legitimacy by emphasizing disciplinary rigor and, to my mind, exaggerating the dispassionate objectivity of our methods and approaches.[6] In either case, we intone a dreary litany, one that I have chanted as much as the next person. I will argue here that service-learning is one means of transforming an institution's mission that offers religious studies an opportunity to claim a leadership role within the pluralistic context of most institutions.

First, a caveat: We should not choose the pedagogy of service-learning for any but intrinsic reasons. From a faculty member's standpoint, the regulative reason must be that a service-learning course promotes learning. "Is any of this real?" a student in my Liberation Theology course asked some time ago. This question arose regarding a syllabus that I had reconstructed because I knew the difficulties students had connecting with abstract theological discourse. Students were reading a novel set in the context of the Salvadoran civil war, journalistic accounts, ethnographies, and sociological studies of Christian "base communities" and were viewing documentaries of Latin American religious life. Yet the question still returned, "Is any of this real?" When I began the process of turning the course into a service-learning course, things changed. Students never questioned the reality of their service context, but they did begin to question all kinds of other things: What does service have to do with liberation? Does it aid or impede it? What is liberation anyhow? What do these utopian dreams have to do with the daily struggles of the people I serve? What are the limits of charitable actions? What are the limits of action in pursuit of social justice? And on and on. The course became "real" because the questions — each one of them directly related to the core issues of the course — arose out of an actual struggle on the part of the students to learn while serving.

My students' experiences in Liberation Theology, while highlighting the intrinsic reason for adopting service-learning as a pedagogy, also illustrate a distinctive contribution of religious studies courses, first, to a service-learning program and, second, to the mission of an engaged university. What transformed my Liberation Theology course was not simply that the students were able to do something, to apply their skills to real problems. More fundamentally, they were asked to engage in a process of transformation that took place over time and demanded both internal and external change. The students I taught had to confront themselves as much as they questioned their social context; they had to challenge their own level of commitment to lasting change as much as they did the more utopian elements of the course's theoretical framework. In Buddhist terminology, the service context demanded of these students that they engage in a *practice* (a term that may be Buddhist but will be familiar to many traditions). For our purposes, any coherent set of actions that flow from an internalized value framework and not merely from instrumental goals, that impose a discipline upon the self, and that link interdependently inner and outer transformation may be called a *practice.*[7]

> *A monk asked Dong-shan: "Is there a practice for people to follow?" Dong-shan answered: "When you become a real person, there is such a practice." (Snyder 1990: 185)*

Gary Snyder's version of a traditional Zen aphorism is one more Coyote trick up his Buddhist sleeve. If religious studies as a field has something distinctive to offer, it is this sense of the subtle dynamics of genuine transformation, an awareness of its paradoxes. Conversely, service-learning offers students in religious studies classes an analogue to the forms of ultimate transformation that we study — without asking them to engage in an explicitly religious practice. I have discovered that my students think more clearly about religiously motivated change when they themselves are engaged in practice.

Reinhabiting the University

Coyote moves on and leaves us — most tenured and tenure-track faculty, that is: So where are we? What about us? What does this understanding of practice and service teach us? In the late 1960s, Snyder moved with his family to the Sierra Nevada to a place they called Kitkitdizze. They and others engaged in an environmental practice called *bioregionalism*. Bioregionalism is a multigenerational approach to reworking the relationship between people and place. It entails creating communities, engaging in political action, developing forms of right livelihood and sustainable practice; it entails the "field sensing *samadhi* of our neolithic forbears" (Snyder 1980: 107-108): "People are challenged to become 'reinhabitory' — that is, to become people who are learning to live and think 'as if' they were engaged with their place for the long future" (Snyder 1995: 246-247). From this standpoint, the traditional model of the teacher-scholar engaging in a set of academic behaviors without any regard to institutional location is a form of mindlessness.

At our 1999 American Academy of Religion conference on the future of service-learning in the field of religious studies, Barbara Patterson of Emory University raised some very trenchant questions. In my rough paraphrase she asked, Whose voices will begin to question our narrow mission statements? Will we include the voices of our community partners when we reshape those statements? What actions are necessary to be able to reaffirm our identity as institutions of higher education and not as poor replicas of a social service agency or a soup kitchen? In other words, can we stay "on the path" while moving "off the trail," and, for that matter, how far off the trail can we go? (Patterson 1999)

To raise these questions with the seriousness that Patterson does is already to answer her first question. Who else but those for whom Weber's "free floating [read: *disembodied*] intellectual" is an illusion? Rather than bemoaning the lost forms of religious engagement of the confessional college or lamenting the lack of respect for religious studies as a valid field of scholarship, why should religious studies scholars not lead the struggle to create a university in which a multitude of practices (the practice of teaching, the practice of scholarship, the practice of community service — all grasped in their spiritual dimensions) illuminate one another?

If we assert our own voices and create forms of partnership with the various communities that surround us, of course we will need to include the voices of our community partners. Service-learning can lead the way here as well. The experiences of colleagues in many disciplines suggest that faculty will slowly let go of exclusive control over their courses as they work with their community partners. They build their relationships and trust grows. If we begin our work with this lever, we can gradually find meaningful ways to include community voices in strategic thinking and decision making at the university level.

Finally, I must confess that I do not worry overly much about higher education's losing its identity. More precisely, the possibility of losing one's academic identity is not tied to experiential forms of education any more than to any other pedagogical form. Do we retain our identities as educational institutions if we adhere to traditional pedagogies whose effectiveness in terms of student learning is called into question by empirical research? The passion for disciplined inquiry, the commitment to critical reflection, and the habits of a probing intelligence are either bred in our individual and collective bones or they are not. If they are, then we carry them with us as we go off whatever historical trail has been blazed before us. If they are not, even if we stick to the path we are headed nowhere.

A "field sensing" mindfulness that balances these multiple considerations is a form of moral agency. However, let me add one more twist to this moral perspective on the practice of teaching. In the spring of 1996, a collection of articles in *The Chronicle of Higher Education,* called "The Widening Gap," argued that higher education, which for an entire generation had been a vehicle of social mobility, had turned in a different direction. The argument referred not just to challenges to affirmative action but to two interlocking studies. According to the first study, the clearest indicator that you will attend college is household wealth. According to the second, the clearest indicator of your eventual level of wealth is your level of education (Burd et al. 1996: A10-A17). The self-reinforcing feedback loop implied by this research leads to the conclusion that the university, whatever its other functions, has become an agent of inequality, a wedge institution separating the haves and the have-nots. It consolidates one group's hold on wealth as that group crosses generational divides, while becoming an increasingly remote and faint beacon of hope to the most disadvantaged members of our society. Even as many of us maintain our ideals and aspirations for a just world and strive to communicate them to our students, the very ground under our feet has shifted. Like tectonic plates, the universities within which we labor are moving relentlessly in a morally different direction. In this context, persistence in traditional roles as if we were neutral arbiters in a system of equal opportunity, rewarding students on their own merits, becomes a culpable form of mindlessness. Unless we are willing to accept the "widening gap," we have no choice other than to apply some lever to the fulcrum of institutional engagement.[8]

Engagement with multiple communities is a challenge to all institutions of higher learning, public or private, research universities or small liberal colleges, religious and secular schools alike. To meet this challenge, we faculty need to reinhabit our institutions and reclaim their traditions. Reinhabitation is a form of practice. Like Snyder, we need to form multigenerational communities within our institutions, work politically to steer them in new directions, and develop sustainable forms of engagement with the large community that will change our colleges and universities into agents of social transformation.

In the Liberation Theology course I taught, we began to discuss the forms of inequality that prevail in our own place, our own institutions, our own university. As the students discussed the forms of practice that we followed in the service context, we also talked about the forms of practice we would need to create were the university truly to become engaged. Practice and place became interlocking concepts whether we were studying *communidades de base* in Latin America, reflecting on our service context, or reconsidering the meaning and task of higher education. The vision of service-learning in relationship to institutional mission that I have outlined arises out of these classroom experiences. It arises out of practice and place. It is about staying put, mindfully, and moving on.

Notes

1. Snyder's poem is entitled "Old Woodrat's Stinky House." My debt to Gary Snyder is reflected in Strain 1999.

2. Along with numerous other efforts such as internship programs, problem-based learning, learning communities, collaborative learning projects, and faculty-student mentoring, I view service-learning as part of a broad-based movement to transform higher education that entails a reconceiving of faculty roles and faculty work.

3. Boyer's speech to the American Academy of Arts and Sciences (1995), "The Scholarship of Engagement," is cited in Cambridge 1999: 175.

4. *Academic Affairs Quarterly* is a DePaul University newsletter. For a public statement of this position, see also Meister 1998.

5. I owe the notion of "bridge" to my colleague Frida Kerner Furman (1989: 103-104, 113-114).

6. For a recent lament of our lack of recognition as a discipline, one tempered by a graceful irony, see Wentz 1999.

7. For the contemporary classic Western conception of practice, see MacIntyre 1984. On the connection in the Buddhist context of inner and outer transformation, see Thurman 1998. On socially engaged Buddhism's concept of a practice, see Kraft 1999.

8. For the most recent discussion of the selective university as an agent of inequality, see Reich 2000.

References

Boyer, Ernest L. (1990). *Scholarship Reconsidered: Priorities of the Professoriate.* Princeton, NJ: Carnegie Foundation for the Advancement of Teaching.

——— . (March 9, 1994). "Creating the New American College." *Chronicle of Higher Education:* A48.

Burd, Stephen, Patrick Healy, Kit Lively, and Christopher Shea. (June 4, 1996). "The Widening Gap in Higher Education: A Special Report." *Chronicle of Higher Education:* A10-A17.

Cambridge, Barbara L. (1999). "Effective Assessment: A Signal of Quality Citizenship." In *Colleges and Universities as Citizens,* edited by Robert G. Bringle, Richard Games, and Edward A. Malloy, pp. 173-192. Needham Heights, MA: Allyn & Bacon.

Furman, Frida Kerner. (1989). "The Prophetic Tradition and Social Transformation." In *Prophetic Visions and Economic Realities,* edited by Charles R. Strain, pp. 103-114. Grand Rapids, MI: William B. Eerdmans Publishing Co.

Holland, Barbara. (1997). "Analyzing Institutional Commitment to Service." *Michigan Journal of Community Service Learning* 4: 30-41.

——— . (1999). "From Murky to Meaningful: The Role of Mission in Institutional Change." In *Colleges and Universities as Citizens,* edited by Robert G. Bringle, Richard Games, and Edward A. Malloy, pp. 48-73. Needham Heights, MA: Allyn & Bacon.

Jencks, Christopher, and David Riesman. (1968). *The Academic Revolution.* Garden City, NY: Doubleday.

Kerr, Clark. (1991). *The Great Transformation in Higher Education: 1960-1980.* Albany, NY: State University of New York Press.

Kraft, Kenneth. (1989). *The Wheel of Engaged Buddhism: A New Map of the Path.* New York: Weatherhill.

MacIntyre, Alasdair. (1984). *On Virtue: A Study in Moral Theory.* Notre Dame, IN: University of Notre Dame Press.

Marsden, George. (1994). *The Soul of the American University.* New York: Oxford University Press.

Meister, Richard. (Spring 1996). "Expectations and Visions." *Academic Affairs Quarterly* (a publication of DePaul University): 1-3.

————— . (Fall 1998) "Engagement With Society at DePaul University." *Liberal Education*: 56-61.

Patterson, Barbara A.B. (November 1999). "Response to 'Creating the Engaged University.'" Presentation at the "A Future of Service" Conference, Boston, MA.

Reich, Robert. (September 15, 2000). "Selective Colleges Fuel Our Age of Inequality." *Chronicle of Higher Education*: B7-B10.

Snyder, Gary. (1980). *The Real Work: Interviews and Talks, 1964-1975*. New York: New Directions.

————— . (1990). *The Practice of the Wild*. San Francisco: North Point Press.

————— . (1995). *A Place in Space: Ethics, Aesthetics and Watersheds*. Washington, DC: Counterpoint.

————— . (1996). *Mountains and Rivers: Without End*. Washington, DC: Counterpoint.

Strain, Charles R. (1999). "The Pacific Buddha's Wild Practice: Gary Snyder's Environmental Ethic." In *American Buddhism: Methods and Findings in Recent Scholarship*, edited by Duncan Ryuken Williams and Christopher S. Queen, pp. 143-167. Richmond, Eng.: Curzon Press.

Thurman, Robert. (1998). *Inner Revolution: Life, Liberty and the Pursuit of Real Happiness*. New York: River Bend Books.

Wentz, Richard E. (October 1, 1999). "The Hidden Discipline of Religious Studies." *Chronicle of Higher Education*: A72.

Making Meaning: Reflections on Community, Service, and Learning

by Keith Morton

Community Service in Context

We could begin a discussion about the relationship between service-learning and the study of religion at many places, but I would like to focus here on the relationship between service-learning and the ways in which students make meaning. As a number of thoughtful scholars have observed, we have a reasonably adequate language for describing stages of cognitive, moral, and faith development in young college students (Chickering and Associates 1981; Fowler 1995; Gilligan 1982; Kohlberg and Turiel 1971; Parks 1986; Perry 1970). Recently, however, Sharon Daloz Parks and some of her colleagues, notably Laurent Parks Daloz and Jim and Cheryl Keen (Daloz et al. 1996), have posed the question, What goes on in between the moments or plateaus we call "stages"? That is, what happens as someone moves from relativism to committed relativism, from committed relativism to faith? I would like to describe here something of what I think happens in these "in between" spaces and times.

I am primarily a cultural historian and storyteller and thus would like to ground my analysis in three types of stories and then attempt to draw them together. The first stories are brief sketches of the lives of Jane Addams and Dorothy Day, the second ones are stories based upon my experience and interviews with a number of people about their understanding of community and service, and the final stories are drawn from the experiences of students with whom I have worked. My use of stories is deliberate and related to what I think service can introduce into scholarship: It is an attempt to work from the particular to the general; it is an attempt to suspend judgment and leave room for paradox, mystery, and contradiction; it is an attempt to establish a link between the ways in which I believe people make meaning — through stories — and their lived experience; and finally, it is an

Much of this chapter was originally prepared for a presentation at "A Future of Service: A National Conference on Service-Learning in Theology/Religious Studies," November 18, 1999. I wish to thank Joe Favazza and Michael McLain for their invitation and assistance.

argument that we might usefully see service as a "text," written concurrently with a course.

I want to place Addams's and Day's lives in context by noting that the phrase *community service* does not appear in American English vernacular until the late 1930s or early 1940s, despite work (much of it school based) that looks like what we would now call service-learning.[1] Where does this phrase, this work, come from?

My guess is that *community service* appeared in common language precisely at that moment when people could feel their sense of organic community — the densely layered place of roots and histories and relationships — shifting profoundly. Such a sense of community gave way to a logic of the marketplace, where people were defined by their individual roles as consumers and public problems were increasingly treated as challenges for individual consumption. Between 1910 and 1945, the economy was transformed from one in which the primary problem was how to provide enough for everyone into one in which the problem was how to consume the surplus that was produced. People experience life as increasingly fragmented when perceived gaps between values and work, work and family, family and public life, grow. The thought I want to develop here is that the idea of community service represents an attempt — vestigial or not — to hang on to, or experience, or create, an authentic experience of community at that moment when people sense it is slipping away. In other words, people come to community service, in part, seeking a transformed understanding of themselves and the world they inhabit through experiences that will help them to make a whole out of a fragmented life.

Service as Charity or Project: The Stories of Addams and Day

Jane Addams and Dorothy Day[2] are the founders, in 1889 and 1933, respectively, of Hull House, a settlement in Chicago, and the Catholic Worker, a "house of hospitality" in New York City. While each of their stories is complicated and the women differ profoundly from each other, what is striking is that they each created a new institution that has become an archetype for the places in which some of our students now serve, and that they created these institutions as ways to reknit what they perceived as deeply fragmented lives.

Addams, attempting to deal with the reality of large-scale urban poverty, helped invent the multiservice community center, social work, and the nonprofit organization; she contributed greatly to sociology, to the theory and practice of community-based action research. Day invented, in the Catholic Worker, an intentional community of voluntary poverty that offered hospitality to anyone who asked for it and practiced a politics of witness: speaking truth to power. She combined direct service and political activism around a core of personal integrity for more than 50 years, profoundly influencing generations of people, including Daniel Berrigan and Robert Coles.[3] I want to explore how Addams and Day came to their work, consider what their decisions meant to them, and ask how their experiences inform my and/or my students' experiences today.

In her semiautobiographical *Twenty Years at Hull House,* Addams describes an inner and outer journey from college graduation to the founding of Hull House that took her eight years to complete, eight years of indecision and wandering, punctuated by periods of debilitating physical, mental, and spiritual struggle (Addams 1910: 61). At the end of this period, Addams decided to escape what she later termed the "snare of preparation" and act. "It was not until years afterward," she wrote, "that I came upon Tolstoi's phrase, 'the snare of preparation,' which he insists we spread before the feet of young people, hopelessly entangling them in a curious inactivity at the very period of life when they are longing to construct the world anew and to conform it to their own ideals" (1910: 74). She decided to step into the leading problems of the age and experience them firsthand, not as a dilettante but as someone committed to living the problems and being constantly aware of the suffering they caused. Twenty years later, she recalled:

> *I had made up my mind that next day, whatever happened, I would begin to carry out my plan, if only by talking about it. I can well recall the stumbling and uncertainty with which I finally set it forth. I told it in the fear of that most disheartening experience which is so apt to afflict our most cherished plans when they are at last divulged, when we suddenly feel that there is nothing there to talk about, and as the golden dream slips through our fingers we are left to wonder at our own fatuous belief. (1910: 73-74)*

What is most striking is the degree to which Addams's resolution was framed as a response to a single moment in her life, an experience she carried with her as a metaphor around which she composed her life. Early in her journey, she visited a poor section of East London and witnessed "two huge masses of ill-clad people clamoring" for food. A man's hand reached up and caught a cabbage, and Addams watched him devour it. She describes him in language that makes it clear she understands that the man has been reduced to a feral, animal state. Her vision turned back to the mob, and her "final impression was not of ragged, tawdry clothing, nor of pinched and sallow faces, but of myriads of hands, empty, pathetic, nerveless, and workworn, showing white in the uncertain light of the street and clutching forward for food which was already unfit to eat" (1910: 62).

How does one respond to an image so powerful that it calls into question the integrity of every other element in one's life? "I have never since been able to see a number of hands held upward," Addams confessed near- ly 30 years after the experience, "without a certain revival of this memory, a clutching at the heart reminiscent of the despair and resentment which seized me then" (1910: 62). This vision of the hands animates her subsequent decisions, becomes a metaphor for what is making a moral claim on her, and makes it a subjective necessity that she create something like the settle- ment as a way of making herself whole again.

The particulars are different for Dorothy Day.[4] Her childhood was com- plicated and hard. As a young adult, she lived a bohemian life in New York as a writer, suffered an abortion, was divorced, had a friend die in her arms of a heroin overdose, and had a child as an unmarried mother, among other experiences. In 1923-24, following a period of deep depression and perhaps as an attempt to write herself into wholeness, she wrote and published an autobiographical novel, *The Eleventh Virgin* (Day 1924), describing many of her travails. It was a modest success, and she moved to Staten Island with her lover, Forster. They had a daughter together, and Day, marginally a Protestant and practically a nonbeliever, determined to have her daughter baptized a Catholic. This decision cost her Forster, an atheist and anarchist. She con- verted to Catholicism at the age of 31 and three years later, in 1933, found- ed the Catholic Worker with Peter Maurin. As different from Hull House as the Catholic Worker was and is, Day's purpose in inventing it, I would argue, was much as Addams's had been: to find a life of integrity through a com- munity consistent with her emergent spiritual values, one that integrated all the vocations she had tried: writer, journalist, nurse, activist, mother. It gave her a loving and platonic relationship with Maurin, and it literally allowed her, I would argue, to pull herself together.

Yet another dimension of these stories speaks powerfully to us in the present: Addams and Day offered up sharp and powerful critiques of chari- ty. Addams, who anguished over what she referred to as "the charitable rela- tion," claimed that "there is no point of contact in our modern experience which reveals more clearly the lack of that equality which democracy implies" (1899: 163). "The very need and existence of charity," she cautioned, "deny us the consolation and freedom which democracy will at last give" (1899: 163). Charitable activity, in other words, grows in inverse proportion to genuine democracy. Hull House was not an experiment in human services but an experiment in democracy. Day said it more bluntly: "In our youth our hearts burned with the desire for justice and were revolted at the idea of doled-out charity. The word *charity* had become something to gag over, some- thing to shudder at" (1952: 87). She did not know then, she continued, that she would come to define her life by her attempt to know "the true meaning of the word" (1952: 87).

How can care for others, or *caritas,* become something inimical to democracy, something to gag over? How did Day and Addams come to choose lives of service when they held these powerful concerns? What does this mean? It suggests that the economy and institutions of modern American culture, which have centralized power to an enormous degree, were felt to be inimical to democracy. The new inequalities created the conditions that necessitated, in Addams's view, human service organizations and the institutionalization of caring through new professions such as social work. In her houses of hospitality, Day explicitly rejected modern economic values and culture in favor of a radical embrace of persons and community.

Addams and Day usefully raise some questions for us who consider service to the community a dimension of our teaching: What would it be like to lead a life that is whole and integrated? What is the nature of suffering? What is meaningful work? What is faith? What does it mean to "walk humbly with God," Addams wondered in 1899,

> ... which may mean to walk for many dreary miles beside the lowliest of his creatures, not even in peace of mind that the companionship of the humble is popularly supposed to give, but rather with the pangs and misgivings to which the poor human understanding is subjected whenever it attempts to comprehend the meaning of life? (1899: 178)

Addams and Day also ask us, Where do I find belonging? How, as an educated outsider, can I be in a relationship with people whose life experiences are so different from mine? How can I find peace when I am conscious of injustice and conscious that I am implicated in that injustice? "We have all known the long loneliness," Day noted at the conclusion of one of her three autobiographies, "and we have learned that the only solution is love and that love comes with community" (1952: 286).

Service as Process: The Story of Bart Shaha and Bangladesh

I turn now to a story from my own life.[5] In September 1989, I was working as executive director of a YMCA in Minneapolis and in that capacity traveled to Bangladesh for training in community development. One of my teachers, Bart Shaha, director of the YMCA in Bangladesh, argued that all service has two fundamental dimensions: the quality (depth and continuity) of relationships and commitment to getting at the root causes of a problem. Bart's argument was that minimal commitment to either relationships or root causes was a definition of service as charity, middle commitment to either defined what he called *project approaches to service,* and a fully engaged commitment led to process or change. Bart argued for a linear understanding of these terms. The common argument is this: Give a man a fish and he eats for a day — charity; teach him to fish and he eats for a lifetime — project. Not quite, Bart argued, especially in Bangladesh. Who owns the pond, the stream, the shoreline? How do you get access to the fish? Process. Consider drinking water, he invited us: If you are thirsty, I give you a glass of water, but I control the resource and determine who will get it. This is charity. A coalition of churches looked at the same problem of water in Bangladesh and determined that access to potable water would likely reduce infant mortality and improve the health of millions of people. They planned their program carefully, developed an appropriate technology, raised funds, and launched a multiyear effort to dig 80,000 tube wells throughout Bangladesh. Forty thousand wells into the project, they discovered an unintended side effect: The landowners in rural areas (most of them absentee) were now able to grow a third rice crop. The landowners got richer while the peasants worked harder for virtually no increase in income. Economic inequality was increased in a country where, at the time, a peasant earned perhaps $60 per year. Bart argued, "There are always unintended consequences. It never works when you try to fix something for someone else." This is the fundamental insight of the mythic community and labor organizer Saul Alinsky, who established an Iron Rule of organizing: "Never do for someone else what they can do for themselves" (Rogers 1990: 15).[6]

I tell this story not to make Bart's case but to suggest that this linear perspective — charity to project to process — is a dominant motif in the literature of community service. It suggests that our goal as teachers is to move our students along this continuum. For a number of years, this is what I taught my students. In turn, many of them kept telling me that, while they understood Bart, he wasn't describing their lived experience. When I asked one young woman what the most important thing was in her experience tutoring at a nearby elementary school (a place with 750 students from 40 countries in a building designed for 450 and where statistically only 250 would go on to graduate from high school), she said, "Susan [a fourth grader] remembers my name and is glad to see me." I responded in a predictable way: It's important for you to think about root causes, to think about why Susan needs you in the first place. "I understand what you are saying," she responded. "But what is important right now is that she likes me." Slowly, and thanks to their patience, I began to hear what my students were telling me, and I came to an alternative description of service. We might still usefully understand service as charity, project, or process, but it might be that these forms of service are paradigms or worldviews: deeply internalized beliefs about human nature, the nature of reality, the meaning of life. The point here is that any one of these types of service, when done with enough integrity and courage, can be transformational. Allow me to explain what I mean by way of an image.

As I have discussed this problem with students, colleagues, and community partners over the last five years, I have arrived at an image of the forms of service as "thin" or "thick." Thin forms of service have little or no integrity; that is, they diminish the dignity of one or more of the persons involved. Thick forms of service have deep integrity; that is, they affirm or increase the dignity of everyone involved. As an attempt to differentiate the charity, project, and process paradigms of service, it is helpful to summarize the "thick" forms of each. (See the table on the next page.)

This description has three purposes. First, I have been thinking about Bart's story of service for 10 years, and it still demands my attention. It is what John Dewey called a "problem": not something bad needing to be fixed but a perplexity demanding my attention until such time as I have answered it satisfactorily. The question *what is service?* is, for me, a life-shaping perplexity. Second, it suggests how much care we must take in choosing the story or stories that we tell about service. And, finally, I believe the story speaks to us as educators: What does success look like? Is it that my students move from charity to change? Or is it that they — and I — find greater integrity and depth in the work that we claim as ours?

Service as Making Meaning: Students' Stories

How do students make meaning of their service? Consider what it is like for a student reading Jonathan Kozol's *Savage Inequalities* to realize that only three in seven of the fourth graders she is coaching in an after-school program will graduate from high school. She expects the poverty she encounters to be overt — angry, abused children in an ugly, decrepit school. Instead, the parents of these children care for them; the school building looks pretty good to the casual eye; the children and teachers are, for the most part, nice. How can this observed information be reconciled with the school's dismal performance statistics, she asks. She becomes interested in the politics of school budgets — this school spends slightly more than half what her school at home spends per student — and begins to understand the role of property taxes. She also begins to appreciate, for the first time, what Langston Hughes meant when he asked, "What happens to a dream deferred. . . . Does it dry up like a raisin in the sun . . . or does it explode?"[7]

Another student working in a Providence school reports that a teacher yells at the kids all the time. I convince her to ask the teacher, whom I trust, why she yells. The teacher tells her, "In this culture, that's how I let a child know that I see him, that I care about him. It's not like the place where you grew up." Does this mean, the student wants to know, that it's alright to yell at children? Her perplexity is a study in the limits of relativism.

A third student does his internship one summer supervising a commu-

Paradigms of Service

	Charity	Project	Process/Change
Focus	Individual (person, self), "private"	Individual, mediating institution	Public, collective
Form	Being fully present to another person	Helping someone to define and achieve a goal	Organizing individuals to have and use power; collective action in "public" settings
Time	Time is cyclic; "hope is out of time"	Time is incremental, bounded	Time is historic; "stepping into a river of history"
Expression	Knows the essence of another person's reality; aims to cross/dissolve the boundaries that separate persons	Respects boundaries that differentiate server and served in order to maintain the dignity of both	Differentiates public and private; focuses on public; organizes around (1) common values and (2) self-interest (self among others); uses creative conflict among differing interests
Effect	Change of circumstances not a necessary or even sought-after outcome; to experience wholeness of relationship	Change is incremental: sharing and development of skills that should ensure access to resources sought	Seeks change in balance of power — and so in the institutions that organize power; longer-term goal punctuated by shorter-term, strategic goals
Community served by	Affirmation of persons' place in it	Increased equality of opportunity for members	Accomplishing strategic goals and increasing ability of the oppressed to exercise power
Examples	Dorothy Day	Jane Addams	Bart Shaha

nity garden project: A large vacant lot has been transformed by a neighborhood coalition into a 10,000-square-foot organic garden, run as a small business by six high school students, two of whose parents are from Cambodia, two of whose parents are from Laos, two African-American. Three of the gardeners are also in or on the edges of gangs, and their "boys" like to come and play basketball next to the garden or sit and watch the gardeners work, teasing them none too gently. The college student is white, and the jokes are often about "working the fields for the man." The college student learns to defuse conflict, learns to talk with the gardeners about drug use and selling, learns to be in a relationship with the gardeners even as he opposes some of what they are involved in. A city boy, he also discovers in the garden an ecological and spiritual metaphor that captures for him the essence of interdependence; he becomes committed to principles of sustainability. He now lives simply and works for an urban land trust, directing a city farm and running youth education programs.

Another student works for four years at a local community center. In a class I teach on the history of service, she helps gut and rehab a 110-year-old workers' cottage in a neighborhood near the school. In one semester, we raise $10,000, recruit 100 volunteers, and put in another $10,000 of sweat equity. We research the history of the house, of the street, of all the families who have lived there, where the surnames have changed from Irish to Eastern European to Southeast Asian to Hispanic. She is one of several students who continues coming back over the summer so that we can complete the project. A family moves in, renting from the local community development corporation with an option to buy. Domestic abuse forces the mother and daughter to leave the house, suddenly. A couple of months later, the student from our class graduates and purchases the house. When she moves in, all of the neighborhood children she has known from the community center come and help her dig a flower garden. Like Addams and Day, this student is finding for herself a way to live an integrated life.

I suppose one could say these are success stories. They describe young people committed to relationships and places and community. They are about people who are finding ways to make lives for themselves and take risks in order to pursue what they believe gives their lives meaning. They describe people who have what I would call vibrant and searching spiritual lives.

The institute in which I teach at Providence College offers a major in public and community service. We have graduated three classes and an average of 15 majors per class per year. For all of this "success," one of the most difficult things I participate in with my students is their feeling of being set apart from families and friends as they claim their identities. One student, a junior responsible for a group of first-year college students serving at a local community center, talks poignantly about race and class and identity:

> *Two of the students in my group have skipped their service a couple of times and I called them on it. They have people counting on them at the site, and call 10 minutes beforehand to say they have to study. They don't care about the site or the people there; they think it's enough that they have good intentions; they don't have a work ethic. And they are angry at me for holding them accountable. I know I'm doing the right thing [a question in her voice] but it's hard. . . . I'm struggling with self-confidence and I'm finding it hard to stand up to them.*

And they struggle with relationships: Another student recently described being at a local shelter, serving a meal. The lunch crush was over, and they had served some 200 meals. One of the guests came up to her and asked for a second helping of something. She gave it to him. The head cook came out, angry, telling her and the guest loudly that they both knew seconds were in violation of the rules. "If someone asks for something and I can give it to him," she says, "I'll give it to him. I know it's breaking the rule, but I'll do it again." This sparks a lively argument in class: Do you follow the rules as a relative newcomer, even if you think they are wrong? How do you strike a balance between the anarchic hospitality of a Catholic Worker and the structure of a human service organization? The incident also causes the student to begin reflecting on the assumptions and values she was expressing, exploring some of the ways in which they could set her apart.

It is common, too, for students in our major, who by their choice have publicly claimed an identity of service, to report how much it confuses their relationships with peers and parents. "They say things to me," one of these students reports after a visit home over a weekend, "like, 'she wants to help the poor,' and they wag their fingers in quotes around 'the poor' and roll their eyes." She describes prodding her mother to volunteer and her mother's resistance. "I'm sure you think I'm not a good person because I don't," her mother said. Perhaps, we wonder, it is not so much that she needs her mother to volunteer as it is that she wants her mother's understanding and affirmation of the journey she has undertaken.

Conclusion: Service and Knowing

I tell these three types of stories — Addams and Day, Bart Shaha, the students (and implicitly a fourth, about my ongoing transformation) — because they illustrate both what I see happening between the "stages" of moral and intellectual development and the role of service in education. Service-learning can be an experience that offers an opportunity for the integration of knowledge and the integration of knowledge with values and vocation; it is an experience grounded in relationships with others. To borrow Parker Palmer's language (1998: 106), service and service-learning offer us an opportunity to "dance" between objective and subjective ways of knowing. While it is not only service that can do this, service offers one important way to raise to the surface fundamental values and beliefs and understandings about reality. It can offer an experience of community, in the experience itself or with peers similarly engaged, that gives permission and opportunity to create new knowledge and to test the limits of that knowledge. These are, as I understand them, opportunities to find out, as Lawrence Kohlberg and others have subsequently asked, whether I am loved, whether I will have meaningful work, and what I believe to be the foundation on which the world rests. In short, community service and service-learning are ways of knowing, ways of making meaning. In their "thick" forms, they can transform a life from relativism to committed relativism to faith. To borrow the language of religious historian William Clebsch, they are attempts to "be at home in the universe" (1973: 187).

Notes

1. For example, a wonderful book written by Paul Hanna in 1936 is about students from 600 high schools who combine service with learning. But the phrase *community service* never appears in the book.

2. For a fuller version of this argument, see Morton and Saltmarsh 1997a.

3. A fascinating and revealing account of Berrigan and Coles meeting, useful for understanding their subsequent work, is Berrigan and Coles 1971. See also Coles 1987 and Coles 1993, the latter of which is dedicated to the memory of Dorothy Day.

4. Most of this argument was first developed in Morton and Saltmarsh 1997b.

5. This story and argument are described more fully in Morton 1995.

6. It is this rule that informs Kretzmann and McKnight's (1997) current ideas about asset-based community development.

7. Jonathan Kozol cites this poem in his introduction to *Savage Inequalities: Children in America's Schools,* a text used in class with this student. See also Rampersad 1994: 426.

References

Addams, Jane. (1899). "The Subtle Problems of Charity." *Atlantic Monthly* 83(496): 163-178.

———. (1910, 1981). *Twenty Years at Hull House.* New York: Macmillan.

Alinsky, Saul. (1989). *Rules for Radicals: A Practical Primer for Realistic Radicals.* New York: Vintage Books.

Berrigan, Daniel, and Robert Coles. (1971). *The Geography of Faith: Conversations Between Daniel Berrigan When Underground and Robert Coles.* Boston: Beacon Press.

Chickering, Arthur, and Associates. (1981). *The Modern American College.* San Francisco: Jossey-Bass.

Clebsch, William. (1973). *American Religious Thought: A History.* Chicago: University of Chicago Press.

Coles, Robert. (1987). *Dorothy Day: A Radical Devotion.* Reading, MA: Addison-Wesley.

————. (1993). *The Call of Service: A Witness to Idealism.* New York: Houghton-Mifflin.

Daloz, Laurent A. Parks, et al. (1996). *Common Fire: Lives of Commitment in a Complex World.* Boston: Beacon Press.

Day, Dorothy. (1924). *The Eleventh Virgin.* New York: Albert and Charles Boni.

————. (1952, 1981). *The Long Loneliness.* San Francisco: Harper Collins.

Fowler, James W. (1995). *Stages of Faith: The Psychology of Human Development and the Quest for Meaning.* San Francisco: Harper San Francisco.

Gilligan, Carol. (1982). *In a Different Voice: Psychological Theory and Women's Development.* Cambridge, MA: Harvard University Press.

Hanna, Paul R., and Research Staff. (1936). *Youth Serves the Community.* New York: Appleton-Century.

Kohlberg, Lawrence, and Elliot Turiel. (1971). "Moral Development and Moral Education." In *Psychology and Educational Practice,* edited by G.S. Lesser, pp. 410-465. New York: Scott Foresman.

Kozol, Jonathan. (1994). *Savage Inequalities: Children in America's Schools.* New York: Harper Perennial.

Kretzmann, John P., and John McKnight. (1997). *Building Communities From the Inside Out: A Path Toward Finding and Mobilizing a Community's Assets.* Chicago: Assisting Christians To Act Publications.

Morton, Keith. (Fall 1995). "The Irony of Service: Charity, Project, and Social Change in Service Learning." *Michigan Journal of Community Service Learning* 2: 19-32.

————, and John Saltmarsh. (Fall 1997a). "Addams, Dewey, and Day: The Emergence of Community Service in America, 1885-Present." *Michigan Journal of Community Service Learning* 4: 137-149.

————. (October 1997b). "A Cultural Context for Understanding Dorothy Day's Social and Political Thought." Proceedings of the Dorothy Day Centenary Conference, Marquette University, WI.

Palmer, Parker. (1998). *The Courage to Teach: Exploring the Inner Landscape of a Teacher's Life.* San Francisco: Jossey-Bass.

Parks, Sharon. (1986). *The Critical Years: The Young Adult Search for a Faith to Live By.* San Francisco: Harper & Row.

Perry, William. (1970). *Forms of Intellectual and Ethical Development in the College Years: A Schema.* New York: Holt, Rinehart & Winston.

Rampersad, Arnold, ed. (1994). *The Collected Poems of Langston Hughes.* New York: Vintage.

Rogers, Mary Beth. (1990). *Cold Anger: A Story of Faith and Power Politics.* Denton, TX: University of North Texas Press.

On En/Countering the Other[1]

by Elizabeth M. Bounds, Barbara A.B. Patterson, and Tina Pippin

> *Without practice there's no knowledge. (Paulo Freire, cited in Horton and Freire 1990: 98)*

Tina Pippin: In the dictionary definition, *encounter* has negative connotations of brief, unexpected, and sometimes hostile or contentious meetings. All who work in service-learning know the contexts in which such "encounters" take place: where the meeting is one of shaky acknowledgment of difference. *Encountering* is perhaps an apt word for meeting *the other*; there is always a risk, an unknown in connecting the classroom theory with lived practice in an organization. Connections often succeed, but they can also fray or fizzle. There is always something "counter" in service-learning as we cross the space of the unknown and encounter the difference and distance of the others.

Bobbi Patterson: My first service-learning experience was in divinity school. I have sharp memories of early lectures and exercises meant to help us begin to identify and engage cross-cultural differences. It was very useful and necessary work. But even then, I kept wondering why we were not talking about how odd this course was in the midst of my Ivy League education. I felt as alien in this course as I felt in my work with the students of South Boston High. I developed a mantra to help me: "The *other* is also us." My mantra guided me through my service and learning, but it also helped me begin to realize how "other" service-learning was in the academy.

Many publications about service-learning continue the tradition I experienced. When we speak of the *other*, we focus on the different knowledges, languages, and practices within our partnering communities.[2] The good news is that we are genuinely trying to attend to this crucial dynamic in experiential learning. But usually, we spend more time analyzing these "identified others" through language and methodologies we know such as feminism, postmodernism, and postcolonialism. We have colonized them rhetorically and epistemologically.

Service-learning or experience-based learning begins in conversations, with storytelling, sharing ideas and fears, and exploring possibilities for individual and communal change. This paper represents our conversations over the past several months. As teachers at a research-based university and a small liberal arts college, we discussed the ways we encountered the *other* in community placements, in our students, in our academic institutions, and in ourselves.

Liz Bounds: Acknowledging the need to engage with "others," those who are not like us, is a key starting place in thinking about the pedagogy of experiential learning or service-learning. For many of us and for many of our students, it is a new recognition, an acknowledgment that the world is larger and more complex than we assumed. And for a liberal, democratic, multicultural society such as our own, the challenge of engaging others is central. Experienced-based education is a laboratory in which to practice these engagements, where the classroom setting provides a framework within which risks can be taken.

Yet engaging others has many levels. We — both our students and ourselves — move through processes of similarities and differences, mediated by structures in which we encounter others. In addition to simply identifying the "otherness" with which our classes engage, we need to interrogate the ways in which we construct the engagement, making sure we do not imagine ourselves and our universities as invisible or benign partners in the enterprise. The discussions of "othering" within literary criticism and anthropology have taught us that the focus on the *other* with no acknowledgment of the location of the *self* conceals the relationships of power that govern the interaction (Spivak 1988).

Tina: Is a concern for social justice and change possible for those of us who work within academic institutions? Is it possible to be an "activist educator" with tenure?

Making the Road by Walking: Engaging Students

Tina: If Myles Horton is right about how "we make the road by walking," then when learners walk back and forth from social justice experiences to the university, the university has to create new spaces for its own humanness to emerge. Horton explains the process:

> *The thing to do was just find a place, move in and start, and let it grow. . . . I just needed to have a vision and that I shouldn't know. You should let the situation develop. And of course you've got to use anything that you've learned in the process. (Horton and Freire 1990: 53)*

Paulo Freire tells of his own work as an activist educator: "We have more space outside the system, but we also can create the space inside of the subsystem or the schooling system in order to occupy the space" (Horton and Freire 1990: 203). For Horton and Freire, theory and knowledge are "always becoming" (1990: 101).

One often stated goal of service-learning is that it should be life changing. The professor helps students assimilate the experience through raised awareness and compassion. Experiences in and out of class are mediated through conversations between faculty and students. We build relationships with the "outside" so that these spaces become familiar. But we need to ask, Are we merely managing the strange, the foreign? How do we control the site/sight of the experience? What gives us the right to such control? What knowledge do we bring back to our campuses, and how do we manage that knowledge? At its best, service-learning allows space for a human face to be put on the *other*. Often this knowledge is counter to institutional forms of knowledge.

In their own way, institutions agree that service-learning should bring about personal change or individual transformation in our students. Their assumptions echo the ideology of certain mediation training groups that emphasize how we all are oppressed as the basis for personal change. In the institutional view, students are not activists, and learning should neither lead to activist work nor be conceived as a site of student protest or where activist professors decide the students' journeys and manipulate their encounters with the *other*.

In contrast to this model of learning, liberatory pedagogies provide important "counters," highlighting the ways our knowledge is institutionally structured. Students and teachers can pay attention to systemic power and begin to understand how knowledge is strictly regulated by forms and requirements and by the boundaries of academic terms. The People's Institute in New Orleans has an instructive definition linking the personal and the structural: Racism equals personal prejudice plus systemic/institutional power.

The possibilities for systemic change cannot be simply ignored. Another way of helping students access systemic understanding is to encourage them to construct their own knowledge based on their own encounters.[3] According to Maxine Greene, "Learners are asked consciously to impose . . . orders that defamiliarize (as literary works may do), that clarify, highlight, render problematic" their usual assumptions (1998: xxxix). Teachers, students, and community partners are all cosubjects, not only in the task of unveiling reality, and thereby coming to know it critically, but also in the task of re-creating knowledge and practice. As they attain this knowledge of reality through common reflection and action, they discover their shared possibilities for change. In this way, the presence of the oppressed in the struggle for liberation will be what it should be: not pseudoparticipation, but committed involvement.

In his discussion of *otherness* in a service-learning experience with the homeless in Washington, DC, and New York City, Robert Rhoads focuses on the importance of mutuality in such work: "Mutuality applied to an understanding of representation of otherness involves creating a mutual space and opportunity for the creation of diverse identities" (1997: 107).

Liz: Dealing with the other requires dealing with the self, interrogating the self's social location and the ways this location forms fractures and contradictions in the self's worldview. Such self-interrogation is always hard to do, especially when we are doing service-learning. Embedded in the idea of service is often an impoverished idea of charity, of a gift given from a superior position to one in an inferior position that validates the moral worthiness of the giver and the moral unworthiness of the recipient. Ruth Smith helpfully sums up this dynamic within the modern Christian discourse on poverty and charity:

> *It is worthy to give to the poor to entrust them with your soul, and the poor have nothing of spiritual worth to give; the poor are of value only if they can fulfill middle-class spiritual needs, and the middle classes are of value only if they can feel superior. (Smith 1989: 73)*

When service-learning is understood within this discourse, the recipient is constructed as an *other* and defined by the characteristics of his or her need. Joan Tronto remarks that "those who receive care are often transformed into the 'other,' and identified by whatever marks them as needing care: their economic plight, their seeming physical disability, and so forth" (Tronto 1994: 145). In our culture, with its stress on independence, any form of dependency marks failure. And for those who offer help, the moral distance from those identified as dependent reinforces our own worthiness.

In working with both public university students and private seminary students, I have detected this self-positioning, which enables the "servers" to resist looking at their position and to continue to view the "servee" through their own interests. Sharon Parks helps clarify this attitude in her study of Harvard Business School students. She found that they saw ethical questions as issues of interpersonal morality to be satisfied in their private relations, from personal ties to some forms of volunteering. They were rarely able to look at ethical issues embedded in the structures of the careers and institutions for which they were preparing; they tended "to separate the 'how' by which success is generated from an ethic of care for a wider public" (Piper, Gentile, and Parks 1993: 30). Such a split between private and public, morality and institution, enables an innocence about one's own location and participation (which is actually not innocent at all, but what Tronto so accurately calls *privileged irresponsibility*) (1994: 121). Parks remarks that she finds this divided mind-set a "signal that these young adults have been upwardly mobile in a culture that is both individualistic and pluralistic . . . in a context in which articulating the full substance of one's value commitments might create tensions that would inhibit the upward flow of success" (Piper, Gentile, and Parks 1993: 25).

The underside of our success-oriented culture is "a culture of charity that normalizes destitution and legitimates personal generosity as a response to major social and economic dislocation" (Poppendieck 1998: 5).

The Site/Sight of Meeting: Engaging the University

Tina: The economics of academic systems (for example, those funded by megamultinationals such as Coca-Cola) supports personal change in students that will help them and their professors become better institutional citizens. But, ideally in this economics, the university (and the multinational) are left unscathed. Institutions are right to be suspicious of any pedagogy that is open to such change. The change in each student is different, the change in each professor is different and changes with each class, and change in the institution is always a possibility. There is the possibility for personal change, but the institution is also at risk.

The university has been known as the *ivory tower,* separated and disengaged from the issues and dilemmas of society, but experience-based education can provide windows or doors leading out into the world (the Internet, distance education, community service). Work with the community can be dangerous, but as long as it is contained on the outside, the university's interest can remain unchallenged. When students encounter structural injustice on the outside, the risk is fivefold: (1) that the *other* will be invited onto campus, breaching the wall in a real sense; (2) then more people will have knowledge of structural injustice; (3) perhaps leading to a connection of students wanting to organize around those who know how to create new structures; (4) which may impact the university's own being in the world, its economics, its ideology of corporate power; and (5) illuminate the existence of the *other* who dwells also on our own campuses and is in our midst (in workers' rights, in gender equity, in all institutional *isms*).

Some colleges define service-learning and other types of experiential learning as *community outreach* that helps market the college to the community while doing some good by enlisting volunteers for worthwhile causes in the process. *Outreach* implies there is an *inreach,* but of course the *other* is not "in" our camp or within our gates. Service-learning is where the *other* is met. Most academic institutions see this learning as off campus, at a site different from the university, so that students can experience the "real world." But the myth that the "customers" want a four-year break from reality can become strained. Student protests over just the last 30 years provide evidence of how students make connections with justice issues globally (e.g., Vietnam, South Africa, sweatshops) and locally (racism, sexism).

One recent example of making connections is the Students Against Sweat movement (connected with the National Labor Coalition). Both large universities and small colleges have experienced student protests against institutional complicity with goods made in Third World sweatshops (mostly by women workers). The result of this activism has been to create "anti-sweat" documents holding accountable the academic institution and the companies. Students attend national and international conferences, travel to worker sites in the Third World, bring workers to appear at conferences in the United States, and push for full disclosure. In these activist discourses, the universities involved have resisted change. Freire proclaims that "a capitalist-based educational system can never be truly liberatory," but there can be visions of a just, democratic society (Shor and Freire 1987).

Bobbi: The number of ethnic, minority, and international peoples on our campuses is growing daily. Added to them are disabled, lesbian, gay, and bisexual persons — all now "in the house." We have made accommodations or provisions for them, often in the form of "centers." Certainly, these centers create visibility, budgets, and a safe space for self-expression and advocacy. But they also isolate; they work against integration where and when it is desired by members of various communities. The *identified others* are given space, but they may not be very liberated.

It is easier to talk about and even with such others. We have developed a way to save our epistemology and language while feeling that we are open to others in our midst. But most of those others actually are not here. The opposite can be true of service-learning and some other types of experiential learning. The academy is their natal home, and they have the potential to dramatically shift the furniture through their transforming and liberating knowledges and practices about teaching and contributing to the common good. They are the unspoken, unrecognized, unidentified *others* in the house, and this dynamic of non- and misrecognition has serious effects on the advocacy and implementation of such learning in our schools.

If institutional responsiveness to the *identified other* is talked about beyond its "centers," it often is in the service of a larger goal such as fundraising, reporting to a dean's council of alumni, or presenting the "nice" contributions of our schools to the media. But discussion at the service of such goals is not genuine discussion. Service-learning becomes a tool, not a living organism in itself. To speak of it on its own terms would be to open ourselves to the realities included in this pedagogy. This is fearful because service-learning, as mentioned above, anticipates not just change in ideas but change in reality, change in our community.

Interestingly, even the prestigious, effective, and progressive service-learning programs are often housed in a "center." Again, there are positive organizational and budgetary elements to this. But the isolation that comes with most "centers" signifies that experiential education, including its subset service-learning, is also an *other* — an *other* that was born and raised right in our midst, fed through the umbilical cord of our own mission to teach and, in the United States, to contribute to the common good.

Liz: To interrogate the university requires some attention to just what universities do. We need to be aware that we participate in the formation and assimilation of persons into modern capitalist society. It is vital to realize that more than two-thirds of all current jobs being created are in the information and knowledge sector:

> *An advanced corporate economy requires the production of high levels of technical/administrative knowledge because of national and international economic competition, and to become more sophisticated in the maximization of opportunities for economic expansion, for communicative and cultural control and rationalization, and so forth. (Apple 1995: 100; see also Sasson 1998)*

Our students understand very well that they stand in the midst of such an economy, quickly developing into a dual market — college educated at one end, low-wage service at the other.

Many of us, of course, understand our work as far removed from these abstract economic structures. But we need to analyze simultaneously the context in which we teach and the skills and processes we promote. The goals of experience-based education are not the same at, for example, Georgia Tech and Emory University, as each positions its students for different places in management. At the most prestigious universities, resources, both human and material, have been put into programs that provide research and services for the corporate elite. Indeed, on most campuses the resources devoted to such programs would dwarf the resources that go to programs devoted to grappling with the problems of impoverished rural or urban communities, even if those are the very problems facing the communities where those institutions are themselves located and where many of their support and custodial staff live.

Within our classrooms, discourses of specialization, professionalization, and consumerism are dominant among both faculty and students. Universities easily accept professional, technical, and even civic knowledge, but resist political knowledge. Thus, it is very acceptable to talk about the pragmatic value of experiential work, something students translate into competitive advantage in the job market. And it is also acceptable to present experiential work as promoting citizenship, a sense of obligation toward others unlike oneself. But it is much more challenging to ask students to learn politics — why some have resources and some do not, how communities negotiate their needs, how to work with others toward solving seemingly intractable social problems. Such political capital can be engaged in any religious community if we understand how to look, ask, and act. Doing this is the only way to begin to escape from the deadly dualism of self and other.

Interrogating Ourselves as Faculty

Bobbi: Service-learning always has the possibility to deconstruct the status quo, internally as well as externally. So it can become threatening to think about teaching and learning as participatory, as evolving and transformative, as less concerned about — even rejecting of — traditional classroom hierarchies. To begin to question some of the foundational dimensions of traditional teaching is part of service-learning's dynamic. It is not satisfied with knowledge deposited and then regurgitated.

Hence, externally, we try to control this in-house *other* by keeping it "centered" and by silencing its reconstructive potential. Internally, we control our anxiety or rage by calling service-learning trendy, loose, touchy-feely, a cover for a liberal agenda. We hope to recover our balance for rigor and theory by reminding advocates of this approach that students do not have knowledge, professors do. Certainly, there are institutional issues at stake, but before we can get to those, we need to look at what is at stake for our self-image as teachers. How might our reactions to service-learning reveal fears about *otherness* in ourselves? Can we do something other than be afraid, angry, or resistant?

All types of experiential learning, but especially service-learning, challenge the way we have been disciplined as faculty, and it can be very threatening to act against or beyond this disciplining. In the Theory Practice Learning Program at Emory, we are trying to think together about this question. One response has been to create small conversation/study groups that meet regularly. We call them Colleague Groups; they are composed of faculty and graduate students who want to learn about experiential education and service-learning and simply to be together to think and feel through the use of these pedagogies. As emerging kinship groups, they have been willing to talk about the risks they feel in trying to practice service-learning. Early on, the discussion turned to our own idealized hopes and self-images as teachers. Some had hoped that their teaching would reflect current issues and needs, but found themselves rarely able to do that. Some realized how deeply they were bound to traditional notions of a "real professor." It felt entirely too risky to leave those notions behind, because doing so would be to abandon a central self-image.

Others raised a different set of themes, describing how, even when using traditional modes of teaching, they felt vulnerable in the classroom. Classroom teaching is risky even when controlled. To take on more vulnerability, as service-learning classes require, put some professors on too much of an edge. The idea of taking that vulnerability into local communities was even more disturbing. They had no training for that, no resources, and certainly there were no serious rewards for this kind of activity from the administration. Moreover, we became aware of the unfinished business inside ourselves about racism, classism, ethnocentrism, sexism, and homophobia. We also discussed the difficulties of student resistance. If we were not prepared and supported, how could they be? Though we all realized that service-learning could be joyous and intellectually and morally passionate, we also understood that it could be hurtful, angry, and upsetting.

Although not all participants were that open, those who were helped us begin to explore the *otherness* inside ourselves that was a source of fear and resistance. Part of us was ready to commit to some type of experiential learning. Part of us was not, and, aside from these few Colleague Groups, there was no place to begin to face and deal with that fear and anxiety in a safe, resourced, and supportive place.[4] All of us were well aware of the institution's expectations and accountabilities. But we had not been so aware of the more internal issues looming larger than we knew.

There were other fears, more external but still in house, that hindered our endorsements of experience-based pedagogies. Some colleagues considered and named these pedagogies stupid and a waste of time better devoted to research. How would we deal with the accusation of misspent time and energy, since many faculty are not aware of the ways in which research and experiential learning can converge?[5] Furthermore, were we even prepared to include the formerly excluded, denied, marginal *other* — from our own campus and beyond — in the academic heartland of research? And how could we do that with genuine reciprocity and appropriate respect? We were realizing what Paulo Freire so often says: These pedagogies are fundamentally about shifting values and perspectives for liberation.

Even on the level of individual classes, we had realized that reciprocal relationships with our community partners destabilized existent statuses of power and authority. But this destabilization was also necessary for transformative creativity. One would be foolish, notes Freire, if he or she believed these concerns were "abstraction[s]" (Shor and Freire 1987: 55). They are not, and they engender real consequences: loss of promotion, loss of funding, loss of tenable publication topics, and loss of power and prestige. Beginning to talk about this silenced *other* in the house is not easy, but it was crucial if we were to move on.[6]

Learning to Question

Liz, Bobbi, Tina: Perhaps what we have said has seemed to have little to do with courses in religious studies and theology. Our academic area seems so marginalized that we cannot possibly be part of the reproduction of an oppressive structure. Our courses, located within humanities and liberal arts programs, are minor to the curriculum. And, beyond this, service-learning employs languages such as those of service and theory/practice that are themselves marginalized within the dominant liberal arts tradition. Nevertheless, we need to grasp our location as contradictory: both marginalized and powerful. When we are interacting with external communities, we need to recognize that our schools have a material presence in those communities — as employers, landlords, taxpayers, providers of services, educators. That presence creates a lens through which the *others* we encounter understand us. Furthermore, institutional power and prestige create a lens through which we understand ourselves, fearing losing privilege, status, and standing among our colleagues.

Through our conversations, many questions have emerged. We have discovered they can be roughly grouped into four categories: (1) understanding the university context; (2) assessing the university-community relationship; (3) analyzing classroom practices; and (4) interrogating ourselves as teachers. Asking these questions helped us identify more clearly what forms of knowledge could be incorporated within our academic institutions and what forms are actively resisted. We must become more sensitive to the nuances of resistance.

• *Category 1:* What kind of academic institution am I part of (mission, size, type, location, etc.)? What are the funding structures of the institution, and how do the institution's investment history and future affect its ethical commitment, locally and globally? What is the institutional investment in different types of experience-based learning? What are the institutional constraints, boundaries, and barriers? How does my academic institution view the purpose of my particular courses?

• *Category 2:* What, if any, are the deep, long-term relationships between the university and the community? Are any of these relationships with the *other* — the poor, the survivor-victim, the convicted criminal, anyone who would be excluded for whatever reason from ever attending the university? How might these relationships shape the community group's perceptions of my institution? Of me? The students? How have I negotiated my relationship with this group? Have they been part of my planning process? What is my stake and goal in this? How do I see my role? Have I begun to restructure my understanding of learning to include ongoing community partnership as essential?

• *Category 3:* How do I view the purpose of my courses? What kinds of knowledge do I want my students to produce during these experiences? What kinds of knowledge do I hope community persons will produce? What are the intersections of these knowledges? Are there conflicts? What needs are being served? Whose needs are they? How do my students understand themselves in relation to the community and its members? What would a transformative experiential education program look like — that is, one based on a radical democratic model (such as participatory action research)?

• *Category* 4: Have I learned to take full advantage of the insights of academic and community critics of service-learning as we implement this pedagogy? What does the teacher need to be doing to be open, continue in the process of personal and professional growth, and take risks in crossing (institutional) boundaries? Am I aware of my biases and blindnesses? Do I know about the "fearful" places in the curriculum I have designed? How have I dealt with these places?

As we have discussed these questions with each other, we have realized how easy it is to be limited by our everyday programmatic needs. Being in dialogue has helped us to go deeper by asking each other the harder, riskier questions about our journeys as teachers and learners.[7] Antonio Faundez reminds us that real knowledge lies in questioning:

> *I would want to stress that education as it is consists generally in finding answers rather than asking questions. An education that consists in asking questions is, however, the only education which is creative and capable of stimulating people's capacity to experience surprise, to respond to their surprise and solve their real fundamental existential problems. It is knowledge itself. (Freire and Faundez 1989: 40)*

It is this element of surprise that challenges and sustains us.

Notes

1. In this paper we are presenting the mainstream understanding of encountering the *other* in various placements off campus (internships, practicums, extended volunteer work sessions, seminary contextual education) and are also pushing the standard definitions to ask what these encounters have to do with systemic, not only personal, social change. Our basic understanding fits with our commitment to the tenets of liberatory pedagogies — that the starting point in educational discourse is the sharing of knowledge, especially the knowledge of the oppressed (Horton and Freire 1990: 55). Theorists who have influenced our understanding of the *other* are Benhabib, Freire, hooks, Horton, Levinas, Shor, and Spivack. This dialogue is influenced by the different locations we have experienced: a small private religiously affiliated college for women, a large public state university, a small private liberal arts college, and a seminary within a midsize private university.

2. Some important materials include Harkavy and Puckett 1995; Harrison and Hopkins 1967; Jensen and Kolb 1994; Palmer 1987.

3. Robert Rhoads asks several questions of students involved in his service-learning experiences. Two of them are these: What have you learned about yourself through your participation in community service in general? What have you learned about others through our participation? (1997: 108).

4. Harry Boyte remarks that "service does little to connect students' everyday concerns with the political process. . . . Volunteers usually disavow concern with larger policy questions, seeing service as an alternative to politics" (1991: 766).

5. Pema Chodron, in her book *When Things Fall Apart* (1997), talks about the necessity of facing one's fear as directly and thoroughly as possible. She also emphasizes the importance of a community, or *shanga,* that can provide supportive listening and teaching, and offer suggestions.

6. There are a number of resources addressing this issue, but one of the classics is the National Society for Internships and Experiential Education's publication of material from a Wingspread conference in 1991, *Research Agenda for Combining Service and Learning in the 1990s* (Wingspread 1991). Although this booklet focuses on researching service-learning itself, the research design and methods are good models for thinking about the potentials of service-learning courses and any research project.

7. At Emory, one strategy we have developed, among others, is the creation of a *metalanguage: meta,* because it lies between the languages, perceptions, and actualities of experiential learning and the more traditional languages, perceptions, and actualities of academic teaching; and *language,* because much of what we do in the academy depends on language, not only to literally convey ideas but also to indicate sources of meaning and power and ways of thinking. Our metalanguage in Theory Practice Learning is helping us build connections where they have not been and share the story with those who have been confused, hesitant, or oppositional. From these bridges, we hope to create a form of service-learning whose actions, ways of thinking, and language are deeply interwoven with Emory. We turned to our community partners to help us develop our metalanguage and reimagine our pedagogy.

References

Apple, Michael. (1995). "Cultural Capital and Official Knowledge." In *Higher Education Under Fire: Politics, Economics, and the Crisis of the Humanities,* edited by Michael Berube and Cary Nelson, pp. 91-107. New York: Routledge.

Boyte, Harry. (June 1991). "Community Service and Civic Education." *Phi Delta Kappan:* 765-767.

Chodron, Pema. (1997). *When Things Fall Apart: Heart Advice for Difficult Times.* San Francisco: Shambala Publications.

Freire, Paulo, and Antonio Faundez. (1989). *Learning to Question: A Pedagogy of Liberation.* New York: Continuum.

Greene, Maxine. (1998). "Introduction: Teaching for Social Justice." In *Teaching for Social Justice,* edited by William Ayers, Jean Ann Hunt, and Therese Quinn, pp. xxvii-xlvi. New York: Teachers College Press.

Harkavy, Ira, and John Puckett. (Summer 1995). "Lessons From Hull House for the Contemporary Urban University." *Service:* 9-20.

Harrison, Roger, and Richard L. Hopkins. (1967). "The Design of Cross-Cultural Training: An Alternative to the University Model." *Journal of Applied Behavioral Science* 34: 431-460.

Horton, Myles, and Paulo Freire. (1990). *We Make the Road by Walking: Conversations on Education and Social Change,* edited by Brenda Bell, John Gaventa, and John Peters. Philadelphia: Temple University Press.

Jensen, Peter, and David Kolb. (1994). "Learning and Development." In *Perspectives in Experiential Learning: Prelude to a Global Conversation About Learning,* edited by Morris T. Keeton, pp. 80-112. Chicago: Council for Adult and Experiential Learning.

Kolb, David A. (1984). *Experiential Learning: Experience as the Source of Learning and Development.* Englewood Cliffs, NJ: Prentice-Hall.

Palmer, Parker. (September-October 1987). "Community, Conflict, and Ways of Knowing: Ways to Deepen Our Educational Agenda." *Change* 19(5): 20-25.

Piper, Thomas, Mary Gentile, and Sharon Daloz Parks. (1993). *Can Ethics Be Taught? Perspectives, Challenges, and Approaches at Harvard Business School.* Cambridge, MA: Harvard Business School.

Poppendieck, Janet. (1998). *Sweet Charity? Emergency Food and the End of Entitlement.* New York: Penguin Books.

Rhoads, Robert A. (1997). *Community Service and Higher Learning: Explorations of the Caring Self.* Albany, NY: State University of New York Press.

Sasson, Saskia. (1998). *Globalization and Its Discontents.* New York: New Press.

Shor, Ira, and Paulo Freire. (1987). *A Pedagogy for Liberation: Dialogues on Transforming Education.* New York: Bergin & Garvey.

Smith, Ruth. (1999). "Decentering Poverty." In *Welfare Policy: Feminist Critiques,* edited by Elizabeth Bounds, Pamela Brubaker, and Mary Hobgood, pp. 60-76. Cleveland, OH: Pilgrim Press.

Spivak, Gayatri Chakravorty. (1988). "Can the Subaltern Speak?" In *Marxism and the Interpretation of Culture,* edited by Cary Nelson and Lawrence Grossberg, pp. 271-313. Urbana, IL: University of Illinois Press.

Tronto, Joan. (1994). *Moral Boundaries: A Political Argument for an Ethics of Care.* New York: Routledge.

Wingspread Conference. (1991). *Research Agenda for Combining Service and Learning in the 1990s.* Raleigh, NC: National Society for Internships and Experiential Education.

Service-Learning and Community Partnerships:
Curricula of Mutuality

by Peter M. Antoci and Sandra K. Smith Speck

Service-Learning Curricula

An increasing number of students, faculty, and administrators are having discussions about the nature of the engaged institution (VanDer Werf 1999), the scholarship of service (Boyer 1987), and service-learning (Kellogg Commission 1999). Often, these conversations include some concern about the last of these: service-learning. Certainly, the notion that higher education provides a vital public service is neither radical nor novel. So why does the integration of service into the learning experience cause consternation among some faculty members and administrators? Is this just a function of institutional lethargy and aversion to change? Assuredly, one encounters these in any bureaucracy. It would seem, however, that if service-learning's advocates want to claim a distinctive value for this approach, they must clarify and articulate its particular contribution to achieving the ideal of an engaged institution. For even though the majority of institutions of higher education are officially committed to the public good, that commitment alone does not guarantee that faculty and administrators will appreciate the value of service-learning as one important means to that end. The discipline of religious studies, which explicitly considers historical answers to questions about the public good and the means to achieve it, is uniquely positioned to offer thoughtful reflection on the public good and the promise of a service pedagogy to prompt such reflection.

A beginning point for advocates of service-learning is to show how it coheres with the mission and history of higher education. The late Ernest Boyer traced this history (1987). He characterized it as a movement from a scholarship of vocation in the Middle Ages to a scholarship of discovery in the centuries following the Enlightenment. In the former type of scholarship, universities tied learning to society's demand for a trained cadre of elite practitioners in the law, medicine, and the church. In the latter type, universities tied learning to the goals of what is usually called "pure research." Along the way, other social needs began to be integrated into the mission and activities of higher education as it sought to serve the public good.

In America, we have seen several phases in the effort to connect the university with the public good. The earliest institutions of higher learning in

America defined their mission as one of ministerial preparation; a literate and articulate clergy was the goal. In the late 18th century, institutions of higher learning began to frame their mission in response to the nation's desire to have an informed and educated, albeit restricted, electorate. By the mid-19th century, new institutions began organizing learning around the agricultural needs of society. Thus, the land-grant system of public colleges was born. By the mid-20th century, higher education was increasingly called upon to supply research for the security needs of modern America. Service-learning is a pedagogy that builds upon this heritage of addressing the public good.

The Engaged University and Its Public

According to the February 1999 Kellogg Commission on the Future of State and Land-Grant Universities, an engaged institution is one that has redesigned its teaching, research, and service functions to be ever more productively involved with its community. The report, however, allows that an institution has great latitude in defining who constitutes that community. It would seem that an understanding of just who constitutes an institution's public and how that public can best be served is crucial in determining the nature of institutional engagement.

Answers to this question are often implicit, escaping thoughtful consideration. Depending upon one's niche in the academy, one may define the public served as one's students or as registered students or as alumni. Some may define their service responsibilities with regard to the institution, peers, or the administration; others seek to fulfill their responsibilities through service to a faith community or an immediate geographic community or specific units of civil society such as the city, county, state, or nation. Thus, we find not only a variety of opinions about the nature of the public good but also very concrete differences of opinion about the identity of the public to be served. Since there is nothing novel in the notion that the academy serves the public good and since service-learning clearly falls within this tradition, perhaps resistance to it stems in part from a general confusion over who the academy's public is.

It is critical that religious studies professors attend to this issue as they develop curricula that integrate service into their pedagogy. A promising place to begin is with the mission statement of one's institution. Examining such a statement is a useful exercise in discovering how that institution defines its public. Since, moreover, the rhetoric of self-definition often invokes the language of sectarian or civil religion — or a mixture of both — religious studies faculty can historically situate such discourse and subject it to critical analysis.

Whether one's institution grounds its mission in the vision of a humane society or virtuous individuals or some other ideal, the way in which it identifies its public may very well determine how it values both the scholarship of service and community-based "interdependent" learning. Indeed, the latter notion, which will be explored more fully below, complicates the entire discussion by suggesting that community agencies, integral to most forms of service and engagement, bring to the table their own missions and publics. Whether their missions and publics and those of their academic partners clash or blend will depend largely upon the character and frequency of the collaborative efforts between them.

Ideally, service-learning should lie at the place where the mutual interests and reciprocal hopes of the academy and the community intersect. Both the learning and the service facilitated by service-learning should take into account the learning and service goals of both community partners and faculty/students. Indeed, to do so well is the particular challenge of service-learning. Hence, one can identify it as a form of interdependent learning that brings into high relief the contours and distribution of cultural power; that is to say, where and with whom one reads, trains, studies, and reflects affects how and what one learns.

The Role of Religious Studies and Theology

Faculty members in religious studies and theology can assume a special responsibility for developing coherent service-learning curricula and make a unique contribution in offering such courses. It is no secret that good service-learning experiences provide opportunities not only for solid research and relevant service but also for focused reflection on the integration of study and service. Throughout history, the religious experience and reflective traditions of human cultures have traditionally provided individuals and communities with such opportunities for reflective service. Religious studies faculty are uniquely equipped to contribute to discussions of human and humane values, both of which are at stake in a quality service-learning experience. Such faculty can introduce and suggest a variety of cultural and epistemological responses to questions concerning human good, qualifications for community membership, and meaningful personal identity (for meaningful identity, see Boyer 1987). They can also help students become acquainted with a variety of historical and cultural responses to the question, What is the purpose of my life and work?

Interdependent Learning

As the academy begins to move from a 19th-century scholarship of discovery to a 21st-century scholarship of service, service-learning is demonstrating the vitality of learning that is derived from the interdependent experiences of learners, whether they be faculty, students, or community partners (Boyer 1987). Since the academy is increasingly being called upon to demonstrate its relevance to the community, faculty are being challenged not only to respond but also to recast their traditional roles (Fairweather 1996; Rothman 1998). For example, engaged teaching and learning, by their very nature, resist attempts to compartmentalize the three traditional forms of faculty work as discrete activities. If the point of teaching, research, and service — indeed the point of higher education in general — is to create and promote learning experiences (Krahenbuhl 1998), should this not be done in as effective and efficient a manner as possible? And do not such considerations lead naturally to service-learning? How else can the academy focus not only on knowledge generation and teaching but also on expanding its public and helping to provide appropriate direct services (VanDer Werf, 1999)?

But for service-learning to make such a contribution, it is critical that all involved appreciate what makes it distinctive. As a subset of experiential or field-based learning, service-learning is not a new pedagogy; what is unique to its practice — and especially suitable to the task at hand — is its insistence on the equal rights and responsibilities of students and clients, the academy, and the community (Ayers and Ray 1996). Indeed, one of its primary goals is the creation of what has been called *interdependent learning relationships* (Boyer 1987).

The way in which partnerships between the academy and community groups are constructed reveals much about how colleges and universities understand their educational mission and identify who qualifies as a learner and who may benefit from learning. When community partners are engaged in the teaching enterprise, the sense and locus of agency, for both individuals and institutions, can be radically challenged. It may very well be that service-learning as a teaching method has the greatest capacity among current pedagogies to foster interdependent learning. Normative notions of difference enshrined in our social understandings of service can, and should, be challenged by substantive collaborations with community partners. In fact, participants' own sense of agency should be transformed by these experiences as the discrete identities of student, teacher, and community member become diffused, blurred, and ever more contingent.

The importance of religious and theological reflection for interdependent learning is obvious. Cultural understandings of service are deeply shaped by religious institutions and theological assumptions. Religious ways of construing the *other* can only be understood by appreciating the historical circumstances out of which such constructions arise. Judgments about their adventitiousness require a thorough knowledge of the social origins and changing interpretations of a particular religion. If a key challenge for the academy is to avoid perpetuating traditional, patronizing experiences of charity or more contemporary experiences of giver-receiver codependencies in the context of service, the discipline of religious studies is well equipped to provide intellectual guidance and resources to help meet this challenge (Boyer 1987).

If there is to be a partnership between the academy and community in a manner that is directly related to learning, it would seem that this partnership necessarily needs to be mutual, reciprocal, and interdependent. This, in turn, will require both flexibility and creativity on everyone's part, but particularly on the part of faculty and especially among those trained to understand the dynamics of meaning making within social groups. Since a community partner may become the locus and voice of *otherness* — socially, economically, and culturally — within curricula planning, the significance of *otherness* for and its analysis in religious studies make this discipline an important ally for those who would promote interdependent learning through a pedagogy of service.

In summary, through service-learning religious studies faculty can help higher education institutions come to respect the unique contribution to student learning that community partners bring to the educational enterprise. Indeed, without such respect, community partners themselves may fail to appreciate the key role they play in facilitating deep and potentially transformative student experiences. The figure on the next page represents a model developed by one institution to graph the interactions and relationships of all participants engaged in its service-learning effort. Development and utilization of conceptual tools such as this can help to ensure that all members of a partnership understand and value each other's unique contribution to their common work.

References

Ayers, George E., and David B. Ray, eds. (1996). *Service-Learning: Listening to Different Voices*. Fairfax, VA: The College Fund/UNCF.

Boyer, Ernest L. (1987). *College: The Undergraduate Experience in America*. Princeton, NJ: The Carnegie Foundation for the Advancement of Teaching.

Service Learning Guiding Model

Central Tenets of Model's Vision:

- Relationship is central to this model. This implies mutual respect from all parties and a concerted, intentional effort to do no harm.

- We all community members. Agencies, faculty and students are all life-long learners. As such, we share a common journey, preparing, serving (each other), and reflecting on our experience of mutual service. We seek transformative learning experiences, ones that challenge all stereotypes and other impediments that get in the way of true relationship.

- Faculty are important mentors in this model and as such, are necessarily engaged in the service experiences with agencies, community members, and students.

- The characteristics of Jesuit Vision of Education (James A. Donahue, S.J.) document the connection between service-learning at Loyola College in Maryland and the college's mission. In particular:
    - a commitment to developing in students [all learners] a "taste for the other" and a sense of justice
    - the belief that theirs ought to be a life of service to [with] others
    - a commitment to the education of leaders, those who will occupy positions of power and influence in the world in all walks of life through whose everyday action in the world the life of faith might find concrete expression.

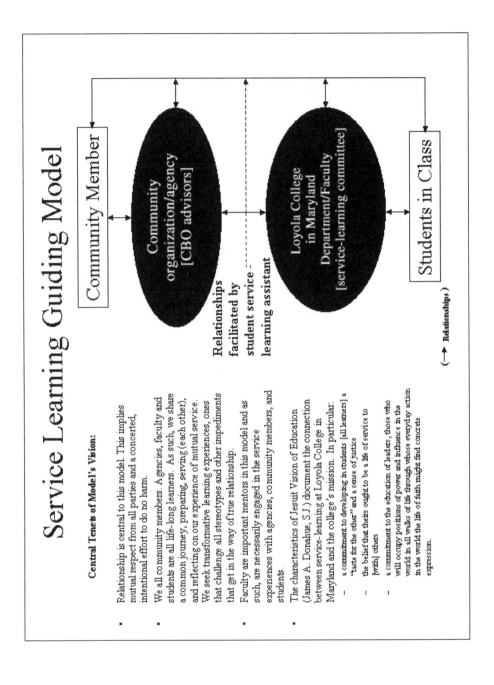

Community Member

Community organization/agency [CBO advisors]

Relationships facilitated by student service-learning assistant

Loyola College in Maryland Department/Faculty [service-learning committee]

Students in Class

(→ Relationships)

Fairweather, James S. (1996). *Faculty Work and Public Trust: Restoring the Value of Teaching and Public Service in American Academic Life.* Needham Heights, MA: Allyn & Bacon.

Kellogg Commission on the Future of State and Land-Grant Universities. (1999). *Returning to Our Roots: The Engaged Institution.* Washington, DC: National Association of State Universities and Land-Grant Colleges.

Krahenbuhl, Gary S. (November-December 1998). "Faculty Work: Integrating Responsibilities and Institutional Needs." *Change* 30(6): 18-25.

Rothman, Michael, ed. (1998). *Service Matters: Engaging Higher Education in the Renewal of America's Communities and American Democracy.* Providence, RI: Campus Compact.

VanDer Werf, Martin. (April 30, 1999). "Urban Universities Try New Ways to Reach Out to Communities." *Chronicle of Higher Education:* 37-38.

Expanding the Horizon of Engagement:
Pioneering Work at the University of Denver

by M. Elizabeth Blissman

In an ecological age, the university must expand its horizon of engagement beyond the social to include the wider ecological context. In order to respond adequately to a context that is not only social but also ecological, higher education needs what Happel and Walter refer to as *creative imagination*:

> *Creative imagination is the supreme faculty of moral humanity. Through it persons perceive the possible that is latent in the actual but that would be unseen by any less exalted consciousness. Because the process of moral decision making is not just a process of passing judgement on the goodness or badness of persons or of the rightness and wrongness of actions, moral thinking at its best must perceive values that do not yet exist and must bring them into being through productive acts. (1986: 68)*

Specifically, those of us working to expand and enact Boyer's concept of a scholarship of engagement (1990) must recognize that this scholarship and this service both take place within a complex *ecosocial context*. Ecosocial context refers to a societal context that also includes attention to the ecosystem(s) in which a society exists. Social context as most often referred to — i.e., without regard to bioregion or the ecological ramifications of human activity — is simply not adequate to the many challenges students, community members, and scholars must currently confront. Given phenomena such as environmental racism and the extinction of whole groups of both human and animal life, it is now appropriate to add the prefix *eco* to any discussion of social context or social location.

Support for such a step also comes from current scientific knowledge regarding the origins of the universe. We are the first generation of humans to live with the concept of an emergent universe, i.e., the realization that all matter in the universe was created out of a singularity commonly referred to as the Big Bang. Based on this view of cosmogenesis, Ruether notes "both earth science and astrophysics give us extraordinary and powerfully compelling messages about our kinship, not only with all living things on earth, but even with distant stars and galaxies" (1992: 48). Especially as scholars

---

This essay began as a panel response delivered at "A Future of Service: A National Conference on Service-Learning in Theology/Religious Studies," November 18, 1999.

(and sometimes even practitioners) of religion, do we have a moral obligation to explore this interconnection? As Harrison suggests:

> *Our theological and moral perspectives must accommodate the deepened
> sense of human interdependence that we gain when we place ourselves
> and our societies in an emergent ecological perspective. Such a perspective
> enables us to envision, more radically than ever before, our relationship to
> the full cosmos. We human beings and our societies are an interlocking and
> interdependent part of a wider environmental system. We no longer dare
> perceive nature merely as something inert, "out there," capable of whatev-
> er "use" we may choose to make of it. . . . To use a traditional ethical
> metaphor not usually extended to inanimate or nonhuman entities in ear-
> lier moral philosophy, our environment turns out to impose moral claims on
> us. (1985: 17)*

Hence, new moral insights are necessary at both religious and secular
institutions, as well as new opportunities for thinking and reflection that
allow us to articulate values that do not yet exist and invite them into being
through creative action.

At the University of Denver, three conceptual frameworks have been
used to move from a human-centered worldview to a broader view of an
ecosocial context. The first concept, *ecosocial location,* helps us each recognize
and understand our own normative frameworks. The second, *communicative
ethics,* suggests that moral decision making is more responsive to a complex
context when it is done across communities of difference. The final idea,
working alliances, puts forth the questions raised in other essays in this volume regarding mutuality and reciprocity, and underlies the importance of
evening out power differentials among participants in an alliance. At this
point, these frameworks are in early stages of development and have been
employed only at a single ecosocial location. Hence, these tools, which have
served as a starting point for reflection and action, need to be employed and
experimented with more broadly.

Ecosocial Location

One essential piece of a service-learning model that responds adequately to
an ecosocial context is sustained reflection on who one is and where one is
coming from in the effort to "stand with" those in community settings. Such
reflection should be part and parcel of any liberationist learning experience
(Spencer 1996). Scholar-activist Eleanor Haney develops this line of thinking
in the idea of ecosocial location, a tool for self-reflection. Haney reminds us
that "we are shaped by our participation in racial/ethnic, gender, sexual, age,
national, ability, and biological groups and geographic settings" (1998: 7).

Thus, each of us is simultaneously limited and enriched in our understandings relative to the cultures and institutions that have shaped us, or, rather, the location from which we speak, act, and think. Careful attention to one's ecosocial location helps, for example, those in the dominant culture resist the temptation to participate unconsciously in the racist and individualist legacies of the United States. It will be essential for those of us working with and in communities different from our own to have a thorough understanding of our own ecosocial location if we are to engage others in a sustainable manner.

Communicative Ethics

Sharon Welch, in her work exploring what she terms a "feminist ethic of risk," advocates intercultural dialogue as a way to expand intellectual and moral horizons. This dialogue leads to what Welch calls *communicative ethics*. Communicative ethics goes beyond the communal ethics supported by Stanley Hauerwas and Alistair MacIntyre, which argues that solid moral reasoning can occur only within a cohesive community with shared principles, norms, and mores. Instead, Welch argues "that material interaction between multiple communities with divergent principles, norms, and mores is essential for foundational moral critique" (1990: 124). Within such a system, moral discernment is a collective, historical process, with the goal being not merely consensus but mutual critique, leading to more adequate understandings of solidarity and justice.

Welch's theorizing does not go beyond the dialogue among human beings to address the challenge currently being presented by the biospheric community. Humans are an integral (and usually destructive) part of many biotic communities, but how is it possible to participate in communicative ethics with the other 99 percent of the species with which we share this planet? Can human beings speak for oppressed areas of the Earth without our own agendas getting in the way? Where might the arenas be located for biotic discourse to take place?

At the University of Denver Service Learning Program, opportunities for communicative ethics across human communities of difference have led to creative service-learning work. Both undergraduate and graduate students have tackled complex descriptive and normative projects addressing challenges such as environmental racism. These projects, however, have not been able to move beyond human communities to a dialogue that embraces the other species of life with which human beings share the bioregion. Welch does not address such complexities associated with communicative ethics, yet for this idea to be applicable in our complex ecosocial context, at least some of the questions raised above must be worked out. This is important for service-learning practitioners and other communities interested in ecosocial praxis.

Working Alliances

A final concept for moving into an ecosocial context emerges again from the work of Eleanor Haney, who proposes the concept of long-term alliances. Alliances are defined as "sustained commitments among groups and individuals to share experiences and insights, pain and rage, dreams and fears, and to engage in collective action for justice. Alliances create a larger power base for action than individual groups can offer" (1998: 2). Action through alliance building can be transformational as part of a service-learning program, because it emphasizes the necessity for those of us who experience both privilege and oppression to focus on more than our oppression. It puts us into conversation with other women and men whose history is more tilted toward victimization, survival, and resistance to not only social and economic injustice but even genocide. An example of the impact of these conversations can be seen where Haney shares self-reflection on how these interactions help Euro-American women:

1. Action through alliance building keeps us honest about the contours, or geography, of our own oppression and privilege, reminding us that we still live with a great deal of social power.

2. It helps us to clarify where our agendas both fit and do not fit with those of others, thus granting us even more opportunities and directions for change.

3. It helps us to focus on a broader base of support for specific goals and a more comprehensive understanding of social change.

4. It enables us to hear the experiences of the oppressed and develop better vision regarding oppression.

As Haney notes, alliances help "white" people to turn our gaze from outward (on the *other*: African Americans, the poor, Chicanos, lesbians and gay men, indigenous persons, etc.) to inward, asking ourselves, "Who are we, and how have we benefited from the disenfranchisement of others? Then we can ask, What must we do to challenge such unjust patterns?" (1998: 182). The act of alliance building thus shows promise as a tool to help persons recognize and act upon an interconnected worldview while shaping liberationist ecological ethics.

According to Haney, the call to alliance building involves much more than mere collaboration, or the coming together of groups and organizations with different, sometimes even conflicting, agendas around specific issues. Alliances go much deeper, and encompass four special characteristics: commitments to breaking down hostilities, addressing inequalities of power and unearned social advantages, creating a broader and more coherent challenge to oppression and violence, and setting the context and condition for faithful theological and ethical reflection.[1] At their best, alliances allow partners both to turn toward one another and stand together, facing structures of injustice in the larger society, for "the more marginal partners in the alliance articulate goals and needs and work with the more privileged partners to determine where they justly fit into those goals and needs. Together they work out an action plan for change" (1998: 14).

The concept of alliances gets a bit less clear when one examines the possibility of living in solidarity with the larger Earth community. However, Haney does model some approaches to living in such an alliance. She speaks to the need to pay attention to, listen to, and learn from nonhuman *others* as well as human *others*. This might take the form of appreciating plants and animals for their very being and not only for what they can provide to humans. Plants, animals, and the Earth itself are not just resources for human use, and Haney suggests that one's daily decisions about one's life and habitat should be made in relation to the lives and habitats of plants and other animals. Among other beings, Haney notes that "wolves, weeds, and spiders become part of the company of 'significant others' that shape my day-to-day existence" (1998: 115).

Conclusion

Through conceptual tools such as ecosocial location, communicative ethics, and long-term alliances, we are beginning to move toward an understanding of our ecosocial context. However, as was stated earlier, these tools are in their elementary stages. To meet the challenges of our ecosocial context, we need to experiment widely with these concepts while at the same time developing additional tools. Most important, we must begin to see the human community as only a part of the overall Earth community and examine how such a view changes and shapes the criteria with which we think, judge, and act.

Note

1. See pp. 11-15 of Haney 1998 for more detail on each of these four characteristics. It is worthy of note that Haney's concept of alliance building puts flesh on the skeleton of Welch's proposal of a communicative ethics and suggests how the communication in a model of communicative ethics could be achieved.

References

Boyer, Ernest L. (1990). *Scholarship Reconsidered: Priorities of the Professoriate*. Princeton, NJ: Carnegie Foundation for the Advancement of Teaching.

Haney, Eleanor H. (1998). *The Great Commandment*. Cleveland, OH: Pilgrim Press.

Happel, Stephen, and James Walter. (1986). *Conversion and Discipleship: A Christian Foundation for Ethic and Doctrine*. Philadelphia: Fortress Press.

Harrison, Beverly, with Carol Robb, eds. (1985). *Making the Connections*. Boston: Beacon Press.

Ruether, Rosemary Radford. (1992). *Gaia and God*. San Francisco: Harper.

Spencer, Daniel T. (1996). *Gay and Gaia: Ethics, Ecology and the Erotic*. Cleveland, OH: Pilgrim Press.

Welch, Sharon D. (1990). *A Feminist Ethic of Risk*. Minneapolis, MN: Fortress Press.

Toward an Assessment-Based Approach to Service-Learning Course Design

by Thomas G. McGowan

Service-learning may be defined as a pedagogical strategy that utilizes authentic community service[1] to enhance academic learning. The essays in this volume illustrate that there are different ways to design and implement successful service-learning courses in religious studies and theology. One of these is to follow a service-learning design logic based on principles of assessment. Several of the essays in this work were directly influenced by an assessment-based approach to service-learning, and I would like to present an overview of this approach in order to provide a context for interpreting these examples and their implications. I call this approach *assessment based* for the simple reason that it is based on an assessment of service-learning courses designed and taught by college professors. The assessment suggests that course-based service-learning is an effective pedagogical strategy but one that is difficult to implement due to its conceptual and logistical complexity. However, by following guidelines based on practices associated with successful outcomes, the likelihood of designing and implementing successful service-learning courses can be greatly improved. My goal in this essay is to describe the findings of the assessment I conducted and to summarize their implications for practice.

From Skepticism to Responsible Practice

Religious studies faculty members proposing to use service to advance curricular objectives are likely to encounter a wide range of responses from their colleagues and campus administrators. In my experience, these responses have ranged from unbridled enthusiasm to downright disdain, depending on one's experience and pedagogical leanings. Service-learning enthusiasts argue that service-learning is a win-win proposition that contributes to the common good and improves higher education by building student character and bridging the divide between town and gown (Howard 1998; Jacoby 1996; Kupiec 1993). Unfortunately, this argument is often advanced without careful consideration of the demands and concerns asso-

I would like to thank Alan Lummus for assisting me with the interviews completed in this study.

ciated with service-learning, and such an omission leaves many skeptical regarding service-learning's purpose and quality. Skeptics argue that few advocates can give a concise, clear definition of service-learning, and without a clear definition, how can service-learning be employed effectively? Some also question the type of "learning" provided by service and how, specifically, such learning is advanced through service activities. In some cases, skepticism takes the extreme form of an unequivocal rejection of service-learning on the grounds that it confounds academic learning and voluntarism, undermining the quality of the former while promoting the latter. Service-learning opponents typically argue that while community service and voluntarism promote student development, both are extracurricular activities and hence belong outside the classroom.[2]

These are some of the arguments I encountered when I first began practicing service-learning in the early 1990s, and they are prevalent still. A considerable degree of skepticism continues to surround service-learning in spite of a growing body of research evidencing its general effectiveness. Be this as it may, I nevertheless believe that service-learning practitioners must take the concerns of the skeptics seriously. Faculty members with experience in programming, grant making, or applied research are well aware of the importance of assessment and the evaluation of project outcomes. In such cases, assessment is required in order to ensure project quality and to improve practice by providing evaluative feedback. Similarly, we who practice service-learning have a responsibility to assess our efforts in order to ensure their quality.

Assessment, of course, has long been a consideration of educators and those concerned about the design and management of different pedagogical strategies. For their part, service-learning enthusiasts have been quick to cite studies that demonstrate service-learning's positive impacts on students. In the case of course-based service-learning in higher education, however, assessment has largely been outcome (student-impact) based with little attention paid to the evaluation of service-learning course design and implementation (Eyler and Giles 1999). It is, therefore, worthwhile to consider what might be learned from a process evaluation of course-based service-learning — an assessment that focuses on the design of service-learning courses and their implementation.

With this consideration in mind, I conducted an assessment of the design and implementation of service-learning courses at Rhodes College. My intention was to generate empirical data that could be used to ensure quality practice, thereby addressing the more substantive concerns of service-learning skeptics. By evaluating outcomes and analyzing the practices associated with particular outcomes, I sought to design an inductive, empirically grounded strategy for successful service-learning course design.

Service-Learning's Particular Relevance to Religious Studies

Before proceeding with a discussion of assessment-based guidelines for service-learning course design, it is important to ask why instructors and, in particular, religious studies instructors should even consider practicing service-learning. These volumes in AAHE's Series on Service-Learning in the Disciplines are rich in narrative accounts of the reasons why instructors have come to pursue this approach. The instructors I have interviewed at Rhodes have cited three main reasons for their pursuit of service-learning — reasons consistently found throughout the service-learning literature: (1) helping students to learn in a more holistic and engaged way, (2) making teaching more meaningful by combining it with activities that contribute to the common good, and (3) trying something different in the classroom in order to make teaching more interesting.

In addition to these generic reasons, I believe one key feature of service-learning also makes it uniquely appropriate for religious studies courses, especially in cases in which basic ontological questions such as *what does it mean to be human?* or *how ought I conduct myself in relation to others?* are relevant curricular concerns. Inherent in the structure of service-learning is the experience of a unique type of *otherness*. Encountering *otherness* requires students to experience something outside of their taken-for-granted world of everyday experience. By forcing students outside of their comfort zone, encounters with *otherness* often stimulate reflexive consideration of implicit presuppositions that are rarely resident to consciousness.

However, service-learning typically provides a rather unique experience of *otherness*. Service often involves encounters with people who are situated in a categorically different social and ontological situation, namely, a situation of need. Experiencing the ontological discrepancy between one's own position (a person not in need) and another's position (a person in need) challenges students on a variety of levels. Those of us who have placed students in soup kitchen serving lines or in programs working with underserved children have witnessed the difficulty students have reconciling the feelings produced by their encounters with ontological discrepancies. Such encounters challenge students in unexpected ways regarding the nature of their own existence, their taken-for-granted reality, and the profound discrepancy between their reality and the reality of those whom they serve. My students report experiences of guilt, embarrassment, awkwardness, frustration, and/or anger as a result of such encounters. Processing these experiences through a variety of means (for example, journaling, group discussion, or essay writing) helps students to appropriate course concepts and to utilize them to make sense of their experience.

The ontologically challenging experience that service provides creates a profound and fertile terrain for exploring a wide range of ontological, moral, ethical, spiritual, theological, and religious concerns. In one of my service-learning courses, students explore the significance of Gadamer's notion of "effective historical consciousness" by critically examining their ongoing interaction with homebound elder companions whom they visit and interview throughout the semester. Focusing on their interactive experiences, students are encouraged to describe statements or interactions through which they have become aware of their implicit projection of age-based assumptions. In other words, through service, students are able to experience the phenomenon of "effective historical consciousness" that Gadamer describes.

Religious studies instructors should be able to see how the ontological discrepancy inherent in many service experiences provides a fertile reference point for their own students' explorations. And when combined with sound design and assessment strategies, service-learning presents itself as an even more promising pedagogical strategy.

Assessment Findings

With the assistance of a colleague, I conducted in-depth interviews with 10 faculty members who had each taught a service-learning course at Rhodes during a particular academic year. The interviews were dialogic and open ended and followed themes deduced from the basic principles of assessment. The logic and purpose of assessment is to determine the extent to which project objectives are realized through practice. Such a rationale presupposes that objectives are made explicit during a project's design stage and that procedures have been established in order to achieve those objectives. In the case of service-learning, the logic of assessment presupposes the objective of facilitating or enhancing learning by way of service and the establishment of procedures for achieving this objective. This means that the key criteria for evaluating the quality of service-learning are (1) the conceptual link between the service and the learning and (2) the effectiveness of procedures designed to effect this connection through practice.

These basic assumptions anchored the 10 interviews. Each interview focused on the following question-themes and continued to the point of saturation:

1. What was the professor's working definition of *service-learning?*

2. Had a clear conceptual connection been drawn between curricular objectives and hypothetical service experiences?

3. Was the service activity feasible and effective in advancing learning?

4. What types of reflective activities were used to sustain the connection between service and learning throughout the semester?

5. What was the nature of the agency/service organization relationship, and how did it impact the quality of both service and learning?

6. Did service in fact advance the learning of course objectives?

As a group, the interviews evidenced definite patterns regarding the relationship between the structure of service-learning course design/implementation and the quality of outcomes. On the basis of the criterion that the service experience enhanced learning in an observable way, two of the 10 courses revealed themselves to be very successful, four to be successful, and four to be unsuccessful. The two very successful cases evidenced instructor mastery of what appear to be four key dimensions of effective, course-based service-learning: (1) conceptualization, (2) operationalization, (3) ongoing assessment, and (4) the structure of the agency/organization relationship. In four of the cases, service did advance learning objectives in observable ways, but in each of these, problems were encountered in one or more of the key dimensions, clearly limiting the degree to which the service could advance learning. In the remaining four cases, breakdowns occurred in one or more of the dimensions, rendering unsuccessful the attempt to advance learning through service. A detailed look at each of these dimensions will clarify their respective importance and their relationship to outcomes.

Conceptualization refers to the process of specifying the way in which course objectives will be advanced through different types of experiences. Successful conceptualization provides a clear answer to the question, How will the student's service experience enhance the learning of course material? The research illustrated that effective conceptualization is a crucial step in the process of successful service-learning course design. In two of the four unsuccessful cases, no clear connection had been established between course objectives and the types of experiences provided to students by way of their service activity. Lacking this clear connection, the service performed failed to provide a basis for learning and analyzing course material. In contrast, each of the successful cases had clearly established a conceptual connection between learning objectives and service. (For example, conducting soil studies for a nonprofit organization needing data for the preparation of a grant proposal provided an experience that allowed botany students to study the interconnectedness of ecosystems.)[3]

Operationalization refers to the identification and utilization of specific activities that provide the types of experiences conceptually associated with enhanced learning. In this way, operationalization ensures that the conceptual connection between experience and learning is achieved in practice. The evaluation study indicated that the most effective service activities were those that produced an intrinsic connection between learning and service. Such activities involved experiences that presupposed the learning of course material as a precondition of the experience itself. However, identifying service activities that facilitate learning as an intrinsic part of the service experience is difficult, and in most cases the connection established between learning and experience via the service activity had been established extrinsically. Extrinsic connections are those that require certain pedagogical activities, such as essay writing or journaling, in order to establish a clear and productive connection between the service activity and learning. Successful outcomes involving extrinsic connections were those in which the professor established reflective practices and sustained them systematically throughout the semester.

The assessment also indicated that when breakdowns occurred at the operational level, they typically occurred because of logistical problems associated with facilitating the service activity in a consistent manner. This suggests that the feasibility of service activities is an important dimension of effective service-learning. For example, the teacher of a course on racism conceptualized that bringing white students from a predominantly white college together with African-American students from a historically black college could provide an experience helpful in exploring communication issues associated with race. The specific activity identified was a series of cross-racial student dialogues that were to be held with the goal of producing dialogues that would then be performed as an educational program for the National Civil Rights Museum. This design was conceptually clear (it established a clear connection between course objectives and service experience), and the activity chosen had the potential of facilitating an intrinsic connection between service and learning through practice. However, facilitating the dialogue-building sessions proved infeasible due to logistical constraints and schedule conflicts. For this reason, the goal of advancing course objectives through the service activity was not met. In contrast, successful cases involved the use of predictably consistent service activities that provided students with the experiences that had been conceptually identified.

Ongoing assessment of the reflective practices used to establish extrinsic connections between service and learning also proved to be an important component of successful cases. For example, one professor used guided essay writing to facilitate analytical reflection on the meaning of basic service activities (for example, serving a meal at a soup kitchen) and the philosophical meaning of community service. These exercises proved highly effective in helping students to mine the value of their service experience for understanding one of their key course concepts. In contrast, the use of journaling in another case proved ineffective, because the journaling process lacked focus and the professor did not review the journals frequently enough to provide the students with feedback on the relationship between service and learning.

In addition to effective conceptualization, operationalization, and ongoing assessment, successful service-learning requires *an effective relationship* with the service agency or organization responsible for facilitating the service activity. In several cases, efforts to secure the commitment and consistent participation of the host organization broke down, obviating the use of service to advance learning. This emphasizes the importance of establishing a quality partnership based on dialogue and a clear understanding of respective interests and needs, and doing so well in advance of the scheduled beginning of the course.

Implications for Practice

The findings described above have been used to develop a workshop curriculum that assists faculty members at Rhodes College interested in teaching service-learning courses. The authors of the course chapters that follow in this volume were provided with aspects of that training curriculum to respond to in writing their course introductions. The workshop curriculum focuses on the key dimensions of service-learning and advances the following guidelines for practice:

• Conceptualization requires (1) specifying one's course objectives and (2) identifying experiences that will enhance the learning of course content.

• Operationalization requires (1) identifying a specific activity that provides students with the experiences conceptually associated with learning, (2) making sure the service activities are feasible and sustainable, and (3) implementing reflective practices to connect service and learning.

• Ongoing assessment requires (1) monitoring the quality of the service experience and (2) monitoring the reflective practices designed to effect an analytical connection between service and learning.

• Establishing an effective agency relationship involves (1) specifying one's needs regarding the agency's role in the service activity identified and (2) negotiating with the agency in a manner that ensures that the service activity will be authentic and will advance the interests of the agency, as well as meet course objectives.

In light of these considerations, I have compiled a list of questions that will prove helpful to faculty members interested in designing a service-learning course (see the list on the next page).

The guidelines presented above may be used to develop a work plan for religious studies faculty designing and implementing service-learning courses. As some of the essays in this volume demonstrate, considering these guidelines in advance allows one to address important design and logistical questions on the front end of service-learning course design, improving the likelihood that service will enhance learning in a demonstrable and coherent way. This is one way to take responsibility for the quality

Questions to Be Considered by Faculty Members Designing a Service-Learning Course

Conceptualization

- What are the key objectives of your course?
- Which of these objectives may be advanced by integrating service and learning?
- Can you identify experiences that will enhance learning and advance course objectives?

Operationalization

- Can you identify specific service activities that facilitate the experiences conceptually associated with learning? Are these activities likely to enhance learning and provide an authentic community service?
- Is the connection effected between service and learning intrinsic or extrinsic? If it is extrinsic, can you identify exercises that may be used to connect learning and service through reflective practice?

Ongoing Assessment

- What monitoring strategies might you use to ensure that the connection between service and learning is sustained? Ask yourself how you can determine whether the service activity is enhancing learning.
- How will you grade the service activity of your students?

Agency Relationship

- How will you identify a host agency and establish a partnership with it?
- What kind of supervision, monitoring, and documentation do you expect the agency to provide with regard to student activity?
- How will the service activity benefit the agency? Are you willing to modify your view of the service activity in order to accommodate the interests of the agency?

of our efforts and to rise above the skepticism some still associate with service-learning as a pedagogy.

Notes

1. *Authentic community service* is service that advances the interests and goals of community service organizations through tasks performed by students.

2. An important distinction must be made between *course-based* and *non-course-based* or *institutional* service-learning. Course-based service-learning involves the use of service as a course component in a way that advances specific course objectives. In this way, the student service activity provides an experiential reference point for learning specific course content and advancing curricular objectives. Institutional service-learning also involves service, but the service activity takes place without the support of a formalized curriculum. Instead, institutional service-learning typically involves informal reflective practices (for example, group discussion) that allow students to analyze the significance of their service for understanding social issues and other topics.

3. Activities connecting service and learning may take place inside or outside the classroom. Inside-the-classroom operations include briefings, discussions, presentations, exercises, and exams. Outside-the-classroom operations typically include journal writing, question-guided essays, research papers, and reports.

References

Eyler, Janet, and Dwight E. Giles, Jr. (1999). *Where's the Learning in Service-Learning?* San Francisco: Jossey-Bass.

Jacoby, Barbara, and Associates. (1996). *Service-Learning in Higher Education: Concepts and Practices.* San Francisco: Jossey-Bass.

Kupiec, Tamar Y., ed. (1993). *Rethinking Tradition: Integrating Service With Academic Study on College Campuses.* A publication of Campus Compact. Denver, CO: Education Commission of the States.

Rhoads, Robert A., and Jeffrey P.F. Howard, eds. (1998). *Academic Service-Learning: A Pedagogy of Action and Reflection.* New Directions for Teaching and Learning, no. 73. San Francisco: Jossey-Bass.

Service-Learning in an Introduction to Theology Course

by Robert Masson

Marquette University's Introduction to Theology: Theo 001 is part of the core program for all students at the university and is usually taken in the first or second year. Generally, 75 percent of the students in a section are freshmen. The course is offered every semester, and the average enrollment for a section is 38. In the fall 1999 semester I taught three sections, the following semester two, and for the first time I added a service-learning option. Students in my class must choose one of three experiential learning options. Hence, although service-learning is not required, all students in the class are involved in experiential projects with analogous tasks and equivalent assignments. About one-third of the students chose the service-learning option each semester. Since this is the first time service-learning has been made a component in one of the university's predominantly freshman core courses, I envision a secondary goal of the course as providing an introduction to service-learning itself. Because there are many upper-division courses at Marquette where students can continue this option, I am content that the service-learning component in my course be rather modest.

Why Add a Service-Learning Component?

There have been courses with a service-learning option at Marquette for many years. Since 1994, they have been supported by an outstanding, and funded, Service-Learning Program.[1] Many of the most time-consuming aspects of this sort of endeavor are ably handled by the program's administrative staff, assisted by a corps of about a dozen student coordinators. This office has developed and maintains relationships with an extensive network of community organizations. It provides orientations to service-learning for students and ensures that they have appropriate orientations at the sites where they serve. It coordinates student placements and troubleshoots when difficulties arise. Every year, it runs a workshop for faculty interested in service-learning, and the program administrator, Bobbi Timberlake, has put together a comprehensive faculty handbook. Over the course of each semester, the office also runs several workshops for students on topics such as working effectively in minority and multicultural communities. With that kind of institutional support, the question of whether to adopt service-learning hinges primarily on how well it suits a course's learning objectives and the teacher's pedagogical style.

Although I have taught variations of the first theology course for 25 years, I had been reluctant to introduce a service-learning option because I had assumed it would mean adding an additional component to the syllabus, analogous to units in colleagues' courses in Ethics, Peace and Justice, Family and Society, and Theology in Global Contexts. The syllabus for our introductory course already aims to do too much; even those colleagues who included service-learning in their upper-level courses did not offer the option in their sections of Theo 001.

The particular challenges of teaching an introduction to theology aimed at freshmen, especially in the first semester, reinforced my concern about adding something more to the course. A crucial and pervasive difficulty for many entering students is their passive learning style. Rote learning worked well for them in high school. Precisely because this had worked so well in the past, many are slow to catch on to our expectation in college of more active and engaged inquiry, in which they are responsible for generating their own questions and in which learning how and when to generate such questions is a central course objective. Memorization is secondary to analysis and argumentation. Understanding how one gets to conclusions is every bit as important as knowing those conclusions or recalling data. Unfortunately, this is a new agenda, even for many of the most promising students. The difficulty is further compounded by their too frequent assumption that theology is not much different from the sort of catechesis many received in their earlier religious education. From this, they have concluded that "classes" about religion do not require or reward questioning and active inquiry. All these difficulties are exacerbated by large sections. The numbers make individual engagement with students in class difficult and make such dialogue outside of class very time-consuming. Finally, the challenge is compounded still again by the difficulties that first exposure to more abstract kinds of analysis and concepts poses for many freshmen. Even those who can follow a nuanced argument often find genuinely appropriating such analysis and concepts a considerable challenge. Likewise, I think it is more difficult than we generally acknowledge to assess how well students have actually appropriated the skills and concepts to which we intend to introduce them.

Although these difficulties made me reluctant to add a service-learning component, they also led me to experiment with a number of pedagogical techniques aimed at encouraging and rewarding a more engaged style of learning in my classes. I had found especially helpful an approach to group discussion and analysis used in our freshman seminar, Introduction to Shared Inquiry.[2] I attended one of the service-learning program's annual faculty workshops, thinking that I might find some further ideas about how to introduce this shared inquiry methodology into my other classes, since big sections with a service-learning option face a similar challenge: How can a pedagogical strategy that works well in a seminar format be employed in larger classes, where effectively guiding individual student reflection is much more difficult and time-consuming? A presentation by Edward Zlotkowski, the general editor of this series, that included, among other things, an explanation of how he uses service-learning to teach Shakespeare's tragedies enabled me to conceive how service-learning also could be used both to achieve my course objectives in Introduction to Theology and to evaluate more accurately student achievement of those objectives. Most important, his example suggested a way to do this without adding a component that would require dropping something else and without creating a dual and quite separate track for service-learners.

Service-Learning and Course Objectives

As an introduction to theology in a Christian context and as the first of three courses in theology required by most colleges in the university, Theo 001 aims to introduce students to a basic theological vocabulary, key texts from the scriptures and history, some central questions and issues in the field, a few central figures, and a schematic outline of the "received" narrative.[3] We define the objective of the three-course sequence as basic theological literacy. As part of a larger core program, the course also aims to inculcate the kind of engaged inquiry discussed above by emphasizing the critical reading and analysis of texts, the articulation of rigorous argumentation, and the importance of historical contextualization and skill in writing. I tell students that my objective, put simply, is not merely to communicate facts and conclusions but to help them learn how to think theologically and how to inquire in dialogue with others and with faith traditions about God and the religious dimension of life. So although my objective, in part, is to communicate substantial information about how theologians deal with such questions and about the resources they use, the ultimate and primary objective is to introduce students to this conversation and provide them with enough of the basic tools so that they can begin to take part in the discussion themselves in a reflective and sophisticated way.

Over the course of the semester, I introduce students to progressively more nuanced notions of *theological anthropology*.[4] This notion serves as an organizing principle for introducing the vocabulary, key texts, central figures, and schematic narrative. It also provides a means of defining a more precise and narrow course objective: By the end of the semester, students should be able to demonstrate that they have understood and appropriated the conceptions of theological anthropology discussed in class by explaining some connections between these ideas and their experiential learning project.

In the initial presentation of this objective, I introduce the notion of theological anthropology as it is understood in theologies of correlation inspired by scholars such as Tillich and Rahner. I explain that what it is to be human is an open question, at least in the sense that our actions — whether good or evil, mundane or extraordinary — as individuals and as communities determine what we and the human world are and will become. A conception of what is ultimate in life — and so a notion of some sort of "god" — is implicit in our answers to this question. Conversely, our convictions about how we ought to behave and our various understandings of what it is to be human are implicit in our conceptions of this Ultimate Concern (whether God or some other ideal). As the course develops, key texts and concepts (e.g., sin, grace, incarnation, sacrament) are presented that more precisely articulate a Christian theological anthropology.

Acknowledging that the notion of theological anthropology just sketched is broad and abstract, I explain that the aims of the experiential learning projects are to help my students appropriate this idea in a practical and concrete way and to create a context other than mere repetition in which they can demonstrate their understanding and application of the concepts discussed in class and in the course readings. One question on the final exam will ask them to demonstrate their achievement of the course outcomes by reflecting on the connection between the understandings of theological anthropology presented in the class and the readings, and their experiential project. In other words, they will be asked to explain:

1. How reflection on their experiential projects helps them understand or explain a key notion in theology.

2. How a key theological notion discussed in the course gives them some insight in reflecting on what they have experienced in their projects.

For a service-learner, this means working at an agency for 20 hours over the course of the semester and analyzing the agency's mission statement (or other documentation that explicitly or implicitly articulates its vision and identity). The student then reflects on the theological anthropology articulated in the mission, compares that theological anthropology with the notions discussed in class, and evaluates both theological anthropologies in light of his or her experience with the agency's work, staff, and the people and community served. Hence, from the start of the semester, students have a set of questions that require their own critical reflection and dialogue with the course material. Can they discover how the ideas discussed in class might illuminate the agency's mission? Can they uncover a significant connection between the agency's theological anthropology and the theological anthropology presented in the course? Can they show how experience with the agency might illuminate the notions discussed in class? Can they show how the notions discussed in class might illuminate their experience with the agency, its mission, staff, clients, or community?

I noted earlier that students do not have to choose service-learning. They have two other alternatives. One option requires attendance three to five times over the course of the semester at a worship service of any religion. Students are strongly encouraged to attend worship services of a religious or cultural tradition different from their own, but this is not required. The third option requires experience and analysis of a cultural artifact (for example, a novel, short story, movie, play, myth, fairy tale, work of art, song, biography or autobiography, or cultural, political, historical, or social event) that can be seen as a significant expression of a theological anthropology. The learning objectives and requirements for these other two tracks closely parallel those for service-learners. This allows for a freedom of choice that would be precluded if service-learning were required of all. This also avoids the inequities in requirements and pedagogical schizophrenia sometimes entailed in dual-track approaches that add service-learning as an extra component or that allow service-learning to substitute for another component required of those who do not choose service. All three tracks in my course require students to discover and then demonstrate connections between the ideas discussed in class and their experience outside of class.

This has proved to be a very helpful way to enable students to better understand and more fully appropriate the content of the course. Moreover, it has provided a context that enables them to demonstrate on their own ground — that is to say, for service-learners in light of their own experience with the particular agency with which they worked — the degree to which they have actually appropriated some of the ideas discussed in class. This, in turn, provides a vehicle for better distinguishing the achievement between students who are adept at talking about ideas they have not appropriated very fully and students who have a genuine understanding. Likewise, it offers a way of assessing students whose ability to discover connections or apply concepts reveals a depth and quality of appropriation that might not be evident in their response to more abstract questions about the same notions. Used in this manner, service-learning and the two other experiential tracks in my class have required some changes in the way I teach and evaluate students, but they have not entailed adding a new unit or substantially new assignments. One of the exam questions must be posed differently, but I do not have to add more time to the final or require, for example, a special paper.

I particularly encourage students who already volunteer in the community to consider the service option. The level of voluntarism at Marquette has always been very high, and my impression is that most of the service-learners would have been involved in service anyway. The advantage of service-learning is that students are encouraged and given tools to reflect critically on their service work and the social realities of which it is a part. Likewise, students who choose to reflect on their experience of worship or art and culture are allowed, and in fact encouraged, to apply time they would have spent in those activities anyhow — for example, time in worship or going to a movie — to the work of the course. My aim is not to create busy-work or new tasks for the students but to help them find correlations between their classes and their world. I do not consider the "extra" time students spend reflecting on their experience something added to the course, since I have always expected students to devote some effort to finding connections between what we do in class and their lives in the larger world. Having a vehicle to make this intention more explicit for them and a way of acknowledging and rewarding their achievement of it has been well worth whatever it has added to their and my workloads.

Using service-learning in this way also combats the habit of passive learning and confronts the presumption that theology does not require or reward questioning and active inquiry. Since the assignment requires an experiential application, neither I nor the class readings can determine in advance what connections exist between the students' service experiences and the class material or how best to conceptualize them. They can sort such things out only by reflecting in dialogue with me, the texts, and their classmates. To succeed, they have to think theologically; they have to inquire critically, analytically, and seriously about their service experience with the tools of theological anthropology discussed in class; and they have to raise questions or draw conclusions for which they themselves are responsible and for which they get credit.

Pedagogical Tools and Monitoring Student Involvement

Since a major outcome for all students from the first day of the course is defined as making a connection between the themes discussed in class and their lives (between "God talk" and our experience of what it is to be human), much of our discussions and my presentations is aimed at assisting them in discovering such connections. Since, moreover, Marquette has many upper-division courses with a service-learning option and my application of this approach in this introductory course is rather limited, I aim to keep expectations relatively modest. By the end of the semester, I am satisfied if a student can make one or two original and substantive correlations. I am elated, of course, when more happens, but I am convinced that service-learning is most effective when it is cumulative — an option available across the curriculum, in a number of courses, and sometimes in modest doses.

This has affected how I design assignments. The first time I introduced service-learning, I overdid it a bit. I asked students to keep a journal, to report their progress by email (one page) three times during the semester, and to write a short paper (four to eight double-spaced pages) at the end of the term. I published a set of reflection questions on the class website to guide their reflections and to outline what should be included in the summary of their thoughts in the email reports.[5] During the course of the semester, there were a number of occasions when we had breakout discussions focused on connections between their experiential projects and the material covered in class. These are quite important and something that I needed to set up and execute more effectively.

Course evaluations indicated what I had already observed. Many of the students got bogged down in the mechanics of filing their email reports. They perceived the paper at the end of the semester as more burdensome than I had intended. (Most other sections of the course do not require a paper.) Since the same outcome can be achieved just as well with a final exam question, the second semester I substituted one question on the final for the paper. However, students who wished to prepare the question in advance as a take-home portion of the exam were allowed to do so. I have also simplified the reflection questions on the webpage and developed a checklist that, at three designated times over the course of the semester, students download, print, fill out, and hand in. On this list, they check off those reflection questions related to entries in their journals or notes. I review the checklists, but I do not ask them to turn in their journals or notes. Generally, I do not make any response to the checklist as long as the student reports that he or she is making progress. Students can include additional comments or questions with the checklist. If they do, I respond to their concerns by email. The checklists make the reporting a relatively easy task for them. It requires me to provide guidance and response only when students request it, and so it usually does not take much time on my part or theirs. Obviously, the checklist allows some students to slide by without taking the reflection too seriously for much of the semester. But those who do so discover that the strategy does not pay off in the end. Naturally, I advise them of that danger more than once. Interestingly, students who chose the service option generally seem to be the most conscientious about attending to the reflection questions.

Since Marquette's service-learning office monitors student hours and administrative matters with the agencies, there is little I have to do in that respect, aside from collecting contracts the third week of the semester and time sheets at the end and passing these along to the student coordinator assigned to my class. It is a great advantage to have such burdens taken care of so that the teacher can concentrate on student learning. It would have been entirely impractical otherwise to add a service-learning option to an introductory course that already has a very heavy agenda.

Assessment

Discussions of assessment too frequently overlook the fact that the most crucial and obvious tool for evaluating outcomes of well-designed courses is the class assignments themselves. In this case, the degree to which students have been able to make connections on their exam question (or paper, the first time around) has given me a good indication of whether I have created a context that enables them to appropriate some of the concepts and make some of the connections. If students fail to achieve this outcome to one degree or another, then more careful examination is needed to determine to what extent this was due to the course design or my execution, and to what extent it was the result of a student's lack of effort. In cases where students did poorly on other assignments or where their other work and participation showed inattention, it is reasonable to conclude the problem was more with the student than the pedagogy — assuming, of course, that there were a good number of students who achieved the outcome with some degree of success. When students who do well by other measures do not do well on this part of the course, then I have to ask about the effectiveness or execution of my strategy. Likewise, I think there is a strong indicator of success when a number of students who otherwise have been struggling with one or another aspect of the course do exceptionally well by demonstrating how reflection on their service helped them to explain a key notion in the course, how a key notion in the course enabled them to reflect on their service experience, or how, in the context of their service, they could make connections between course ideas that were not made explicitly in class or in the readings. I have had enough positive indicators of this sort to make me confident that the service-learning option is worth the effort it requires of me and the students. I have had enough negative indicators to keep me working at improvement. In this regard, I have developed an evaluation form I give students at the end of the semester. Comparison of this form with the results of the standard university student evaluation appears to confirm my judgments.

Conclusions

Although my approach to service-learning as a vehicle for helping students appropriate some key concepts of theological anthropology is in the context of a theology program at a Jesuit university, I do not see any reason why it could not be altered to work in a religious studies program within a different or broader context. I am convinced, however, that the value of sharing syllabi and pedagogy in volumes such as this one has less to do with offering ideas that someone else might adopt in their classes than it does with offering examples that stimulate colleagues' imaginations about how to encourage students to make connections between what they learn in the classroom and what they learn through service. At one level, what I do in my introductory course is quite different from how Edward Zlotkowski uses service-learning to teach Shakespeare's tragedies, but hearing how he found a natural and very fruitful connection for his students enabled me to envision a quite new and different path for my own course. It is my hope that someone else's imagination might be roused by my own experiments. I also hope to have shown at least one way to conceive of offering service-learning as an option without necessitating quite separate and unequal tracks for others in the class. My approach requires that all of the options have an experiential dimension, but if I myself could happen on to this device, I do not doubt that others have and will be able to envision other and even better alternatives.

In the discussions among colleagues at the conference that gave birth to this volume, there was some concern about how to devise service-learning courses that can be genuinely transformative and that can lead students to a critical understanding of the social, cultural, and political factors that create the need for service work in the first place. I am very much in sympathy with such ambitions, but my limited experience suggests these outcomes are often more realistic as the objective of a more comprehensive program. More modest objectives in specific courses are worth the effort and are rewarding. There is a place, I think, for courses where the aim is merely to introduce service-learning or to offer a quite modest application of it. Moreover, service-learning can be every bit as appropriate in a theoretical or text-based course with no direct link to what we ordinarily think of as "service" as it can be in areas such as "ethics" or "peace and justice," where the correlation is more obvious.

Finally, the relative ease with which I have been able to introduce successfully service-learning into my course suggests how important institutional support is. We at Marquette owe a great debt to those who made this possible. What can be achieved with such support — and the burden of time and energy borne by faculty who must work without such support — should be a lesson taken seriously by any university or college that claims, or would like to claim, service as a significant arena for its promotion of student learning and growth.

Notes

1. Initial funding was provided by two federal grants secured through the efforts of Dr. Andy Tallon, professor of philosophy, with the assistance of the Marquette Office of Research. In 1996-97, the program was fully institutionalized with funding coming from the university budget. In fall 1999, 727 students in 50 courses taught by 35 professors were involved in service-learning at 123 agencies.

2. The basic rules of shared inquiry at Marquette championed by one of the seminar's originators, Dr. John Pustejovsky are: No one takes part in discussion who hasn't read the text. We discuss only the text we have read. Any opinion must be backed up by the text. The leader/teacher may only ask questions, not answer them. Discussion questions must have more than one defensible answer and must be ones that can be answered from evidence within the text.

3. The department has put together a reader with brief orientations to the scripture selections, a short anthology of historical texts (Augustine, Aquinas, Luther, Julian of Norwich, Dr. Martin Luther King, Jr., etc.) and introductions to them, a time line, a glossary, and other supplementary materials edited by John Laurance and available over the last few years through various custom publishers. The course description is available at http://www.theo.mu.edu/theology/undergrad.htm. Additional readings are assigned by each teacher.

4. One of the books assigned for my sections is a text that I wrote for the course that treats these themes systematically: The Charmed Circle: Theology for the Head, Heart, Hands and Feet (Kansas City, MO: Sheed & Ward, 1987).

5. Readers are welcome to review that material in its current version by following the links to it at http://www.theo.mu.edu/masson/.

		Office Hours	Class Hours			
Office:	Coughlin Hall 211	M & W 4:00-5:00	Theo 001	CU 128	MW	2:25-3:40
Phone:	288-6952(0) 332-0373(H)	Tu 3:30-4:30	Theo 302	DS 442	W	5:45-8:25
E-mail:	robert.masson@marquette.edu	& by appointment	ARSC 007	LL 222	Tu	2:00-3:15
Web page:	http://www.theo.mu.edu/masson					

FIRST DAY HANDOUTS
  Syllabus
  Calendar
  Required & Recommended Texts

1. BRIEF DESCRIPTION OF THE COURSE REQUIREMENTS

The course will require you to read assignments before class. The calendar indicates the day readings are due. There are three announced multiple choice quizzes listed on the calendar that will count for 25% of the grade. There could be pop quizzes at any time that will count in the calculation of your grade for participation. There will be two one page papers. The first will count in the calculation of your participation grade; the second will count 10% of the course grade. There will be mid-term (25%) and final exams (40%). All students will have an experiential learning project over the course of the semester which will be the basis for a final exam question and will count for 1/3 of that test grade. You will have the option of preparing that question in advance as a take-home exam. Participation points will be awarded for various exercises over the course of the semester.

2. SIMILARITIES & DIFFERENCES BETWEEN 001 SECTIONS

All sections of Theo 001 assign the Scripture texts listed in the textbook *Introduction to Theology* (p. v) and the historical texts included there. Other assigned texts vary from section to section. See the accompanying sheet *Required & Recommended Texts* for this course's additional readings. All sections of Theo 001 share the GOALS and OUTCOMES listed below, but each professor uses his or her own expertise and pedagogical strategies to achieve the goals and help you reach the desired outcomes.

3. BULLETIN DESCRIPTION OF THEO 001

The introductory course focuses on key sources and questions of theology as found in Christian tradition and Scripture. This includes an overview of the key concepts and core narrative common to Christian worldviews and an orientation to the academic study of religion.

4. GOALS

The comprehensive educational goal of the core curriculum is theological literacy; that is, an intellectual formation to a level legitimately expected of graduates of a Catholic university. The specific objective emphasized in Theo 001 is: to increase students' awareness of the mystery and religious dimensions of human life, particularly as conveyed in the basic narrative outline, from creation to fulfillment, that characterizes Christian worldviews.

5. GENERAL OUTCOMES FOR THEO 001

1.   Students will have a comprehension of basic theological vocabulary, an historical time line, and important texts of Scripture and the tradition.
2.   Students will get a grasp of the overall terrain of theology as an academic discipline.
3.   Students will have an initial engagement of important issues and figures of the Christian tradition.

6. SHARED INQUIRY AS A PEDAGOGICAL PRINCIPLE

My objective as teacher is not merely to communicate facts or conclusions, but to help you to learn how to ***think theologically*** and to ***inquire with*** you about God and the religious dimension of life. So although my objective, in part, is to communicate substantial information about how theologians deal with such questions, the ultimate and primary objective is to introduce you to this conversation and provide you with enough of the basic tools so that you can begin to take part in the conversation in a reflective and sophisticated way. The three outcomes for this course specify precisely the tools that you will need for this: namely, 1) basic vocabulary, historical framework and key texts from Scripture and history; 2) a grasp of the overall terrain of academic theology; and 3) initial engagement with important issues and figures in the Christian tradition. The ability to take part in the conversation in a reflective and sophisticated way is the meaning of the goals "theological literacy" and "an intellectual formation to a level legitimately expected of graduates of a Catholic university."

Although this course is not intended for majors, its goal is to equip you to think and talk about theological and religious issues in some depth. This means that to accomplish the core requirement in theology, memorization and passive learning will not be enough. You have to become **engaged inquirers** yourselves. You have to acquire the basic skills to take part in this sort of conversation and demonstrate that you can use them to some effect.

The course has been designed to support efforts to engage yourself in this kind of inquiry. All the information which I want to communicate is provided in *The Charmed Circle, The Introduction to Theology, The Shadow of the Galilean* and the readings on the Class Reserves. *Engaged inquiry* presupposes that you study these materials **before** class, and that we use our time in the classroom to clarify and give you practice using the information and concepts discussed in the texts. Participation in the classroom exercises will be very important, because learning is not just a matter of acquiring information. The learned person is one who has acquired skill in using the information, who knows what questions the information answers and who knows how to use the information to advance an inquiry. Those are the kinds of skills which will be taught and which you will have to demonstrate at the end of the semester. Passive learning will not get a good grade in this class.

Some classroom time will be devoted to "shared inquiry" discussions and exercises. These are small breakout discussions which will give some time to practice the art of theological conversation and to test your grasp of the data and concepts discussed in the readings. In the breakout groups, we will follow a variation of the *Rules for Shared Inquiry*. These rules will be explained at the beginning of those discussions. For now it is important that you know rule 1: you are responsible for carefully reading and studying all assignments before class. You can also expect a number of quizzes or similar drills with the same objective: practicing and testing your appropriation of the material. These exercises will help you and I assess your participation and progress over the course of the semester and will be calculated in your participation points.

7. THEOLOGICAL ANTHROPOLOGY: ORGANIZING PRINCIPLE

You should think of *The Charmed Circle* as your lecture notes. There are several organizing principles. A key one is the notion of "theological anthropology." Over the course of the semester, four ways of understanding this notion will be introduced. Each conception will presuppose the former.

Here, then, is a very brief and preliminary explanation of the first way of understanding how many theologians today use the term "theological anthropology."

What it is "to be human" is an open question, at least in the sense that our actions as individuals and as communities determine to a large extent what we and the human world are like. In effect, our actions answer the question "what is it to be human?" and thus determine what will become of us and our world. A conception of what is ultimate in life--and so a conception of some sort of "god"-- is implicit in our answers to this question. Conversely, our convictions about how we ought to behave and our various understandings of what it is to be human are implicit in our conceptions of our "God" or "gods"--or whatever else it is that we take to be of ultimate concern in life.

In this broad sense, every stance a person takes presupposes a theological anthropology, that is to say, presupposes an understanding both of God (i.e. an understanding of what is ultimate, theology) and an understanding of what it is to be human (anthropology).

Since the core conviction of Christianity is that God has become one with humanity in Jesus and, in so doing, calls us to unity with one another, Christian theology necessarily focuses in a very particular way on understanding the connection between the human and divine, or put in other words, between theology and anthropology. As mentioned above, the connection between the human and divine can be characterized in four ways. Describing these four senses of "theological anthropology" provides one way of mapping some of the terrain theology covers. The notion will provide us with a way of summing up the understanding of reality which is expressed in the basic narrative and key texts from Scripture and history to which Theo 001 is introducing you.

8. EXPERIENTIAL LEARNING PROJECT

Needless to say, the notion of "theological anthropology" just sketched is broad and abstract. One aim of the course is to fill in the details and make it a concrete conceptual tool that will be useful to you.

The course hopes to help you appropriate this idea in a practical and concrete way through your semester project. Every student will pick from one of three options described below. Although each of these options involves a different way of learning, the objective for whichever you choose will be the same: a more concrete appropriation and application of the notion of theological anthropology. One of the questions on your final exam will ask you to demonstrate your achievement of the course outcomes by comparing the connection between the understandings of God and humanity (theological anthropology) discussed in *The Charmed Circle* and the course readings with a significant connection between the understandings of God and humanity which you are able to discover through reflection on your experience. In other words, you will be asked to explain:

1. how does your reflection on your project help you understand or explain a key notion in theology?

2. how does one or more of the theological notions discussed in the course give you some insight in reflecting on your project?

You have to declare your option on the date indicated on the class calendar. Note also on the calendar when contracts and reports are due.

•**SERVICE OPTION**

You will volunteer at an area service agency for 20 hours over the course of the semester. The agency need not have a religious affiliation. Placement with the agency and oversight of your volunteer work will be coordinated through Marquette's Service Learning Program. You will keep a journal reflecting on your experience. This will provide the basis for your answer on the final exam. During the course of the semester, you will be asked to report on your progress and keep a time sheet for your service activities. Your objective will be to find out how the agency's self-understanding is expressed in its mission statement (and/or creed, tradition or other expression of its identity) and to reflect on what that tells you about the organization's explicit or implicit understanding of God (or ultimate reality) and humanity. On the exam, you will reflect and compare this with the understanding of God and humanity discussed in the class.

You must attend Service Learning Sign-up Night (**Wed, Sept. 6, 5:30pm-8:30pm in the AMU Ballroom A & B**). Further information for signing-up is available in Books Hall 100.

Because of the time commitment involved in service, 20 points for participation will be awarded with this option.

•**WORSHIP OPTION**

You will attend three religious services over the course of the semester. These may be services at any church, synagogue, or Islamic center, but all three services must be at the same worship site and must be major weekly celebrations of the community. These do not have to be services of a community to which you belong. In fact, you are discouraged from attending services at Gesu, campus liturgies, or your normal place of worship. You will keep a journal reflecting on your experience. During the course of the semester, you will be asked to report on your progress. Your objective is to discover how the worship service expresses the community's understandings of God and humanity. On the final exam, you will be asked to show how something you have learned from reflections on your experience of these worship services sheds light on a key theological notions discussed in class, and how the understanding of God and humanity discussed in class sheds some light on what you observed in the worship services.

In the past, students who have attended worship services of a different tradition have found that experience much more suggestive. To encourage students to make the extra effort to try this, 10 points for participation will be awarded to those who chose to attend and reflect on the worship services of a religious tradition different from their own or who attend a religious service of a culture different from their own. The class web-page has a listing of church services and indicates some Catholic Churches with worship services which have a multi-cultural dimension.

•**ART & CULTURE OPTION**

You will choose a cultural artifact (that is to say: a book, short story, movie, play, myth, novel, fairy tale, work(s) of art, song(s), biography or autobiography, cultural, political, historical or social event) which can be seen as a significant expression of a theological anthropology. Your topic must be approved by me or the teaching assistant. During the course of the semester, you will be asked to report on your progress. Your objective is to analyze the artifact in order to determine what understandings of God and humanity it expresses. On the exam, you will reflect and compare this with the understanding of God and humanity discussed in the class. Students for whom we approve the choice of a difficult or long literary work will be awarded 10 points for participation

9. ASSIGNMENTS & GRADING SCALE

Exercises &	Participation points
Pop Quizzes	The purpose of these is practicing and testing your appropriation of important concepts. These will provide some measure of your participation and progress over the course of the semester.

Quiz 1	5%
Quiz 2	5%
Mid-Term	25%
Quiz 3	15%
1 Page Paper	10%
Final	40%
	100% + participation points

PARTICIPATION POINTS

Over the course of the semester points will be given for a number of exercises, pop quizzes, and to recognize participation or effort displayed by such evidence as perfect class attendance, meeting deadlines, or doing optional assignments. These will always be awarded for opportunities available to all students in the course of regular class assignments. (These are not extra-credit points offered to students individually or to make-up for missed assignments or poor work.) The grading program will calculate the total possible points, the class average, the average for each student and the standard deviation. Points will be added to the final grade based on the following scale.

If the grade for participation is:	points added to the semester grade are:
1 standard deviation above the class average	2.0
2 standard deviation above the class average	1.5
equal to the class average	1.0
not more than 2 standard deviation below the class average	.5

"God and Human Suffering" as a Service-Learning Course

by Chris Johnson

The first time I taught God and Human Suffering, by the end of the semester many students remained frustrated by the "big stuff." Asked to write a concluding paper in which they would pull it all together and craft their own theodicy, the students hedged and hesitated about their ability to come to satisfactory conclusions about, for instance, the nature of God or the possible meaning of suffering. But they did find themselves crafting passionate and thoughtful arguments for the importance of doing something about evil and suffering. They also envisioned that precisely in that doing they would learn more deeply (but still not necessarily solve) the realities and questions raised by the course — the big stuff that so bedeviled them. This two-pronged observation was, for me, an important starting point in choosing to incorporate service-learning in subsequent versions of the course. The students themselves, that is, articulated the rationale for service-learning in this course: They wanted to strengthen their ability to wrestle with complex, troubling issues, and their engagement with those issues could be realized through service. This essay will describe a version of the course that was developed partly in response to students' seeking to make more of their education, for themselves and for the deeply scarred world in which they live.

The Course and Its Context

Features of the course that perhaps make it an instructive example of how and why to try service-learning include its relative infancy and my status as a junior faculty member. I am currently in my fifth year in a tenure-track position in the Philosophy and Religion Department at Buena Vista University (a private, four-year, residential, regional university of some 1,250 undergraduate students[1] on its main campus in Storm Lake, a northwest Iowa farming community of 10,000 people). BVU is affiliated with the Presbyterian Church and has a history and ethos that make it fertile ground in which to grow experiential and service-learning opportunities. In particular, our institutional motto and mission statement highlight "education for service." Since the arrival of our current president in 1995, the university has moved to embrace Ernest Boyer's New American College model of higher education (Boyer 1990, 1994). In recent years, we have accomplished major revisions of the faculty roles and reward system and the entire academic program to bring them both more in line with our mission and New American College values. The latter include an emphasis on excellent learner-centered teaching that fosters connections between theory and practice, curriculum and cocurriculum, knowledge and service, and campus and community in order to address real social problems. Experimentation with, and development of, service-learning and other forms of experiential learning are encouraged, even for those who, like me, have yet to come up for tenure.

Furthermore, the department of which I am a member has long been characterized by a thrust toward social engagement, innovation, interdisciplinary and cross-boundary thinking, and student empowerment. By disposition and training (especially in religious social ethics, with an emphasis on virtue or character ethics, religion and culture, and political/liberation theology and ethics), I was inclined toward such notions as the scholarship of engagement (Boyer 1996) even before I had heard of Boyer's vision of the New American College — or of service-learning, for that matter. Hence, I had already begun to experiment with incorporating some form of service activity into many of my other courses in biblical studies, ethics, and religion and culture, even if in a piecemeal way. I was interested to try service-learning in the God and Human Suffering course because of the content-related, student-driven rationale I mentioned above. It was time for me to get serious about doing it right in my own courses, and the university made it attractive and possible to do so.

One implication of an institutional climate such as ours is that students are increasingly coming to expect, and even to prod reluctant faculty into trying, service-learning in their courses. This, in turn, is beginning to drive faculty development initiatives and other forms of support and infrastructure that have long been part of the fabric at other schools. This course and others like it at BVU, in other words, have been grown in institutional soil that in some ways is still relatively unbroken. Even though we have long been inclined toward connecting theory to practice and institution to community, we are still learning how to use the pedagogy of service-learning well. That the course is new, that it has been grown in an environment where (and by a faculty member for whom) service-learning itself is relatively new, and that it has worked well is testimony to the strong possibilities of service-learning as a pedagogy.

As I write this, we are nearing the end of my third time through the course. Students typically take the course, which is an elective, as part of their philosophy/religion major or minor or toward their general education distribution requirements. This means that the course draws a wide cross-section of students with varying levels of motivation and experience. As a newer and still-evolving experimental course, it has yet to officially appear in the catalogue. In the students' course registration materials, it has a twofold numerical designation (Reli 150/450) that signifies both its experimental status (the 50) and the fact that it is open to the full range of students, from freshman to senior (the 100/400). In practice, this means that the course has been pitched in the upper-200 level or sophomore/junior range. The syllabus includes an active-learning portfolio (worth 20% of the grade) consisting of two components: writing several short critical-reflective essays (which collectively amount to a journal) throughout the semester, and service-learning. Students who register for the 150 version of the course may choose either of those options, and 450 students must complete both. When the course settles into the catalogue as a permanent offering (at the 200 or 300 level), I will most likely require service-learning for all students. Other course requirements, or "opportunities" as I call them, are attendance and class participation (20% of the grade), two papers (20% each), a comprehensive one-on-one 45-minute oral final exam (each student signs up for a time slot near the end of the term, 10%), and a final creative project that each student presents to her or his colleagues when we gather at my home for our last time together (10%).

Course Objectives and Service-Learning

The course learning objectives include standard cognitive aims such as appropriation and analysis of important content and skills acquisition and development (writing, critical thinking, argumentation, etc.). But the objectives also touch on areas of emotional, spiritual, and interpersonal growth on the assumption that *learning* is more than just a matter of the intellect and is certainly not limited to the transfer of information from teacher to student. The syllabus emphasizes the engaged, empowering, and democratic spirit of the course and includes a description of my role as a facilitator/moderator and fellow learner who promotes collaborative, self-directed learning and assumes the ongoing need for flexibility and a variety of pedagogical strategies. One of our first tasks as the semester begins is to negotiate, as best we can, the details of the syllabus so that it becomes a living, breathing, student-owned covenant by which we can all be empowered and held accountable.[2] As the syllabus and our first days of class discussion and team building emphasize, this is a course that will touch participants in some very deep and personal ways and will challenge our whole selves — mind and body, heart and soul, public and private. Service-learning is an important tool in this sort of enterprise because of the ways in which it too engages the whole person in a comprehensive web of learning and growth.[3]

Since another aspect of active learning I employ is the utilization of various information technologies, the syllabus and most other course documents (assignments, etc.) are posted on the course website for the students to access themselves. This, in turn, means that those e-documents can include such features as links to other resources on the Web, instant-access email addresses, PowerPoint presentations, and so on; graphics such as cartoons that have been scanned in (for example, "The Far Side" and "Calvin and Hobbes" — true gold mines of religious studies material!); and animation.

An important means of drawing students from the start into the active, dialogical spirit of the course is the syllabus itself, which I try to make as lively, interactive, and textured as possible. The first page of the syllabus, for example, consists of a clip art sketch of a stick-figure person scratching its head, in a posture that suggests inquisitiveness and perplexity, surrounded by eight or 10 quotations from sources as diverse as the Bible, Elie Wiesel, and a *Star Trek* film. This not only sets an initial tone of active questioning and multidimensional, out-of-the-box thinking (it is likely to be very different from what the students are used to in a syllabus!) but also becomes a resource to which we find ourselves returning regularly throughout the semester. I also include BVU's mission statement in the syllabus in order to help us to think about how this course fits into our larger, shared educational venture at this place and time in our lives. The course texts and resources — representing a variety of genres, including novels, short stories, essays, and films — I select with an eye toward their capacity to engage us as whole persons, to provoke the imagination and exercise our character as moral agents, as well as to challenge our intellect. Such goals, in turn, are related both to the pedagogical implications of narrative theory and character ethics (areas of my academic training) and to the fact that experiential learning has been shown to affect not only cognitive learning but also personal development, spiritual and ethical values, and civic engagement.[4] In a separate (electronic) handout specifically on the service-learning component of the course, I address in more detail the specific rationale and aims of service-learning in general, in this course, and as part of the institutional context.

Planning, Pedagogy, and Assessment

Some features of the "Info on Service-Learning" handout should be noted explicitly. First, I explain why I ask my students to do service-learning in part by explaining what service-learning is (so that they can distinguish it from, for example, *required voluntarism*, an idea they rightly resent), how it fits into their overall educational career at BVU, and so on.[5] Second, I try to use a conversational style to better convey the truth that I take them seriously and want to work with them as real people and fellow learners.

Third, and in a more logistical vein, I let the students know they themselves are largely responsible for identifying and arranging appropriate service opportunities (although I have asked the 450-level students to commit themselves as a group to working with the oncology and hospice units at our local hospital). The university's director of community service and internships and I assist them in selecting their sites, based on the learning objectives of the course and on the needs of the community partners. Once students have identified an appropriate site, they meet with their community partner to discuss training, expectations, scheduling, and so on. They then return a simple one-page form to me that details the results of that contact.

Sites have included local nursing homes and schools, Head Start and Even Start programs, the multicounty Council Against Domestic Abuse, a residential facility for children with special needs, the county historical society, and the county hospital and its oncology and hospice programs. One student who commutes quite a distance chose to create a "coats for kids" program in his home community's school district to gather and distribute warm winter clothing to children from low-income families. Once their service begins, students use a simple log to keep track of their work, including dates, times, and brief notes on what they do, think, learn, realize, feel, and question. These quick jottings provide some of the raw material for their more extended efforts at critical reflection and meaning making through their journals and discussion groups.

These journals and discussion sessions have met with mixed success. In an early version of the course, for example, an assignment called on the students to include letters to themselves at the beginning and end of the semester and regularly to organize their own, out-of-class sessions — neither of which was done well. In-class discussion, however, has been very fruitful when the service-learning students have shared their experiences and reflections with one another and with their non–service-learning colleagues. Written reflection has also improved when it has been regular, guided, and responded to in a timely fashion.[6] Further improvements in this area may come through the use of student facilitators, i.e., students who have had prior experience with service-learning and reflection via alternative spring break trips, other courses, and so on.

Some of the most significant connections students make between their experiences (working with people who are ill, dying, abused, or poor, for example) and course content have had to do with issues such as the following:

• The cause, purpose, and meaning of suffering and evil; sustained and sophisticated thinking about the various theodicies we encounter in the readings and discussion; questions on human versus divine responsibility for evil (Does God intend for an 11-year-old girl to die of leukemia? Why are poor people poor?).

- Questions concerning the existence and nature of God; human apprehension and/or projection of God's attributes (power, goodness, love, justice, etc.); or alternatively, evidence for and implications of the possibility that there is no God (Do suffering and evil prove the nonexistence of God? Is the universe a random, chaotic, meaningless place ruled by Fate, Chance, or Luck?).
- Distinctions between and differing attitudes toward natural, moral, and systemic evil (How, if at all, does the destruction caused by last year's tornado differ from that of the sudden onset of cancer in the life of a young parent or that of the economic and geopolitical realities that force so many families to flee their homelands to seek work in northwest Iowa?).
- Human nature: our capacities for and propensities toward good and evil, individuality versus connectedness, abilities and practices of resistance to or noncompliance with evil, the struggle to live well in the face of violence and despair.
- How human beings ought best to respond to suffering and evil (care for the dying, social activism and advocacy, etc.); the adequacy in specific situations of "standard" responses ("Everything happens for a reason," "Something good will come out of this," "God works in mysterious ways," "We couldn't have or know goodness without evil," and "It's not our place to question").
- Ways in which people who are suffering are regarded by those who are not, including the fears, misconceptions, and anxieties of many students when they first encounter the suffering *other*.
- The possibility and nature of forgiveness (tied in with issues of anger, punishment, justice, and retribution in cases of sexual and domestic abuse, for example).
- The possibility and nature of religious faith after the Holocaust (or after any occurrence of cataclysmic evil or profound suffering, which, of course, raises questions of the "uniqueness" of the *Shoah*).
- The origins and meanings of classic Christian beliefs such as atonement, incarnation, resurrection, the suffering and death of Christ, etc., as they impinge upon issues and realities of suffering and evil.
- More sophisticated and insightful interaction with and connections among the readings and films employed in the course.

While service experiences provide much of the valuable raw material and serve as a crucible of sorts for students to connect course content with real life in these (and other) ways, we engage in active-learning experiences of many different kinds throughout the course. (In some ways, I prefer to think of the course as an "experiential learning" course rather than exclusively a service-learning course.) In addition to the negotiated syllabus and the use of various technologies, other forms of active learning include role play, debate, coloring and drawing, interactive drama, student-led presentations, brainstorming sessions, five-minute reflective writing, adjusting our classroom space and/or moving to different spaces around campus, and so on.

These devices range from the sublime to the (potentially) ridiculous. First, an example of the latter from the second year I offered the course: I wanted to help students better to internalize and ponder the filth and revulsion conveyed by the powerful essay "Excremental Assault" by Terrence Des Pres (in Roth and Berenbaum 1989). In this essay, Des Pres provides narratives and analysis of the ways in which the Nazis sought to humiliate and dehumanize the Jews by forcing them to wallow in their own excrement. The pedagogical challenges of helping students to get it, students who are so far removed from the horrors conveyed in this and other Holocaust accounts, are enormous. Short of taking them on an immersion field trip to the sewage treatment facility on the edge of town, I tried to think of something that would efficiently but vividly, well, repulse the students into allowing themselves to be grasped by Des Pres's text. Thus, I had everyone remove his or her shoes and pass them around the class, deeply inhaling from each shoe as it passed by. As vividly experiential as that was, the key to learning was to then have them write for five minutes about their reactions and how this experience helped them to get what Des Pres discusses in the essay, and then to move into small-group and whole-class discussion.

Of course, the chortles and grimaces the students made as all those shoes traveled their gaseous circuit of the room highlight the risk that we might in fact be violating the spirit of Des Pres's essay and demeaning once again the humanity of those who suffered and died in the Holocaust. And without the purposeful, quiet moments for written reflection and then an entire class period devoted to serious, substantive discussion of the text — now in light of the shoe experience as well as, it turned out, some of the students' service-learning experiences — the risk would have been even greater. But at the very least, this simple, in some ways frivolous, exercise planted a seed in the minds and hearts of most of the students in the room. It helped to break the potentially debilitating gloom that reading the essay casts in the first place. But it did so in a way that equipped us better to internalize and reflect critically on what Des Pres was telling us and thus to honor the gloom rather than simply push it away or, worse yet, become indifferent to it.

A much graver experience involved suddenly relocating the class to a windowless, cramped, stuffy, boxcar-like basement room in another building on the day that we are to begin discussing Elie Wiesel's classic text *Night*. I scheduled this day to coincide with a day of campus-wide events to honor victims and survivors of sexual and domestic assault. (This day comes late enough in the semester that our rapport as a class is by then solid — an important consideration given the risks involved in what we do.) Once we had shoehorned ourselves into that tiny room, I began — suddenly and without explanation — by plunging the room into total darkness and lashing out with abusive shouts and noises of violence: cursing, fists against the closed door, a chair slammed against the wall. After perhaps two or three minutes of this (which, judging by the tense gasps and silence that punctuated the black air, seemed like much longer), I lit a candle and softly read excerpts from *Night*. My focus was on the scenes in the boxcar to Birkenau/Auschwitz where Madame Schöchter goes mad with her vision of flames and has to be beaten into silence while her 10-year-old son looks on (Wiesel 1986: 22-26). With a second candle and the eerie glow of a single exit sign above the still-closed door providing our only light, one of the students, with whom I consulted ahead of time, then began to share with the class some of the statistics and stories of sexual assault from across Iowa — and ended up telling the story of her own sexual assault and her struggle to take back her life, which led others to do the same as we lit still more candles. By the end of that 75-minute period, we had helped one another to explore stereotypes, gender roles, relational dynamics of power and violence, fears of the *other*, obstacles to and possibilities of healing, restoration, and faith, personal/private and public/political dimensions of suffering and moral evil, Wiesel's theodicy of protest, and so much more.

On such occasions, it is powerful and humbling to be a teacher in the presence of persons of such courage, insight, and grace. Together, we transform our learning. We move out of our usual learning space, beyond our usual expectations of one another and ourselves, and into strange and frightening places of mind, body, and heart. We bring the realities of sexual abuse closer to home and push ourselves to see that the realities of the Holocaust are not as far from home as we typically imagine. In doing so, we show that experiential learning, including service-learning, breaks down barriers and builds bridges, connecting learners with content, the university with the community, teacher with student, theory with practice, mind with body and heart, us with them.

While it is tempting to say that experiences such as those I have described are virtually self-validating, the question of assessment still needs to be addressed. Assessment of service-learning's contribution to the course learning objectives and of the students' ability to make connections between their service work and the course content is largely accomplished via attention to the quality of the discussion/reflection sessions, student writing (journals and essays), and one-on-one conversation/interviews with me near the end of the semester. Service-learning–related writing and reflection are evaluated according to the same qualitative criteria (which are articulated in the class-negotiated syllabus) as apply to all dimensions of the students' work: such things as comprehension of material, thorough and accurate analysis and synthesis, sound argumentation, making and articulating connections, being complete, adhering to standards of academic integrity, and exhibiting insight, passion, creativity, and a willingness to take risks.

Student comments on their end-of-semester course evaluations also provide some clues as to the ways in which service-learning contributes to their overall experience, as do the brief, open-ended reports their community partners are asked to submit. But while there exist several avenues by which to discern service-learning's effectiveness in helping students to achieve our wide-ranging set of learning objectives (cognitive, emotional, spiritual, and interpersonal), the best indicators remain the students' own accounts of how their learning has been enriched and made relevant beyond the typical bounds of the classroom.[7]

Conclusion

That, after all, is what service-learning is most fundamentally about: enhancing student learning with/in communities in order to change the world. In a course where the issues can at times be so complex, the material so hard to grasp, the questions so overwhelming while the answers remain elusive, and the realities personally painful, service-learning can make a powerful contribution. My students, I am convinced, were right (as they have been about a great many things) when they helped to plant the seeds for a service-learning version of God and Human Suffering. My attempt to grow those seeds into a lush, organic learning experience has been my way of honoring both their profound struggle to learn well and their desire to heed the call to be of service in a suffering world.

Notes

1. The university currently has one graduate program, in education, and several branch campuses or centers in communities all over Iowa with a special focus on distance learning and degree programs for adult learners. My course, like most of the programs and curriculum at the Storm Lake campus, serves undergraduates.

2. For some helpful treatments of issues and strategies related to democracy-enhancing and liberationist pedagogy, see, for example, Freire 1993; hooks 1994; Maher and Thompson Tetreault 1994; Palmer 1983, 1998; Pippin 1998; and Shor 1996.

3. See, for example, Eyler and Giles 1999, which documents the positive role service-learning can play in personal and interpersonal development; understanding and applying knowledge; engagement, curiosity, and reflective practice; critical thinking;

perspective transformation; and citizenship. See also Kendall and Associates 1990 for several essays that discuss the impact of service-learning on students' social and civic responsibility, intellectual development, cross-cultural learning, leadership development, moral and ethical development, and career development. An outstanding comprehensive bibliography of recent studies that document the benefits of service-learning is to be found in Eyler, Giles, and Gray 2000.

4. Among the rich philosophical and theological literature on the interrelationships of narrative, moral agency, personhood, action, and community, see, for example, Coles 1989, 1993; Hauerwas and Jones 1989 (and virtually everything in the vast body of work by Hauerwas); Jones 1989; MacIntyre 1984; Nussbaum 1990; and Taylor 1989.

5. It is widely recognized that definitions of service-learning abound. A resource I have found helpful in this regard is Furco 1996; see also the first three sections ("Definitions and Principles," "Theory," and "Pedagogy") plus the very helpful "essential reading" bibliographies in Campus Compact 2000.

6. Among the many helpful resources now available to assist with the pedagogy of service-learning, particularly critical reflection, see, for example, Bringle and Hatcher 1999; sections 3 and 5 ("Pedagogy" and "Reflection") of Campus Compact 2000; Eyler, Giles, and Schmiede 1996; and Reed and Koliba 1996.

7. For more on assessment in service-learning courses, see Bringle and Hatcher 1997, 1999; Campus Compact 1995, 2000; and Jackson 1993.

References

Boyer, Ernest. (1990). *Scholarship Reconsidered: Priorities of the Professoriate.* Princeton, NJ: Carnegie Foundation for the Advancement of Teaching.

——— . (March 9, 1994). "Creating the New American College." *Chronicle of Higher Education:* A48.

——— . (1996). "The Scholarship of Engagement." *Journal of Public Service and Outreach* 1(1): 11-20.

Bringle, Robert, and Julie Hatcher. (1997). "Reflections: Bridging the Gap Between Service and Learning." *Journal of College Teaching* 45: 153.

——— . (Summer 1999). "Reflection in Service-Learning: Making Meaning of Experience." *Educational Horizons:* 179-185.

Campus Compact. (1995). *Connecting Cognition and Action: Evaluation of Student Performance in Service Learning Courses.* Providence, RI: Author.

——— . (2000). *Introduction to Service-Learning Toolkit: Readings and Resources for Faculty.* Providence, RI: Author.

Coles, Robert. (1989). *The Call of Stories.* New York: Houghton-Mifflin.

——— . (1993). *The Call of Service.* New York: Houghton-Mifflin.

Eyler, Janet, and Dwight E. Giles, Jr. (1999). *Where's the Learning in Service-Learning?* San Francisco: Jossey-Bass.

———, and Charlene J. Gray. (2000). "Research at a Glance: What We Know About the Effects of Service-Learning on Students, Faculty, Institutions, and Communities, 1993-1999." In *Introduction to Service-Learning Toolkit: Readings and Resources for Faculty*, pp. 21-25. Providence, RI: Campus Compact.

Eyler, Janet, Dwight E. Giles, Jr., and A. Schmiede. (1996). *A Practitioner's Guide to Reflection in Service Learning: Student Voices and Reflections.* Nashville, TN: Vanderbilt University Press.

Freire, Paulo. (1993). *Pedagogy of the Oppressed.* Rev. ed. New York: Continuum.

Furco, Andrew. (1996). "Service-Learning: A Balanced Approach to Experiential Education." *Expanding Boundaries: Serving and Learning:* 2-6.

Hauerwas, Stanley, and L. Gregory Jones, eds. (1989). *Why Narrative? Readings in Narrative Theology.* Grand Rapids, MI: Erdmanns.

hooks, bell. (1994). *Teaching to Transgress: Education as the Practice of Freedom.* New York: Routledge.

Jackson, Fleda Mask. (1993). "Evaluating Service-Learning." In *Rethinking Tradition: Integrating Service With Academic Study on College Campuses,* edited by T.Y. Kupiec, pp. 129-135. A publication of Campus Compact. Denver, CO: Education Commission of the States.

Jones, L. Gregory. (1989). *Transformed Judgment: Toward a Trinitarian Account of the Moral Life.* Notre Dame, IN: University of Notre Dame Press.

Kendall, Jane, and Associates, eds. (1990). *Combining Service and Learning: A Resource Book for Community and Public Service.* Vol. 1. Raleigh, NC: National Society for Internships and Experiential Education.

MacIntyre, Alasdair. (1984). *After Virtue.* 2nd ed. Notre Dame, IN: University of Notre Dame Press.

Maher, Frances A., and Mary Kay Thompson Tetreault. (1994). *The Feminist Classroom.* New York: Basic Books.

Nussbaum, Martha. (1990). *Love's Knowledge: Essays on Philosophy and Literature.* New York: Oxford University Press.

Palmer, Parker J. (1983). *To Know As We Are Known: Education as a Spiritual Journey.* New York: HarperSanFrancisco.

———. (1998). *The Courage to Teach: Exploring the Inner Landscape of a Teacher's Life.* San Francisco: Jossey-Bass.

Pippin, Tina. (1998). "Liberatory Pedagogies in the Religious Studies Classroom." *Teaching Theology and Religion* 1(3): 177-182.

Reed, J., and C. Koliba. (1996). *Facilitating Reflection: A Manual for Higher Education.* Washington, DC: Georgetown University Volunteer and Public Service Center.

Roth, John K., and Michael Berenbaum. (1989). *Holocaust: Religious and Philosophical Implications.* New York: Paragon House.

Shor, Ira. (1996). *When Students Have Power: Negotiating Authority in a Critical Pedagogy.* Chicago and London: University of Chicago Press.

Taylor, Charles. (1989). *Sources of the Self: The Making of Modern Identity.* Cambridge, MA: Harvard University Press.

Wiesel, Elie. (1986). *Night.* 25th anniv. ed. New York: Bantam.

God and Human Suffering

Religion 150/450, Buena Vista University, Fall 2000

You saw it, God. You saw it! The death of an innocent child, and my vengeance. You permitted it, and I don't understand you.
— "Silent Spring," Ingmar Bergman

> *Misery does not come from the earth, nor does trouble sprout from the ground; but human beings are born to trouble just as sparks fly upward.*
> — Job 5: 6-7

Creatures of a day we live like cattle, knowing nothing of how the god will bring each one to his or her end.... Thus evil is with everything. Yea ten thousand dooms, woes, and grief beyond speaking are the lot of humankind.
— Kallinos (6th cent. BCE)

> *The human adventure is just beginning.*
> — Star Trek II

In the Holocaust, not all the victims were Jews; but all the Jews were victims, and all the killers were Christians.
— Elie Wiesel

> *He was despised and rejected by others; a man of suffering and acquainted with infirmity.... He was wounded for our transgressions, crushed for our iniquities; upon him was the punishment that made us whole, and by his bruises we are healed.*
> — Isaiah 53: 3-4

Imagine that you are creating a fabric of human destiny with the object of making [humankind] happy in the end, giving them peace and rest at last, but that it was essential and inevitable to torture to death only one tiny creature... would you consent to be the architect on those conditions? Tell me, and tell the truth.
— Ivan Karamazov

> *All things work together for good to them that love God.*
> — Romans 8:28

Course Description and Objectives:

This is a course about perhaps the most troubling, befuddling set of questions human beings face. These questions have to do with the reality of suffering and evil (personal, natural, and systemic), and the nature of God. Another quote summarizes the problem, at least for people who believe in the Judeo-Christian God (as we'll see, the problem either doesn't exist or takes different form for others):

> *"Is God willing to prevent evil, but not able? Then [he] is impotent. Is [he] able, but not willing? Then [he] is malevolent. Is [he] both able and willing? Whence then is evil?*
> — Epicurus (341-270 BCE)

As a "150/450," this is an experimental course that will rely heavily on your ownership and commitment for its success. My guess is that each of us has had some kind of encounter with suffering and evil (and yet, I'd also guess, we can't even imagine some of the forms of evil that many people regularly endure). Personal experience will feature prominently in what happens both in and out of class. I urge us to covenant together to treat each other with sensitivity and respect while we engage in challenging academic work on a not-at-all-"academic" subject. Some of the course will be "hard" in the usual "this-is-college" ways, but my hunch is that it will also be difficult in ways that you're not likely to experience in other classes. We will need to agree, for instance, on ways to ensure "sacred space" for and with each other (e.g., confidentiality, support, compassion).

I look at myself as a facilitator/moderator and fellow-learner — maybe a "coach" — and not a "lecturer." I want you to succeed, so even when I challenge and push you to work hard I am doing so because I am on your side. I promote collaborative, self-directed learning, which means we'll learn together as we go, employing different learning methods and making necessary adjustments along the way. One of my working assumptions is that the college experience is an incredible gift and opportunity, so I'm thrilled to be able to help you make the most of it.

More specifically, our work together will involve *extensive, informed, energetic discussion;* various forms of writing (including email discussion and two essays; readings and films; minimal lecture and other forms of presentation by me; an exam; and some sort of community involvement. All we do is in the service of:

* developing your familiarity with the subject matter and methods of this strand of academic religious studies;
* helping to equip you to deal well with these issues as they arise in your own lives;
* contributing to your development as persons of good character, compassion, and servant-leadership; and
* helping you to cultivate skills in curiosity, reading, critical thinking, independent learning, collaboration, making connections, writing, listening, speaking, and reflection.

It may be helpful to think of how this course fits into the larger purpose of the institution, as reflected in BVU's Mission Statement:

> *"Buena Vista University is an independent, regionally acclaimed, comprehensive, teaching institution dedicated to 'education for service.' Buena Vista aspires to become the nation's leading 'New American College,' while retaining its Presbyterian heritage. The University prepares students for leadership and service in an information-driven, global society. The traditional disciplines provide a framework for a curriculum which prepares students for the professions and life-long learning."*

One of my aims in all of this is to be as helpful and accessible to you as I possibly can. I want to get to know each of you as persons, and I want each of you to learn and to grow. This means, among other things, that I will help you to do well with the course opportunities, as outlined below. But it also means that you will need to help me to learn your names and faces quickly, seek me out for help, talk to me about course content, problems...anything at all. We're in this together, and I expect serious commitment and hard work (and a desire to have some fun) from each of you.

Texts:

"Rebellion" and "The Grand Inquisitor," Fyodor Dostoevsky
God on Trial: The Book of Job and Human Suffering, Bill Thomason "Shadowlands" (film)
A Grief Observed, C.S. Lewis
"A Small, Good Thing," Raymond Carver
Christianity, Patriarchy, and Abuse: A Feminist Critique, Joanne Carlson Brown and Carole R.
      Bohn, editors (selected chapters: Joanne Carlson Brown and Rebecca Parker, "For God So
      Loved the World?" and Marie Fortune, "A Transformation of Suffering")
"The Problem of Evil" in David Stewart, *Exploring the Philosophy of Religion*, 4th edition
      (including excerpts from essays by John Hick and C.S. Lewis)
"Night and Fog" (film)
Night, Elie Wiesel
Holocaust: Religious and Philosophical Implications, John Roth and Michael Berenbaum (selected
      chapters: Terence Des Pres, "Excremental Assault" and Irving Greenberg, "Cloud of
      Smoke, Pillar of Fire")
"Weapons of the Spirit" (film)
The Sunflower, Simon Wiesenthal
The Giver, Lois Lowry

Course Opportunities:

1) Attendance and Participation (20%) The great philosopher Woody Allen is supposed to have said, "Life is 70% showing up." The most important factor in your succeeding in this course will be coming to and **driving** the class each day; regular attendance and **active involvement** are required (or better said: "necessary"). I will do frequent (basically daily) assessments of your leadership and participation in class. If you need to miss a day for athletic trips, serious illness, death in the family, and so on, please let me know IN WRITING so that I can count it as an excused absence as well as respond to you and your situation in a supportive and helpful way.

2) Two Papers (20% each; 40% total) will provide opportunity for sustained thinking about issues that emerge as central for you, as well as for helping each other to improve as writers (see next item). The first essay will put you in conversation with Ivan Karamazov, and the second will ask you to spell out your understanding of and response to "the problem of suffering," in conversation with other course readings.

3) One exam (10%) near the end of the term will be a comprehensive 45-minute one-on-one conversation with me, focused largely on the connections between your papers and portfolio (see #4) and the content of the course.

4) Active-learning portfolio (20%) will be a compilation of short critical-reflective essays, which cumulatively will amount to a "journal" of sorts for the semester, and service-learning as a hands-on way to extend what we do in class into the real world. **"150" students will need to include your choice of one of the following** (please indicate your choice to me by the end of the second day of class); **"450" students will include BOTH:**

- **"Critical-reflective essays":** Here's a chance to really shape your learning in ways that are meaningful to you. In response to some aspect of the material of your choice, or occasionally in response to a question from me, these quick (about 500 words), personal papers will ask you to connect your in-class learning with the Real World. These are intended to be opportunities for you to seriously *think through* some of the questions, insights, and challenges that arise from the subject matter of the course. You'll be encouraged to review, synthesize, probe, question, or disagree with me, the readings, and each other. Although they are meant to be informal, please do write them *well* (i.e., with consideration for proper grammar, providing support for your views, etc.). You'll submit these electronically, via the drop box in CourseInfo.

- **"Community Involvement"/Service-Learning** may take any shape you like it to. The idea is to take part in some sort of sustained community service activity in Storm Lake or another area community and connect it with the content of the course. You'll need to identify and commit yourself to some sort of meaningful community service project(s) for a **minimum of 15 hours** for the semester (roughly an hour a week). You can do this either as an individual or in groups, but it will be important that your service engage you directly in situations and relationships where you will be enabled to think more deeply about the content of the course while also making a meaningful contribution. You will also need to **bring your experiences to bear on regular class discussion and keep an ongoing journal (you'll submit a new entry to me via email at the end of each week)** on the interrelationships between the service experience and the "academic" content of the course. This is a modest exercise in experiential learning about the issues we tackle in this course: life and death, suffering and evil, the struggle to live well in the face of violence and despair. More details can be found on the handout, "Info on Community Involvement," available on the course website.

5) Creative Project (10%), formulated in consultation with me and presented to the class during our final exam period at my home, which gives expression to your **intellectual and emotional engagement with some important issue or aspect of the course**. Really struggle with this, and then **have a blast — go "outside the box"** in all kinds of ways. If you choose, you may collaborate with as many as two other people. The possibilities are virtually unlimited here, and the initiative is all yours. I'll be happy to talk over possibilities with you ahead of time, and help you as much as I can as you develop your project. But the thematic focus (the content) and the shape it takes (the form) are both up to you.

Assessment and Grading:

Criteria for Evaluation for these dimensions of your work will generally include the following (with variation and/or further detail to be spelled out in connection with individual assignments as appropriate). I'll ask: Does the work:
- ❖ show **accurate knowledge** of the texts read and themes discussed in the course? Are the important "facts" presented correctly?
- ❖ demonstrate good **comprehension** of the material, clearly explaining and connecting the ideas in your own words and in coherent, meaningful ways?
- ❖ show that you have been as **complete** and in-depth as possible, given reasonable restrictions on time or length?
- ❖ provide adequate **support** for its statements, drawing on **evidence** such as detailed, relevant examples or particular facts drawn from class materials and/or legitimate outside sources?
- ❖ adhere to standards of **academic integrity**, including citation of the sources of ideas, information, and materials that are not your own, whether you paraphrase or directly quote? (BTW: thanks to Dr. Jeffrey Carlson for the model for this section.) Academic dishonesty is not only immoral; it is (in some forms) also illegal. Plagiarism, intentional or otherwise, will

be grounds for failing the course. For more information, check out the University Academic Honesty Policy in your student handbook, or <u>on the Web</u>.

❖ **analyze** the material well, breaking it down into its parts and clearly explaining the relationships between the parts?
❖ **evaluate** the material, assessing its usefulness, meaningfulness, or truth, by providing a reasoned judgment based on clearly formulated criteria?
❖ exhibit **creativity, insight, passion,** and willingness even to **take risks,** in both content and expression?

Grading for the course will be on a percentage scale: 90% = A, 80% = B, etc. My understanding is that letter grades, while problematic in all sorts of ways, communicate something like the following.

❖ An A signifies excellence; "this is stunningly good, outstanding, exemplary, cutting-edge, standard-setting achievement."
❖ A B means "this is good, solid work. While it's not among the very best, it does stand out from the crowd."
❖ A C is average; "this is more or less on target but has room for improvement; nothing special but not disastrous either. You did the minimum to meet basic expectations and requirements."
❖ A D means "barely acceptable; big trouble, needs a lot of work."
❖ An F signals that "this ain't even on the planet. Dead On Arrival. Flush it."

[Normally the semester reading & assignment schedule is placed here. The handout "Info on Service-Learning" that follows is an abbreviated form of a separate handout that explains that portion of the syllabus in more detail.]

Info on Service-Learning

"So I'm taking a religion class at a place that aspires to be 'the nation's leading New American College,' where we're into things like 'Education for Service' and the 'Scholarship of Engagement.' So what? What does that have to do with me or this class? What's the deal with that thing in the syllabus about 'service-learning?'"

The Big Picture

Recall that the institutional mission statement (including the bit about "Education for Service") is included in the syllabus. Why? In order to get you to think about how your involvement in this course connects with the big picture of what this place is about, and with the fact that you're a college student HERE. Being in college is at least partly about becoming a leader, and leaders are people who serve. Somehow, your time here does have something to do with connecting you with other people, attuning you to other people's needs and perspectives, breaking you out of that "safe" but often pinched northwest Iowa shell, equipping you to be of some good in the world. All your classes should be helping you to do these things in some way or another. This class just happens to include another important means and opportunity — community involvement — for you to accomplish them. This little slice of the syllabus is a limited-scope experiment in what is often called "service-learning." So what's that?

Service-Learning

Service-learning is just that: the integration of service and learning where each is valued as necessary for the other. It is a way of learning that takes place through and within the performance of meaningful service in a community, *and* a way of enriching service through academic learning. Ideally it takes the form of service that is integrated into the curriculum in specific academic courses — which is, in a rudimentary form, the case with this class. I incorporate service learning into the class in order for you to learn (some of) the course content, in ways you otherwise would not be able to — as well as providing opportunity to grow in some of the "big picture" ways I mention above. Maybe it would help to think of the service as the "lab" for this class, a hands-on way of grappling with and putting into practice the ideas, the theories, the questions of the course.

It might also be helpful to know that service learning differs from other things with which it is sometimes confused. It is not the same thing, for example, as voluntarism (which is designed to benefit the community but isn't explicitly and purposefully connected with academic learning). Nor is it the same as internships (which emphasize the career development goals of the student but don't explicitly and purposefully benefit the community).

The Assignment

"OK, OK. That's all well and good, but what am I supposed to do for this part of the grade? What do you want?"

Here are the basics of the assignment:
1) Develop and commit to a sustained community service project (or small handful of projects) for a minimum of 15 hours for the semester (roughly an hour a week). You must begin your service by the end of the third week of the semester (if I don't hear anything from you — a service agreement form, a journal entry, etc.), I will assume that you are not completing this part of the assignment and you'll receive no credit for it.
2) Keep an ongoing journal on the interrelationships between the service experience and the "academic" content of the course.
3) Bring your experiences and reflections to bear on regular class discussion with colleagues.

Now, more detail:
Your first task will be to identify and involve yourself in some form of **meaningful service** with an organization or agency in the wider community (usually but not necessarily Storm Lake). Your primary aim will be to **connect** (especially via critically reflective writing and discussion) the service experience with the content of the course. The **quality** of the experience (in terms of your learning and their benefiting from your service) is the important thing; the quantity (15-hour minimum) is just a means to an end. Maggie Baker, Director of Community Service and Internships, can help you with project ideas and contacts.

Throughout the semester, keep a **journal** where you briefly describe the work you're doing (with whom, where, for how long, etc.) and, in greater depth, reflect on how that experience connects with what you're learning in class. Please submit your journal entries to me via email each time you perform your service activity. I'd encourage you to use your first entry to tell about your expectations and concerns, hopes and fears for this experience and speculate about how you think it might connect with the course. In your final entry at the end of the semester, critically reflect on how you've changed since the first entry and on how the service has helped you to think about your choice of issues, themes, questions, or insights from the class. (Also, you should identify and reflect on ways in which something you've encountered in class contributed to the effectiveness or meaningfulness of the service — remember the two-sided nature of service-learning, which I described above). I will provide you with additional reflection questions and prompts as the semester goes along.

One place to start might be with simply sketching a list of some of the **big issues** of the class. For example, in God and Human Suffering, these include:

- the cause, purpose, and meaning — the "Why?" — of suffering and evil; sustained and sophisticated thinking about the various theodicies we encounter in the readings and discussion; human versus divine responsibility for evil
- the nature of God, human apprehension and/or projection of God's attributes (power, goodness, love, justice, etc.)
- distinctions between and differing attitudes toward natural, moral, and systemic evil
- human nature: our capacities for and propensities toward good and evil, individuality versus connectedness, abilities and practices of resistance to or noncompliance with evil, the struggle to live well in the face of violence and despair
- care for people who are dying, ill, or in despair
- how human beings ought best to respond to suffering and evil (care for the dying, social activism and advocacy, etc.); the adequacy of "standard" responses such as "Everything happens for a reason," "Something good will come out of this," "God works in mysterious ways," "We couldn't have or know goodness without evil," and "It's not our place to question."
- the possibility and nature of forgiveness (tied in with issues of anger, punishment, justice, and retribution)
- the possibility and nature of religious faith after the Holocaust (or after any occurrence of any cataclysmic evil or profound suffering)
- the origins and meanings of classic Christian beliefs such as atonement, incarnation, resurrection, the suffering and death of Christ, etc., as they impinge upon issues and realities of suffering and evil

Your task will be to ponder those (and other, related) things as you serve, again keeping an ongoing journal that can serve as the basis for your substantive contributions to discussion. Finally, have your site supervisor (when appropriate) complete and sign the evaluation form, and include it in your active-learning portfolio along with your service-learning journal.

"Religion and Social Engagement: Labor and Business Ethics"

by John Leahy and Kim Bobo

Course Specifics

Religion 259, Religion and Social Engagement: Labor and Business Ethics is a 10-week community-based service-learning course, one of many new courses at DePaul University designed to satisfy an experiential learning requirement effective September 1999 for all graduates. Registration is open only to students with at least junior standing. The course is an offshoot of Religion/Management 228, Business, Ethics, and Society, which fulfills the American Assembly of Collegiate Schools of Business (AACSB) requirement for business graduates. Religion 259 received the approval of the Religious Studies Department, the Liberal Studies Council, and the University Office of Community-based Service-learning (CbSL).

DePaul University invited faculty to create community-based service-learning courses. This provided a safety valve for two mounting frustrations with the traditional business ethics course. Quarter after quarter, the general enthusiasm that students exhibited with regard to utilitarianism, Kant, Rawls, and Nozick deteriorated into general apathy when they encountered the religious ethics component of the course found in "Economic Justice for All," the 1986 pastoral letter of the American Roman Catholic Bishops. Discussion of poverty and its causes and the duty of domestic and international assistance embodied in the principle of the "preferential option for the poor" could be characterized as, at best, wooden.

The second source of frustration was the absence of a unit on organized labor in the more prominent business ethics textbooks. Compensatory attempts to introduce organized labor/management issues through plant visits and invited speakers were minimally effective. Since students had less information about the topic than the textbooks did, there was no base on which to construct effective learning.

Still, these frustrations alone would not have prompted the course proposal without two positive personal experiences had by one of us (Leahy). Service on the Chicago Workers' Rights Board brought him into contact with workers and their advocates by way of public hearings, study groups, and direct contact with laborers. He had to find some way to bring their questions and their situation to the business students who would be the managers and the policymakers who would affect those workers' lives.

The second experience had occurred years earlier when he worked with a competency-based M.A. program for adults in the workplace. The philosophy behind the program was firmly rooted in learning from and through experience. For the majority of students in the world of business, experience was the motivator for continued learning. And so, the genesis of this course is itself an example of how both negative and positive experiences can generate learning opportunities, not only for oneself but for others as well.

Why Service-Learning?

DePaul Perspective: DePaul introduced an experiential learning requirement for all undergraduate students as part of a mission-directed educational strategy. Community-based service-learning is one of six forms of experiential learning available to students. Students fulfill this requirement in their junior year, because much of the learning necessitates foundational knowledge and sufficient maturity to manage the independence essential for such an experience. Learning is gained through observation and participation in activities, most often in field-based settings outside the classroom. Learning by doing creates partnerships between the university and community-based agencies: In this case, the National Interfaith Committee for Worker Justice (NICWJ) provides and supervises the service activities.

National Interfaith Committee for Worker Justice Perspective: NICWJ came to this course with two goals. First, it was interested in acquainting students with worker justice issues. NICWJ's experience is that people in general, including students, learn the most when they are actively engaged in talking with and working with real people. Consequently, service-learning was an obvious model for helping students understand worker justice issues.

Second, NICWJ is trying to make real changes for low-wage workers in the city of Chicago. It believes that students, through surveys, research, organizing, and direct action activities, can make a concrete contribution to the efforts to improve conditions for low-wage workers.

Because goal two is the primary mission of the organization, goal one had to be done in such a way as to meet goal two. The educational opportunities offered had to support the work of NICWJ.

Learning Objectives

The course had two sets of learning objectives: skills, and conceptual and applied knowledge, as described in its course syllabus:

Skills: Students should be able to:

1. *Demonstrate interviewing skills, including preparation of questions, transcription of interviews, and synthesis of relevant content.* Because students would be asked to interview workers, we knew they would want to talk ahead of time about their questions and approach. Learning interviewing skills is obviously best learned "hands on."

2. *Produce writing both for academic and general audiences.* Because we wanted the students to prepare a project that would be useful to the National Interfaith Committee for Worker Justice, we needed the students to be able to write in a manner that was comprehensible to the general population. Generally speaking, students do not have these sufficiently strong writing skills. Hence, this became a learning objective.

3. *Reflect critically on their classroom and service activities through journal writing.* We wanted students to combine theory and experience, the abstract and the concrete. The journal is an effective tool for recording impressions and would allow students to think more personally and creatively about ways of creating the desired combinations.

4. *Work as responsible members of a team and as active contributors* — both to the gathering and processing of information (obtained through interviews) and to discussion in the classroom.

Conceptual and Applied Knowledge: Students should be able to:

1. *Understand the structure of low-wage industries.* We believed that students would understand an industry better if they researched it and talked directly with workers, unions, and managers.

2. *Use moral reasoning and apply at least three theories of distributive justice.* Instead of looking at moral questions in the abstract, students would be asked to reflect on real-life moral dilemmas they found in their research and conversations with workers.

3. *Understand the roles unions play in society.* Because most people who are not familiar with unions have negative stereotypes about them, the service-learning model is ideal for introducing students to the actual role unions play in low-wage workers' lives. Students would interview both union and nonunion workers. They also would interview union staff.

Plan to Develop Appropriate Service Activities

Industries Selected for Study: Because the Chicago branch of the National Interfaith Committee for Worker Justice has had active campaigns to improve working conditions for nursing home workers, janitors, and day laborers, the course developers decided to focus on three industries: nursing homes, janitorial firms, and day labor agencies.

Background Information on Selected Industries: NICWJ compiled background resources on the industries selected. This material was then placed on the electronic reserve shelf for students to review.

Interview Arrangements: Because the course began in the fall and we wanted students to get out and talk with workers right away, the staff of the service-learning office and the staff of NICWJ set up interviews with workers and union leaders for selected weeks. By the start of the course, most of the interviews had already been scheduled. The names of all the people to be approached were provided by NICWJ. When problems arose, NICWJ intervened to get the needed appointments. Indeed, many of the appointments were made possible only because of the long-term relationships the organization had with the workers and unions.

Preparation and Distribution of Course Syllabus: The syllabus and calendar that were prepared and distributed in the first class (although minor changes were made at several points throughout the semester) intermingled interviews, participation in events, and outside activities with more traditional coursework and ongoing reflection on the outside activities.

Service-Learning Hours: A simple form was distributed to students to help them account for their service-learning hours. In addition to the hours directly related to their projects (e.g., interviews, research on particular industries), students were expected to attend special rallies, worker forums, picket lines, or other worker events to complete their 25-hour service requirement. Among the activities students participated in were:

• A rally of steelworkers who had been on strike for six months. Students reported conversations they had with workers on the line about why they had gone on strike and how they supported their families. Students were surprised by the joyful reception they received and were urged on by workers to continue their education.

• An event outside a garment factory. At the last minute, the event was canceled, but the students did not know this. They walked inside a garment sweatshop looking for the event. When they inquired about a strike, they were escorted out by management. The students were shocked to learn there were such sweatshops in Chicago and be treated with what they thought were poor manners.

• An evening survey of people in homeless shelters sponsored by the Chicago Coalition for the Homeless about their experiences working in day labor. A group of 30 interviewers (including the students, the faculty member, and a staff member from NICWJ) surveyed approximately 800 people outside homeless shelters about their experiences. The results were used in a report by the Coalition on day labor agencies. One of the agencies was the subject of extensive reporting in the *Chicago Tribune* about misuse of city contracts.

• A Workers' Rights Board hearing about the day labor industry. The students helped set up and attended a hearing on day labor held by the Chicago Workers' Rights Board. One of the students served as timekeeper for witnesses offering testimony.

• Journals. Students were asked to keep journals, which were reviewed at midterm and again at the end of the semester. At midterm, students were given concrete instructions on how to go beyond just listing events to develop a more reflective document.

• Paper/project. The students were asked to prepare a general background on one of the selected industries as well as interview results that could then be adapted into a useful tool by NICWJ. (These should have been started sooner in order to get something truly usable.)

• Class locations. Classes were held both at the DePaul downtown campus and at the offices of the National Interfaith Committee on Worker Justice in order to give students a better feel for the life and work of a nonprofit community-based organization. Travel time between locations was about 40 minutes on the city's train system.

Procedures and Administrative Issues

A service-learning hours form was developed as we got into the course as a means of tracking student service. However, because the class was small, when special learning opportunities (such as rallies or events) arose, students were called directly. Many of them seemed surprised to receive this kind of personal attention. (When the class becomes larger, we will need to develop broadcast email systems to reach everyone quickly.)

Students who came to the first class session were surprised, if not shocked, to learn that the course required an additional 25 hours of service. They were unaware of the requirement, and most dropped the class. This was the first quarter the new requirement went into effect. Now the new university course registration booklet clearly marks CbSL courses and explains their demands.

Success of the Service Activities

The course was extremely successful in reaching the first goal under "Conceptual and Applied Knowledge," that is, helping students understand low-wage worker issues. It was moderately successful with goals two and three (the ability to use moral reasoning and apply at least three theories of distributive justice, and an understanding of the roles unions play in society). It was also moderately successful in achieving goal three under "Skills" (developing critical reflection through journal writing). It was less successful in helping students develop interviewing skills and producing writing for general audiences (goals one and two).

The course was also less successful in helping the National Interfaith Committee on Worker Justice meet its organizational objectives of improving conditions for low-wage workers. Clearly, we must in the future work more effectively to ensure that the educational opportunities provided the students better meet the primary self-interest of the partner organization. We believe this is possible, given the lessons learned this past semester.

However, despite this mixed record of success, the presence of DePaul faculty and NICWJ staff at many of the service activities not only demonstrated interest in the students' experiences but also served as a strong support for and confidence builder in this new form of learning. In addition, NICWJ staff members attended almost every class.

Toward the end of the course, the instructors spent half an hour working with the class on evaluating what worked and what did not. Although some of the service-learning experiences were "scary" for the students, there is no question they learned a great deal from them. Students gained enormous empathy for the plight of low-wage workers. Three-fourths of the students offered to be involved in activities in the future to support low-wage workers in Chicago. Some student suggestions included postponing the interviews until later in the quarter to allow students to get a firmer background on unions and on the relevant industry, and spending more time at the beginning providing assistance on how to do journals. Some students also noted that the double campus commute was confusing.

Lessons Learned

1. Students are unprepared to interview workers. We found that students were scared and ill-equipped to talk with workers. Thus, we must make more of an effort to prepare them. However, the basic activity of having them interview workers was in itself very powerful and useful.

2. Students should begin their projects sooner. If projects are going to be done to benefit the community partner, they must be started by midsemester in order to develop them enough for them to be useful.

3. Students should do some basic service work for the partner organization. In order to ensure that the partner organization gets enough out of the program, students should be required to do some basic service tasks (stuffing envelopes, recruitment calls) as part of their overall hours.

4. Students need more help with their writing skills. Generally speaking, the students' writing skills were poor, and more attention needs to be given to helping them write for a general audience.

5. Classes should be held on campus. In order to give the students a variety of learning opportunities, we held some classes at the community partner's office, and these were scheduled for longer periods. However, this arrangement did not work with students' schedules. In the future, we will respect the class time at the assigned campus location. Then, the service-learning hours can be negotiated directly between the students and the community partner.

6. The class should maintain its diversity of activities. Students really appreciated and learned from the outside activities, such as rallies and hearings. Future classes should encourage students to be involved in a broad range of these activities.

7. The syllabus should explicitly state as a course goal helping the partner organization to research and produce material to meet its organizational objectives.

Course: Religion 259
Religion and Social Engagement: Labor and Business Ethics

Community-based Service-Learning Supervisor:
Kim Bobo, Executive Director, and Kristi Sanford, Organizer
National Interfaith Committee for Worker Justice
1020 W. Bryn Mawr, 4th floor
Chicago, Il 60660-4627
773-728-8400
FAX 773-728-8409
Kbobo@aol.com

Academic Instructor:
John Leahy, S.T.D., Associate Professor
DePaul University (Office SAC 434)
2320 N. Kenmore
Chicago, Il 60614
773-325-7209
jleahy@condor.depaul.edu

Location and time: Academic: 12:00-1:00 P.M. M-W-F
Lincoln Park Campus, Faculty Building, Room LL107

Service-Learning: See address above under Service-Learning Supervisor
Hours to be arranged with Kristi Sanford

1. Content of course. The course will study the relations between labor and management from an ethical point of view. It will take a normative, rather than a descriptive, approach to ethics in accord with the way ethics is studied in Philosophy and in Religion Departments. In particular, the course will study issues of distributive justice, especially in relation to labor organizing, wages, and benefits for workers in our society. The primary readings on ethical theory are taken from John Rawls and Robert Nozick, whose theses dominate the discussion of distributive justice in our society, and from a representative of American religious thinking on these matters, the American Catholic Bishops.

2. Nature of the course. This is a 4-credit course offered as one of the options for fulfilling an experiential-learning requirement. The course involves community-based service-learning -- the community, in this instance, being the Chicago Interfaith Committee for Worker Justice. The goal of the course is student learning through participation in service to the community. The instructors represent the academic side of the University and the community service side of the Interfaith Committee.
 This course is part of a new learning experience at DePaul that combines passive presence with active participation. It puts students in the position of discovering and creating knowledge for the human community through firsthand contact with persons whose work lives generate the issues that are studied in the classroom.

3. New demands. The new learning experience, however, comes with a price. It disrupts the more comfortable situation of sitting in the classroom with other students and exchanging information with them. As irrelevant and tiresome as many students thought this experience to be, at least it was predictable. The cost of relevance and action, which the new learning experience provides, is increased preparation time, the need for flexible scheduling, and even some challenges to the usual daily life plan. To participate in this course, students must take direct responsibility for their learning. They organize their learning by sorting out the raw material of their experiences, by communicating those experiences in a fashion that informs and, perhaps, sensitizes others who have not had a similar experience with the ethical demands of work life. It will not be enough to have opinions. One will also have to support them with evidence and theory.

4. New setting for learning. The course expands the traditional setting for learning from the traditional campus to such locations as the community-based organization, meeting halls hosting public hearings, and the public square entertaining citizen rallies. The Lincoln Park campus and the Interfaith Committee will serve as home sites for theory and reflection. Off-campus sites for interviews with workers, union officials, and company managers, for hearings of grievances, for public demonstrations, and for assisting the Interfaith Committee, Jobs With Justice, and the Chicago Coalition for the Homeless with their daily activities will supply the experiences and reflection on which to build cases studies.

5. Goal. The goal of the course is to produce a reflective journal and an original piece of research on low-income workers in our society. The journal will allow one to keep a record of experiences and, especially, one's critical reflection on them.

The research will:
  a. serve the work of the Interfaith Committee; and
  b. demonstrate the student's ability to combine theory and experience, the abstract and the concrete, in his/her learning.
Students will demonstrate:
  a. understanding of the labor movement in the United States, including an understanding of the purpose and work of the Interfaith Committee, Jobs With Justice, and the Chicago Coalition for the Homeless;
  b. understanding of concepts used in ethical thinking;
  c. the ability to explain and apply at least three ethical theories of distributive justice;
  d. the ability to apply the theories to the resolution of moral issues using the moral reasoning process.
More specifically, the student should be able:
  a. to exercise the moral reasoning process;
  b. to carry out the interview process from the formulation of questions to a synthesis of findings;
  c. to keep a journal reflecting on experiences in service learning, including a critical evaluation of them;
  d. to work as a responsible member of a team and as an active contributor both to the gathering and processing of information obtained through interviews and other participatory service-learning, as well as to discussion in the classroom.

6. Assistance. Four persons will assist in the learning experience: the two instructors, a staff member with the Chicago Interfaith Committee, and a staff member with the Community-based Service-Learning Program (CbSL). Professor Leahy's primary responsibility will focus on conceptual issues in ethical thinking, while Ms. Bobo will provide background on the labor movement and labor leaders in the Chicago area. Both will assist students in reflection on experiences outside the traditional classroom, journal writing, formulating interview questions, and preparing the final product. Ms. Kristi Sanford, Organizer for the Chicago Interfaith Committee, will serve as resource adviser and liaison with the Interfaith Committee. She can be reached at the Committee offices.

7. Resources. The living resources will be the staffs of the Interfaith Committee, Jobs With Justice, the Chicago Coalition for the Homeless, low-income workers, the union leaders, and the company managers. Videos, readings, and other learning resources appear on a separate sheet. Most of the readings for the course are on the Electronic Reserve Shelf (EreS), which can be accessed through the DePaul Library www.depaul.edu. I will give instructions in class as to how you can retrieve the readings. (You will need an Acrobat Reader.) Specific required readings are found in the daily calendar.

8. Grading. Grading will follow the DePaul Bulletin 1999-2001. Grades will be distributed in the following manner:
- A quiz on distributive justice (20% of the final grade) scheduled for Class 21.
- A journal, which will be graded twice, about the middle of the quarter (10%) and again at the end of the quarter (20%)=30% of the final grade.
- Participation in activities, including attendance and the whole interview process=20%
- Project: Case Study research at the end of the course=30%.

I follow the description of grading found in the Bulletin 1999-2001. Numerically, the grades are A=93-100; A-=89-92; B+=86-88; B=83-85; B-79-82; C+=76-78; C=73-75; C=69-72; D+=64-68; D=60-63; F=below 60. For special rules in relation to plagiarism, see the Bulletin 1999-2001.

Presence in class and at service-learning activities is required for maximum benefit in relation to grading. An absence means no contribution for the day or no participation in a required activity. Two unexcused absences will lower the final grade a letter, and three unexcused absences will result in failure for the course. An absence is considered "excused" when Professor Leahy or Ms. Kristi Sanford is informed with reason before class or service activity by phone, in person, or by email. Three "tardies" are the equivalent of one unexcused absence. Please consider another course if you do not intend to engage in the level of involvement this course requires both inside and outside the classroom.

9. Interview Schedule. The interviews will take place with workers, union officials, and managers in two different occupations: janitors and day laborers. The schedule for the interviews will be coordinated by the National Interfaith office and the office of Community-based Service-Learning (CbSL) at DePaul.

10. Time distribution: In class: 30 hours
Service-learning participation: 25 hours. Of the 25 hours, 10-15 will consist of assisting the three agencies in their daily activity, and another 10-15 hours will be dedicated to interviews and settings found in paragraph number 4 above. (A time sheet will be distributed to keep track of the hours.)

11. Journals & Final Exam.

1. Keep all the journals I return to you. At present, you should have three weekly journals and the midterm synthesis that includes the fourth week. Journal schedule from now until the end of the quarter:
Class 19: Turn in a journal for Week 6.
Class 22: Turn in a journal for Week 7.
Class 25: Turn in a journal for Week 8.
Class 29: Turn in the final journal.

- The journal should be 5-6 pages long and follow suggestions that I made on your midterm journal, as well as on the other journals you wrote.
- It should be a synthesis of the previous three journals you will have turned in and include Week 9. (Late journals will be deducted 5 points for each day late.)
- At this time, turn in all the journals. There should be a total of 8 in all. All the journals you turn in should be typed.

2. Final exam: The final exam is scheduled for Week 11, 11:45-2:00 P.M. (The last day of class is Friday of Week 10.)
- The final exam will be a take-home exam that will apply moral theories of distributive justice to the information you gather in your interviews. So, the final works from the interview material. More details will follow.
- Also, more information on how to apply the theories of distributive justice to moral issues will be provided in class.
- At the latest, plan to turn in the exams by 2:00 P.M. of exam day. I prefer that you turn them in earlier, if possible. No exams will be accepted after 2:00 P.M. of exam day.

3. Final journal instructions:

- The final journal is a final synthesis of reflections on your learning through service and course learning.
- The journal may refer to material from the first half of the course, but its major focus should be learning since the last journal. The emphasis, therefore, should be on Weeks 6-9.

Be sure that all of your journals from the beginning of the course are handed in during Class 29 with the final journal.

- The journal will follow the instructions for synthesis and grading criteria handed out for the Midterm Journal, which was due during Class 16. The final journal will differ from its midterm companion by reason of depth. In the second half of the quarter, service has developed into interview and class work involving deeper conceptual issues. The learning from both of these experiences should be the focus of the assignment. Accordingly, the journal will devote less space to description and more to analysis and application. In the application section, one of the items you want to address is the set of issues dealt with in chapter 6 of Coles that is assigned for Class 26.

- The weekly journals you turned in should be of great assistance in tracing your thoughts. Remember, however, that the work of synthesis is to reduce the material by organizing it and shaping it. This is where the journal becomes an exercise in creativity, an exercise that will be only as good as the level of understanding and reflection that you bring to it.

- The Final Journal should be 5-7 pages long, double-spaced, font 10 or 12. Please organize all the other journals so they are easily accessible for me to consult.

Making a Difference With Service-Learning:
"Christian Ethics and Modern Problems"

by Walter H. Schuman

Background

I have taught Christian Ethics and Modern Problems at Ashland University every other year for the last 26 years. It has been an elective course for undergraduate religion majors and honors students, but only since 1995 has it had a service-learning component. Students taking the course know beforehand that they will be expected to complete 30 hours of service with a community project they may select in consultation with the professor and site supervisor.

Although I did not incorporate a service-learning component into this course until recently, I had successfully integrated service-learning into another course, Death and Dying, since 1973 and have continued to teach three sections of that course every year. My interest in service-learning began with a research project entitled "Lessons From the Dying." Students were assigned to residents in a nursing home or to individuals served by hospice programs who were living out the end stages of their lives. The students were to share at least two hours a week with a dying person and listen to his or her story, trying to make connections with their reading assignments in Kubler-Ross, Tolstoy, and Plato and with Hebrew, Christian, and Hindu scriptures. The most important thing I discovered through this project was that learning comes through a series of partnerships between students, teachers, and the community. This experience convinced me that serious academic learning could be achieved through service. Since 1973, I have tried to incorporate a service-learning component in all my courses with the Honors Program and several of the courses in the Religion Department.

Service-Learning Rationale

Rather than speak in generalities about the course objectives for Christian Ethics and Modern Problems, I would like instead to turn to one student as a case study: Valen Jones, a religion and psychology major and academic honors student. Together we coauthored an article for the university newspaper, *The Collegian*. Herewith is an excerpt from the article, "Making a Difference With Service-Learning":

In the fall of 1997, I was a student in Prof. Schuman's Christian Ethics class. One of the requirements for the class was participation in a community service project. I chose to assist the deputy chief of the Barberton Fire Department. He was upset by the total number of fire deaths in his city over the past three years, and he was involved in a project to reduce this total. After contacting him recently in order to follow up, I was very happy to find that we had made a significant difference in the lives of the citizens of Barberton.

Deputy Chief Dennis Eller of the Barberton Fire Department began this project because he was alarmed by the fact that within the past three years, his city had lost nine children and three adults to fire. All of these deaths could have been prevented by fire safety education. He began an applied research project to remedy this problem.

At that time, Barberton had minimal fire education. The only education they provided was during Fire Prevention Week in October. During this week, firefighters only spoke at the schools if requested to do so. Also, those firefighters who did speak at the public schools had no educational instruments to demonstrate the effects of fire on a home. The department provided tours of the fire station; however, these tours often did not involve any fire prevention or safety education.

Senior citizen housing developments in the area were another concern to Deputy Chief Eller. These developments had no fire prevention programs in place.

I helped Deputy Chief Eller in several areas. First, I researched material regarding fire safety education. Deputy Chief Eller was able to obtain a Fire Safety House through the donations of several community groups, including the Red Cross. I then assisted with the education of children in the Barberton Public Schools. Finally, I helped Deputy Chief Eller write a paper, which he presented to the National Fire Academy, regarding this applied research project.

The results of my voluntarism have been wonderful. First, currently, every second grade class in the Barberton City Schools (a total of 21 classes) is now being taught NFPA's Learn Not to Burn program continuously throughout the year. Second, the city now has a Fire Safety House [that] aids in teaching about fire. Third, five preschools now use the Learn Not to Burn program throughout the year. In the spring of 1999, first and third grade classes in all the public schools will begin to incorporate this program. Fourth, all three senior citizen developments now hold monthly blood pressure drives and offer fire safety classes quarterly. Finally, the most wonderful news is that within the last year, Barberton has not had any fire deaths!

Previously, the Barberton Fire Department assigned only one man to fire

safety education. Now, a fire education committee exists, which involves 14
firefighters with an addition of five more firefighters pending.

My involvement with this project was time-consuming. However, it is
wonderful to know that a project that I participated in has actually saved
lives. From my experience, I would strongly suggest that others become
involved with a community project. It is truly a rewarding experience.

What made Valen's project a model for doing service-learning at
Ashland University? First, it was grounded in the academic course objectives. Service was not an add-on. It was a means to learn how we unite individual moral decision making with the moral responsibility of the community. Another course objective was to learn how we form a moral community that is marked by justice and concern for all creation. In Valen's project,
the question was how to protect the lives of innocent children who are being
destroyed by needless fires.

Service-learning is first and foremost a pedagogical model, a teaching-
learning methodology. It may prepare students for active citizenship,
increase moral awareness, develop leadership skills, instill compassion for
those in need — but all these are secondary benefits to the primary function
of service-learning in the curriculum, that is, to learn through service.
Second, service-learning is grounded in a need defined by the community,
not a preconceived project of the course, "a make-work assignment." Valen
worked with community leaders and developed a fire safety education program with the public school system. She was learning not only how moral
consensus is formed but also how to establish moral values that will shape
a community in the future. The Barberton community was her classroom.
Its parents, children, and safety officials were her teachers. Third, in order
for service to be integrated with learning, it must have some form of reflection on the service in light of the course objectives. Valen chose to do a journal that had the form of a progress report; she clearly had certain personal
goals to fulfill in her class project. Fourth, final evaluation of service-learning is not of the service or even the accomplishment of student goals but of
the learning that is demonstrated through the service. Valen clearly demonstrated in her journal how moral decisions are made, how a moral climate
is developed in a community, and how values are sustained to improve the
future common good of a particular group. She learned how to "do ethics,"
which was the primary goal of the course, and her evaluation was based on
these clear academic objectives, not sincerity or even hard work.

When Valen came to me about her project on fire prevention, I must
honestly say I did not think it would work. It appeared to be an educational
project, not a way to do ethics. I told her she would have to convince me that
her service was tethered to the goals of the course. After my first evaluation
of her journal, I was convinced! Valen was caught up in a hornets' nest of

conflicting interests among the mayor of Barberton, who wanted to tear down the housing project as a blight on the city; the American Housing Authority, which was petitioning to save the building; the fire chief, who saw the problem as one of education; the Red Cross, which was already collecting money for fire prevention kits; and the residents themselves, who just felt helpless and powerless. How do you form moral consensus within such a sociopolitical structure? Valen rolled up her sleeves. She wanted to "challenge the bureaucracy," as she put it. She wanted to arouse the moral consciousness of the poor. So, together with the deputy chief, she made weekly visits to the housing project. They formed coalitions with the fire department. Together, they petitioned the mayor. In the end, the housing project was spared; the firefighters were on a crusade to save lives, and the residents felt empowered to change their own plight. How does moral change occur? Valen learned that what she was reading in Niebuhr and Bonhoeffer could take place if one had the courage to act. "Wow," she said. "I didn't think I could make such a difference."

What is most important is that all this took place outside the formal structure of community agencies or campus resources. It happened because one individual, Valen, found the right service opportunity. In her words: "I wanted to save kids' lives." She was a rebel with a cause.

Pedagogical Procedures

If service were to be grounded in course objectives instead of an add-on to learning, a change of pedagogy was needed. The starting point was to design a service-learning project around course objectives. Valen, along with other students in the class, met with me individually to design the service project in a way similar to how students in biology would begin a research project in the lab. We asked questions similar to those that would be asked in lab science; for example, would this experience help me test certain hypotheses?

The second step was to meet with community leaders, in a role not as the students' lab assistants but as their partners, to fine-tune the proposal with what was possible in the context of community need. Ashland, Ohio, is a rural community with social problems, but it has few of the traditional social service agencies to assist in meeting these needs. Students had to look for community service not only with structured agencies but also with individuals and groups. Valen chose to work with the deputy chief of the Barberton Fire Department in designing a fire prevention program in a rundown housing project. We discovered that some of the best community service projects were found not with social service agencies but in working with socially concerned individuals.

The third step was to develop a volunteer service contract (on the next page). We met in the community setting. This was a very important element in the changed pedagogy. The community was the base of operation where professor, student, and community partner were all on equal footing. The contract was more akin to a covenant with promises and commitments than a legal checklist of responsibilities and duties. In Valen's case, the deputy chief had as much to say about the project goals as we did from an academic standpoint. Again, the emphasis on partnership had to be in place if community needs were going to intersect with academic goals.

The fourth step was to create an environment where discovery and insight could take place. Students had to keep a journal with guided reflection questions that emerged from both the service setting and the classroom. More often than not, it was cognitive dissonance — conflicts between what was being read and what was being experienced — that opened the door to learning. Students were also encouraged in class discussion to illustrate their ethical arguments with their experiences in the community. It was essential to treat the insights students had from the service experiences as equal to their reading reflections.

The fifth, and perhaps the most important, step in the changed pedagogical method was arranging meetings with students to discuss what they were learning. It was in that setting that Valen declared she was a changed person through her experience:

> It is not what I learned, but what I have become. I discovered the moral character in me. Church is not just a building you attend on Sunday; it is wherever you go in service, and for me, it was the housing project. This experience forced me to question things I would never have thought of before.

This testimony was repeated over0 and over again by the students that met regularly with me to discuss their projects.

Monitoring Service-Learning

The key to monitoring service-learning is a caring partnership among the site supervisor, student, and professor. I sought out people who had some clinical training experience. Pastors and chaplains were also very helpful in encouraging and modeling service. I asked supervisors to meet with students at least four times during the semester so that in the final evaluation, we could assess the progress that was made throughout the semester. I met with students three times during the semester to assist them in making connections between their service experience and their reading assignments. This seemed to be the most difficult task for them. It required a different

CHRISTIAN ETHICS 401
Professor Walter H. Schuman

SERVICE-LEARNING PROJECT REQUIREMENTS

1. Select an organization/agency to work with for the semester from the list of community service programs or design your own program with approval of the professor. Contact the agency and fulfill its requirement for volunteer work. Thirty hours is suggested as a minimum for the semester. It may be divided as best fits the agency's needs and the student's schedule.

2. A journal must be kept with weekly entries on what you are doing and learning from this experience. Crucial to service-learning is how the experience connects to what you are learning in the classroom. A midterm and final summary of approximately two pages in length must be included in the journal.

3. A Volunteer Service Contract must be filled out and returned by the third week of the semester. A final Student Evaluation Form must be returned before the date of the Final Exam.

kind of textual reading — not for mastery of information, but for questions raised and answers suggested in relation to the service projects.

Each student had to keep a journal with two entries a week to interpret their experiences in light of the reading assignments. Using H. Richard Niebuhr's ideas from *The Responsible Self* (Harper and Row, 1963), students were to ask, What is going on here? What ought to go on here? How am I to interpret this event? Who is responsible, and for what? What is a fitting response to this?

How students answered these questions in their journals clearly demonstrated their ability to integrate service with learning. It was a key factor in monitoring the project.

Assessment in Service-Learning

Assessment is still a problematic issue in service-learning. Although the assessment is of the learning, not the service, the two cannot be completely separated in the final evaluation. Students received academic credit (75 points out of 100) if they completed the community service as it was outlined in the volunteer service contract. In order to move beyond a grade of C, the journal, the two student summary evaluations in the journal, and the final student evaluation form came into play as instruments to measure the learning in the service. Students who clearly demonstrated creative connections in reading text and service, asked probing questions that brought service into dialogue with classroom discussions, and offered observations on their experiences were awarded a portion of the remaining 25 points. This was an imperfect way to value their community service yet grade the learning in the service.

Postscript

Service-learning can be time-consuming and exhausting, and it presents formidable challenges to faculty and administration. So why should we incorporate it into our courses? Because it is fun and exciting! The collaborative partnerships that form between faculty and students, campus and community; the interdisciplinary and multidisciplinary knowledge that is shared; the community of mutual concern that is developed — all make education come alive again. Learning takes place in a larger context than the classroom and offers faculty, students, and the community a vehicle to respond in collaborative ways to critical issues that face our communities, our nation, and our world. It is a form of education that can make a difference — which is why I have included it in my courses.

Christian Ethics and Modern Problems 401
Professor Walter H. Schuman
Ashland University
Fall 1997

COURSE TITLE AND DESCRIPTION:

Christian Ethics and Modern Problems, 401, 3 credit hours. An exploration of moral decision making by Christians as individuals and community.

PURPOSE AND PROCEDURE:

The student will be given an opportunity to develop a Christian approach to personal and social ethics by examining contemporary moral dilemmas. The particular concern of this course is to unite individual moral decision making with the moral responsibility of the Christian and civic community.

COURSE OBJECTIVES:

1. To develop a Christian approach on <u>Doing</u> ethics.
2. To apply this approach to ethical problems in the world today.
3. To develop an appreciation not only for student rights but what is the right thing to do, the moral responsibility of Christians.
4. To broaden the student appreciation of individual responsibility to include the community of faith in moral decision making.
5. To appreciate the difficulty of forming a moral consensus in the civic arena.
6. To make a difference toward the common good in a given community.

INSTRUCTIONAL APPROACH:

Students will be expected to complete 30 hours of service in a community project that may be selected by the student in consultation with the professor and site supervisor.

A journal must be kept with weekly entries on what you are doing and learning from this experience. Crucial to service is how the experience connects to what you are learning in the classroom. A midterm and final summary of your experience of approximately two pages in length must be included in the journal.

A Volunteer Service Contract must be filled out and returned by the third week of the semester, and the Final Student Evaluation form must be returned before the date of the final exam.

The Interweaving of "World Religions" and Service-Learning in a Community College Setting

by Raj Ayyar

I have been teaching World Religions and humanities in the Florida community college system for the past 19 years. During my years at Brevard Community College (BCC), I realized early in the game that the student is not a blank slate/empty container dutifully "filled" by the instructor. Concepts remain in a void of abstraction unless the learner is actively engaged and encouraged to relate concepts to his or her life through journaling, individual and group presentations, and in-class reflective exercises that bridge the gap between the abstraction and that students' lived reality.

This is particularly relevant within the community college setting, since many students who attend a two-year college are into a quick-fix functionalism that discounts the humanities as irrelevant to their career goals, as something they have to take as a necessary condition of graduation. Many of them come into a world religions course or a philosophy course with a martyred, sometimes truculently martyred, attitude. So unless the instructor can kindle their interest by building experiential bridges between abstract concepts and lived reality enlivened by real-life examples, personal anecdotes, and humor, that instructor is likely to face student apathy, attrition, negative evaluations, and sheer disregard for course objectives and lesson plans. In the community college, experiential education is not a cute experiment but, in some definite ways, a bread-and-butter necessity for humanities instruction.

All through the 1980s, I played with different learning strategies, including journaling, in-class group presentations, and end-of-term debriefing sessions. However, I did not move from generalized experiential learning to the specific subset of experiential learning known as service-learning until the 1990s. When I took a sabbatical in 1989, I decided to do research and work with the homeless in the Tenderloin District of San Francisco. I learned a great deal from my clients — about despair, great, sometimes absurd hope, and a gritty flair for survival. This experience was so life-transforming that I wanted to include a service component in my courses.

This essay is dedicated to the memory of Sandy Sheehy, who was an outstanding international service-learning success story. Her groundbreaking volunteer effort with abandoned and homeless children in India and Nepal was a personal, professional, and spiritual awakening for her, an awakening that left its indelible imprint on her life. Sandy died an absurd-tragic death in a car accident that killed her shortly before graduation night.

When I returned to teaching at BCC in 1991, the time was ripe for my newfound interest in voluntarism and service. I wanted to motivate students to get actively involved with the community. One such avenue opened up when I agreed to sponsor the Partners in Community (PIC) club. This club encouraged service and crisis agencies in the community to visit the campus and set up booths and tables in an outdoor picnic atmosphere. At these events, the agencies would share information about their goals and service needs and recruit student volunteers. Participating agencies included homes for battered women and children, a girls' ranch for abused young women, homeless shelters, and hospice representatives and counselors from HIV support groups and organizations. PIC got a major boost when Roger Henry, director of the BCC's Center for Service-Learning, decided to recognize PIC, not just as a service-learning organization on campus but as a full-fledged service agency. PIC was instrumental in helping not only to serve as a bridge between the campus and the outside community but also to create a sense of community at an often alienated commuter campus. Its constitution underlined PIC's commitment to understanding and serving the marginalized or oppressed *other*.

BCC now has an extremely well-organized service-learning center under Roger Henry's leadership. The center recruits large numbers of faculty and students in its efforts to link service and education. Placements are available at 200+ agencies throughout the county. I began my own service-learning adventure modestly enough by just adding an extra credit option to my syllabi, whereby the student could get 20 extra points for documented service at any agency, working a minimum of 20 hours per semester.

Many students jumped at the opportunity to get extra points and thus played the service-learning game to milk the grade benefits of my bonus-points bribe. However, many surprised themselves and their instructor by discovering how life-transforming the experience of service could be. Many changed their majors and careers because of the fieldwork in which they were involved. Some became service "addicts" in that they continued to work at their agencies long after the semester and the 20-point bribe were over.

Through the early 1990s, I developed and transformed the service component from "mere" voluntarism to an integral part of the World Religions course. By the mid-1990s, my students had an array of service-learning options. One such option involved extra points for 20+ hours in the field plus a reflective paper on the same experience. A fourth-credit option developed, whereby a student could get one whole extra course credit by doing 50 additional hours in the field, a reflective paper, in-class debriefing sessions, and an end-of-term debriefing session. The fourth-credit option altered World Religions from a three- to a four-credit course. For students who elected one of these service options, I decided to waive the final examination.

Furthermore, as my course moved from voluntarism to a full-fledged incorporation of service-learning, my own understanding of the students' service work became more discipline specific.

I have learned a lot through dialogic interaction with those students who have chosen one of the service options. I have come to realize that service-learning is much, much more than a comfort zone teaser that provides a channel for the philanthropic student to give back to the community; it is a powerful tool for cultural diversity learning. Whether students work with the homeless or with people who are HIV-positive or with seniors afflicted with Alzheimer's, they are challenged to go beyond the parochialism of their conditioning as far as ethnicity, class, age, gender, sexual orientation, or disease status is concerned. However, whereas *cultural diversity* deals with learning to respect the *other* in general, no matter what the differences are, service-learning is more specifically concerned with the oppressed *other*. Given the fact that one of the stated objectives of my course is that the learner will understand and respect cultural and religious differences, going beyond his or her personal orientation, service-learning provides an ideal discipline-specific tool for teaching about differences and diversity.

The spiritual dimension common to many religions is that of compassion, seen as unconditional respect for the divine spark within the *other* and learning to hear, work with, and forgive the *other*, whatever his or her differences or "trespasses." Many students report that they are able to concretize the concept of compassion, even as the reflective process enables them to work through their own agendas and learn to identify compassion as something distinctly different from mere codependency or their own grade-related interests.

In 1994-95, I decided to extend the ambit of my World Religions course and its service-learning dimension by planning a study abroad program in India and adding a strong international service-learning component. This was unique at the time in the context of a community college. Indeed, international service-learning is still a novelty. In the mid-1990s, it was a challenging and yet rewarding enterprise that entailed working with a nervous BCC administration that had real concerns about possible liability issues arising from the project. The program was structured so that students who simply wanted World Religions credit during their study abroad would receive six credit hours, while those who also elected the service-learning option would get nine credit hours.

The India study abroad program was a success, far beyond my expectations. Not only did my students learn firsthand about several major world religions — including Hinduism, Buddhism, Syrian Orthodox Christianity, and Indian Islam — through the immersion process, but three of them took the service-learning option and worked at Mother Theresa's home for abandoned children in Calcutta (shortly before Mother Theresa passed away), an experience that changed their lives.

World Religions (REL 2300)

Instructor Raj Ayyar

Objectives:
The major objective of this course is to introduce the learner to the mystical and philosophical aspects of the world's major religions. We will emphasize the underlying parallels rather than the dogmatic differences between the faiths that we study. A prerequisite for the course is a willingness to encounter multiple perspectives with an open mind. We will discuss ethnocentrism as a critical block in the way of understanding world religions. We will evaluate strategies for reaching a more transcultural view exploring service-learning as one valuable tool for understanding religious diversity.

Texts:
Huston Smith, The World's Religions
Matthew Fox, The Coming of the Cosmic Christ
Joseph Campbell, Myths to Live By
Cohen and Phipps, The Common Experience

A supplemental text required for service-learning: The Service-Learning Reader, ed. by Gail Albert and others

Requirement: Points
a. Class participation-----------10
b. Research paper---------------20
c. Journals----------------------- 30
d. Four tests--------------------- 40
e. Extra credit------------------- 20
Requirements expounded below.

a. Class Participation: All students are required to participate in class discussions. Disagreements with the instructor and /or fellow students are acceptable provided that they are worded in appropriate "I" statements.

b. Research Paper: (3,000 word minimum, double spaced) Compare, do not contrast, any religion in column A with any in column B.

Column A	Column B
Christianity	Hinduism
Judaism	Buddhism
Islam	Taoism
	Neo-Paganism
	Dhamanic Traditions

Comparisons must include all 4 of these key concepts:

1. An inner self, spirit, soul, or energy
2. The five loves
3. Uses of prayer/meditation for internal focus
4. The universe as an interconnected unity

c. Journals: The journal exercises are for you to reflect on the themes that are taught during each class section. You are required to:

      1. Turn in 3 journals (600 x 3 = 1,800 words) by midterm

      2. Turn in 2 journals (600 x 2 = 1,200 words) by end-term

Define the topic of your choice briefly (1-2 paragraphs) followed by 2-3 pages (double spaced) of personal reflection based on research, reading, life experience, and class interaction.

d. Tests: Four tests will be given during the semester. This includes the final.

Service-Learning Options:

Extra Credit: Students who fulfill the requirements as outlined above are eligible for extra credit by working with the Center for Service-Learning. Students can earn up to 20 points by:

      1. Actively working with a service agency for 20+ hours per semester.

      2. Completing and turning in necessary service documentation forms.

      3. Writing a 3-page journal connecting their service experience with a topic in World Religions course.

4-Credit Hour Option: Getting 1 credit over and beyond the 3 credit hours for World Religions

      1. Actively work 50+ hours with service agency

      2. Complete and turn in necessary service documentation form

      3. Write a 3-page journal connecting service-learning to a theme of World Religions course

      4. Do an in-class presentation (hand in a brief outline) sharing insights with fellow students

      5. Complete the end-of-term debriefing session.

Students who choose either of the above service-learning options are excused from taking the final exam.

Topic List for World Religion:

    Ethnocentrism and beyond

    Explanations of ethnocentrism

    Mysticism compared with "peak" and "plateau" experiences

    Mysticism versus the lower aspects of World Religions

    Hindu Trinity

    Hindu dialogue with Death, the Katha Upanishad

    Brahman, the Atman, and the World

    Three paths in Hinduism compared with similar paths

    Buddhist, Christian, Islam, and Sikhism

    Four noble truths in early Buddhism

    Buddhist and Christian ethics comparison

    Tibetan book of the dead basic themes

    Zen Buddhism

    Taoism, Yin and Yang

Incompletes: Incompletes will be given only in cases of extreme situations.

The Role of Service-Learning in the Transformation of "Islam: Faith and Practice"

by Jonathan Brumberg-Kraus

I was first exposed to service-learning at a faculty workshop conducted by the Filene Center for Work and Learning on our campus at Wheaton College (a small nondenominational, private liberal arts college in Norton, Massachusetts). What intrigued me most about this approach was the facilitators' insistence that our foremost concern when considering adopting service-learning components should be which of our own pedagogical goals would best be addressed by this approach. I found that some aspects and techniques of service-learning indeed addressed the pedagogical goals I had for a new introductory undergraduate course called Islam: Faith and Practice.

So far, I have taught Religion 316, Islam: Faith and Practice, twice: once in the spring 1997 semester and again in fall 1999. The first time, eight students were enrolled (four Muslims and four non-Muslims, all women). Two of the students were religion majors. The second time, enrollment jumped to 26, with a more diverse mixture of male and female students, Muslims and non-Muslims (though this time the Muslims were in the minority), and religion majors and nonmajors. I mention the makeup of the class because it reflects the different degrees of familiarity students had with Islamic religion and culture. Also, some of the Muslim students were motivated to take the class by a personal interest in learning about their own background along with other Muslims. Other students took the course for different reasons. By taking Religion 316, religion majors and minors were able to meet the departmental requirement of taking an advanced 300-level course. The course also fulfilled the Perspectives on the Non-Western World general-education requirement. The service-learning component — conducting oral history interviews with members of the local Islamic Center of New England, in Sharon, Massachusetts — was a required part of the course.

My motivation to adopt a service-learning component based on a relationship with members of the local Islamic Center was due to the convergence of several factors. First, as I mentioned before, Wheaton College provided training and assistance to its faculty to convert regular academic courses to service-learning courses or courses with a service-learning component. We were provided with workshops to familiarize us with the theory and practice of service-learning, stipends and ongoing mentoring, opportunities for collegial exchange with other faculty members doing service-learning, and opportunities to evaluate and assess our activities. Most of this was accomplished under the auspices of the Filene Center for Work and Learning and under the guidance of faculty member Grace Baron. Baron is both a full professor in the Psychology Department and the director of service-learning programs at the Filene Center.

Second, I was motivated by a desire to address what I felt were my limitations as a non-Muslim teaching Islam. As a non-Muslim, I did not have an easy familiarity with the experiential, social, ordinary ritual (not just doctrinal) dimensions of Islam that I feel are so important for getting a full picture of religious faith and practice.[1] I was acutely aware of this need because, as a Jewish rabbi, I could easily draw upon my experiences in order to emphasize these dimensions of religions in my other courses on Judaism, the Hebrew Bible, and the New Testament (in its cultural historical context). Also, I felt very strongly that students would get a truer picture of Islam if they had opportunities to have practicing Muslims present Islam to them. Finally, I was motivated by my pedagogical conviction that experiential learning (the integration of experiences with critical reflection upon them), what I view as the main *learning* strategy of service-learning, is an effective teaching tool in general and for religious studies in particular. Course content informed by direct contact with the practices and practitioners of a religion is more likely to stick than is course content alone.

I conceptualized the objectives for adding a service-learning component to my Islam course in my original proposal in November 1996 to the Filene Center for one of its Shouse Service-Learning Fellowships:

> The principle "content" objectives of this module for the course are (a) to have students learn from Muslims (not just their non-Muslim professor) what it means to be Muslim, (b) to help students understand that Islam is not only a system of religious concepts but also a lived practice, and (c) to expose them to the diversity of Muslim belief and practice (i.e., especially due to differences of gender, ethnic background, age, immigration to America, and conversion). The "skills" objective is to familiarize students with the mechanics and ethics of compiling oral histories — a promising model for experiential learning in religious studies. The "service" objectives are (a) to offer the Islamic Center a forum to educate others about Islam, especially to dispel prejudices about all Muslims being fundamentalist terrorists screaming for holy war, and (b) to establish the personal relationships essential for mutual understanding and respect between Wheaton students and the Greater Boston Muslim community. I note here that I am proposing a somewhat different way of looking at service — the establishment of concrete opportunities for the development and encouragement of multicultural understanding is itself an important form of community service.

Student Requirements

In addition to the regular reading assignments and critical papers, students had to complete the following service-learning assignment:

> All students in the course will be required to participate in this project, though not necessarily as interviewers of members of the Islamic Center. The oral history unit itself will consist of these components:
>
> 1. assigned preparatory readings in oral history, focusing on use of interviews for "thick" cultural description; arranging, preparing, and conducting the interview; asking questions; writing up transcripts; understanding ethical and legal ramifications of oral history; and finding examples of oral histories of Muslims or Arabs living in America
>
> 2. guest lecturer from anthropology or history department (on doing oral history/field studies) or outside speaker
>
> 3. practice assignment interviewing a friend or family member
>
> 4. interview of member of the Islamic Center of New England
>
> 5. transcript of the interview
>
> 6. three- to four-page reflection paper relating their experience to concepts or procedures covered in prior class readings, lectures, or discussions.

Students were to interview one Muslim, chosen from among a group of people representing various ages, ethnic backgrounds, and genders. I allowed the students the option of working in teams of two when course enrollment was eight and in groups of three when enrollment was 25. The labor could be divided: one student conducting and recording the interview, the other transcribing it if some students felt more comfortable with a behind-the-scenes role. Still, whether or not steps 4 and 5 were divided, all students were responsible for steps 1, 2, 3, and 6.

The second time I taught the course, I added two experiential assignments that were not service per se: memorizing and reciting Al-Fatiha (the first Sura of the Qur'an in Arabic) and learning enough Arabic calligraphy to copy the Arabic alphabet and the Basmallah statement at the beginning of Al-Fatiha, a common Islamic artistic motif. Students were also required to write brief critical reflection papers on these activities.[2]

Course Accomplishments

Spring 1997

The project began in the summer of 1996, when I sent a letter to the *imam* (leader) of the Islamic Center of New England (ICNE), Talal Eid (with whom I had made arrangements for a field trip to the ICNE for a different class the previous year), requesting his permission for and input on my proposal to interview members of the Center. When I followed up the letter by phone in the fall of 1996, Mr. Eid referred me to the Center's then director of public relations, Serajel Haque. Though we briefly discussed the proposal by phone, I met with Mr. Haque at the Center in January 1997 to explain my proposal, deal with the logistics, and schedule some possible dates. We agreed to set up two visits from the class: the first a field trip on which students would observe the classes, worship, and other aspects of a typical Sunday morning at the Center (the main meeting day for the community); the second a return trip during which the students would interview individually a cross-range of about 10 Muslims of different backgrounds.

When the course began at the end of January, I stated in the syllabus that at least two Sunday visits to the ICNE outside of regular class time were required and that the students would be interviewing practicing Muslims as part of the course. I emphasized this project at the outset to assuage the students' possible, and my own actual, concerns about a non-Muslim's authentically presenting Islam. We visited the Center as a class twice: on Sunday, February 16, and Sunday, May 4 (the last weekend before class ended). The May 4 date was originally scheduled much earlier in the semester, but Mr. Haque was suddenly called away on business, and we had to reschedule.

On the first visit, Mr. Haque gave us a tour of the center and served food in the social hall, where we had an opportunity to ask him and the imam questions about Islam. Then we divided up to observe the adult classes and the children's Islam classes. Later, we all reassembled to hear the imam conduct a *tafsir* (Qur'an interpretation) class in the main room, where at 1 pm we remained to observe the whole community at prayers. Two of the Muslim students participated; one had even brought her own special white prayer outfit. The women in the class were advised to dress appropriately — hair covered with scarves during the prayers, arms and legs covered — though pants were acceptable and *chadurs* (head coverings) were hardly required (much to some students' surprise). We all took off our shoes to enter the prayer room. I mention this because it is precisely these sorts of cultural expectations that are best learned through an on-site visit rather than a lecture, film, or reading. Students wrote one- to two-page papers the following week in response to their visit.

For the second visit, Mr. Haque arranged to have a diverse group of Muslim men and women available for student interviews. Some were from Arab backgrounds; some were from India, Pakistan, and Bangladesh; one woman was from the former Yugoslavia; two women were converts (one from an American Catholic background, the other from a Filipino Catholic background); another woman was an African-American Muslim by birth. Several of the interviewees were students, but most were professionals —

doctors, teachers, journalists, engineers. Wheaton students prepared for the interviews, first, by doing a reading assignment from James Hoopes's *Oral History: An Introduction for Students* (University of North Carolina, 1979) that focuses on interviews that derive "cultural information" and the logistics and ethics of creating oral histories; and, second, by doing/observing a "practice interview" with fellow Wheaton students. For the practice interviews, students were instructed first to compose appropriate questions about the religious beliefs and practices of their interviewee and then to interview a Wheaton student of their own choosing (but not someone in the class). I also devoted two class sessions to discussing the practical and theoretical issues prompted by the readings and the students' experiences with the practice interviews. In these sessions, I myself modeled interview questions — e.g., constructing open rather than "loaded" questions. I had the students do this because I did not want them to go into their interviews with the Muslims at the Center with no direct or indirect experience of what might occur in their efforts to collect cultural information from their informants.

Before the actual interviews began, Mr. Haque and I made a few opening remarks to the Muslim group to explain what we were doing, and I asked all participants to sign a waiver to allow the use of their interviews. There were more interviewees than interviewers, so after we went around to introduce ourselves, we had to negotiate the best way to proceed. I had already sacrificed the benefits of a one-on-one interview for those of diversity when I originally requested more interviewees than we had students. We formed into three groups, with two to three students interviewing and taping interviews of three to five interviewees at a time. I left once the interviews got under way. The students produced three transcripts, and each student wrote a two- to four-page evaluation of the interview experience. One group had technical difficulties with their tape recorder, and at first feared their tape was too inaudible to be transcribed. Since this happened at the end of the term, one student in this particular group was left doing the bulk of the work, including all of the transcription.

Fall 1999

While the service-learning component in fall 1999 was basically the same as in the spring 1997 iteration of the course, I implemented it a bit differently this second time around. First, I had a student teaching assistant (a member of the class) whose job it was to organize the logistics of setting up interviews and to help me with other administrative tasks, which facilitated coordination of the conventional academic and service-learning components of the course. Incorporating a service-learning component into a course can be like having to direct two courses in one, so I was grateful the Filene Center provided me with an assistant. I also had an opportunity to meet with a consultant the Filene Center hired, Jeanne Hubelbank, who helped me and other faculty members with service-learning courses to evaluate our ongoing projects. Second, the class on this occasion was much larger, so we had to arrange for more interviewees. Instead of practice interviews outside of class, I had the students do an in-class assignment (taking about two class sessions) on asking effective questions about religious beliefs and practices, using a worksheet I designed for this purpose.[3] Also, by this time, the imam at the Islamic Center of New England no longer had a public relations committee or chairperson (such as Mr. Haque) to handle the arrangements on his side, so Imam Talal Eid took on this responsibility himself.

Another change involved the interview arrangements. I did not want the students to conduct group interviews at the Islamic Center as they had done in the past. I preferred that they work one- or two-on-one at the interviewees' homes or offices so that the students could learn about their subjects by observing where they lived or worked. As it turned out, several groups did end up with three students interviewing one Muslim participant, since all the students wanted to have face-to-face contact with an interviewee. As a result, we arranged only one visit to the Islamic Center itself, where we again had an opportunity for the imam and other members of the community to speak informally with the students and for the students to observe prayers. At the same time, the imam spoke to a number of people and then gave me a list of Muslims interested in being interviewed. Indeed, he himself consented to be interviewed, as did one of his daughters, Marwa, a student at Northeastern University. I assigned the students to nine groups of three, assigned one of the Muslims the imam selected to each group, and made it the students' responsibility to contact their interviewee and set up their interviews on their own time. Scheduling, however, proved to be a problem. Several of the students were not able to set up interviews before the term was over and either had to find other Muslims outside the Islamic Center on their own or do an alternative assignment. One student was able to take an Incomplete and set up her interview during Wheaton's January term, because she happened to be on campus then. The interviewees were not as diverse a group this time (e.g., eight out of 10 were male), but the opportunity to interview Muslims as knowledgeable about Islam as the imam and his daughter was definitely a compensating advantage. Students ended up interviewing four members of the Islamic Center and three Muslims from other venues.

Evaluation

Successful Components

The course's content objectives were easily met by this project, namely,

(a) to have students learn from Muslims (not just their non-Muslim professor) what it means to be Muslim, (b) to help students understand that Islam is not only a system of religious concepts but also a lived practice, and (c) to expose them to the diversity of Muslim belief and practice (i.e., especially due to differences of gender, ethnic background, age, immigration to America, and conversion).

All of this occurred as a result of the visits.

For example, as evidence that students came to understand that Islam is not only a system of religious concepts but also a lived practice, one of the Muslim students commented:

> *I went in, I admit, with the attitude of thinking that I knew everything, and thinking that I wouldn't learn anything new. . . . We started with the question of whether practicing Islam in America is different from practicing Islam back in the specific countries from which they come. The answer I received surprised me, because they all said that there wasn't a difference. . . . For me there is a big difference. I know that when I am back home I pray more, and the whole outlook of things seems so much more different. Celebrating the holidays and things like that seem so much more meaningful. Perhaps we had different outlooks because of generation gaps — most of these people were in their middle ages — so this could have resulted in the differences of opinion. It was also very interesting to see the differences of opinion in the group.*

I also believed that the service objective to "offer the Islamic Center a forum to educate others about Islam, especially to dispel prejudices about all Muslims being fundamentalist terrorists screaming for holy war" was met. Thus, one of the non-Muslim students commented in her evaluation:

> *I was really excited about how diverse the group was. I must say that I was surprised that there were doctors, molecular biologists, free-lance journalists, communication specialists, and businessmen in the group. My false assumption had been that Muslims were either wealthy oil tycoons or small convenience store owners, and I was glad that the array of their professions showed me my own prejudice.*

Nearly every student interviewer commented on the diversity of the Muslims we interviewed.

To a certain extent, the service objective of establishing contacts to build relationships between the local Muslim and Wheaton communities was met in that several of the Muslim students expressed interest in returning to the Center on their own to pray or celebrate holidays and could not wait to tell their parents that such a resource was available in the area. The second year

I taught the class, one of my students, an African-American Muslim, attended the services at the Islamic Center regularly and did volunteer work there. He was one of the students who interviewed the imam (actually it was this student's suggestion to ask for the interview), and he commented to me later what a great opportunity it was for him to get to have a conversation with the imam. For all the time he spent at the ICNE, he had not had a chance to make this personal connection.

Comments from the students' critical reflection papers were generally enthusiastic, even if they expressed initial misgivings. Typical was this admission:

> When Professor Kraus first assigned this assignment, I wasn't very excited. I thought it would be one big hassle to try and contact the Imam's daughter. . . . Once we did talk to each other . . . I honestly think it was one of the best experiences I've ever had as far as finding out more about another person's religion. Marwa enlightened me on topics such as her experience as a woman in the United States, and how she personally feels about Sufis. . . .

Less typical, but no less instructive, was another student's comment:

> Basically, the end of the conversation was the interviewees questioning us, the interviewers. I was offended, and this is not a personal offense towards anyone, but one of the people in our class [a Muslim Wheaton student] referred to the non-Muslims in the class as atheists. This upset me because it basically gave a reputation to our group.
>
> Anyhow, the interview went well overall but I would like to be honest with you and say that if I were to have the choice to go back and visit, I would not because I did not leave feeling comfortable. However, this was an extremely interesting project that has actually enlightened me because it was interesting to see how Muslims from all over felt and their reactions to certain issues.[4]

These examples make it clear that the postinterview reflection papers not only were pedagogical opportunities for the students to synthesize critically their experiential encounter and research about Islam but also were evaluative tools. Did they offer evidence that the service-learning component of my Islam course was successful? It depends on the criteria for assessment. If success means that the service project was a transformative experience for the students or a learning experience that "sticks" or that the specific objectives I set out were met according to the students' own comments, yes, for most of the students, it was. But in my own written self-assessments required by the service-learning fellowship I was awarded and in the conversations I had with the supervisor of Wheaton's service-learning program, Grace Baron, and the evaluation consultant, Jeanne Hubelbank, I also had opportunities to point out areas that I thought were less successful.

Areas Needing Improvement

First, I would have to conclude that the interviews definitely could have been better organized. The first time I taught the course, the group interviews, while exposing students to the diversity of Muslims, also prevented them from exploring more deeply the experiences of individual Muslims. Time was short, everyone needed a chance to speak, and some interviewees tended to dominate the conversation. I changed that the second time that I taught the course. However, scheduling the interviews at the end of the term did not leave much room for error or technical failures. Had we been able to conduct the interviews earlier, we could have done follow-up interviews, redone the interview where the tape recorder did not work, or pursued one-on-one interviews in addition to the group ones. This continued to be a problem the second time I taught the course. The benefits of postponing the interviews until later in the course, when students had a more thorough grounding in Islam to inform their questions, were outweighed by the logistical difficulties of having students do them too late in the semester. In addition, the timing did not give students enough time to work with the finished product, even though I had a student assistant the second time around. Once the interviews had been handed in, we did not do much to archive them or make them accessible to others. In that sense, I think the oral history skills objective and the service objective to educate the broader Wheaton and southeastern New England community about our Muslim neighbors were only partially met.

More difficult, deeper content issues were hard to address within the limited framework of this project. Of great concern to the non-Muslim students in the class were the issues of Muslim prejudice against women and non-Muslims. Raising such issues tended to put either the Muslim students or the Muslim interviewees on the defensive and create an us-against-them situation. Some of the Muslim students commented that in their interview, when this situation became the case the interview went off the record. Also, it was difficult in the group interview setup to question what seemed to some students as pat answers or to pursue a line of inquiry that went beyond the superficial and opened up an exchange of ideas. Contrary to the service goal to improve mutual understanding between Muslims and non-Muslims, in some cases the course may have exacerbated misunderstandings and distrust.

I also was concerned that as a community service project, this seemed too one-sided. We at Wheaton initiated the project, and our interviews of

Muslims from the Islamic Center sometimes felt to me as if we were taking something from our community partners without giving much back. My guilty conscience was assuaged somewhat the second time I taught the course when I set up a follow-up meeting with Imam Eid to get his feedback on the project. It was good to be able to bring up my concerns about the apparent one-sidedness of our service relationship directly and candidly with him. When I shared these concerns, he said, in so many words, that he had no problem with our Wheaton classes continuing to visit the Islamic Center and interview its members. I objected, "If we keep doing this, won't it start to get a bit old?" But to this he replied that it would not get old for each year of new students who visited the Islamic Center and interviewed its members for the first time. Nevertheless, I would like to see more opportunities to get ongoing feedback from the imam and the other members of the ICNE who participated in the interviews.

On a more personal note, perhaps I was overly ambitious in adding a skill I am new at (conducting oral histories) to a course I was teaching for the first time. Because so much was new, the course became an organizational nightmare. I constantly changed assignments and requirements; and although I partly addressed this flux by using an electronic discussion to keep students up to date, student evaluations commented on the lack of good organization both times I taught the course. Still, I am convinced that I could not have achieved the educational goals I did without the service-learning component.

Where to Go From Here

My experience of transforming my course Islam: Faith and Practice through a service-learning component has led me to consider practical ways to enhance that course specifically in the context of Wheaton College's program and more general, theoretical questions about the use of this pedagogical strategy in religious studies courses. One of the practical directions in which I would like to take the service-learning component of the course is to publicize the work we did beyond the 30 or so students, teachers, and members of the Islamic Center who actually participated. The service we do in this type of project requires consciousness raising about religious diversity and cooperation beyond the few who are directly involved. One possibility would be to edit and post the interviews on a website (a project I have begun). A Wheaton/Religion Department website that archives oral histories of leaders and members of local religious communities compiled by our students might prove to be a useful resource for heightening multicultural awareness in the surrounding area. Finally, it makes sense to import this type of service module into other religion courses, both as a requirement for single-tradition courses (e.g., Judaism) and as an option in advanced courses (e.g., Scripture in Judaism, Christianity, and Islam; or Faith After the Holocaust). I have already transferred this service-learning oral history module to my Judaism: Faith and Practice course.

I am utterly convinced that oral history projects are especially suitable for teaching religious studies. But the opportunity to reflect on my experience implementing the service-learning component of my Islam course in a presentation for the "A Future of Service" conference held before the 1999 American Academy of Religion annual meeting has also pushed me to raise what I think are some important questions for a service-learning pedagogy in religious studies:

- Is heightening multicultural awareness a form of service?
- If so, is this not accomplished more by "being there" and listening than by "doing something"?
- Do students have to view what they are doing self-consciously as "service" for it to be service?
- Can or should we assess the success of service-learning beyond the personal transformation of the students involved? Would public dissemination of our interviews (e.g., via a website) be "service"?
- Treating community partners as equal members "at the table" seems to be a fundamental value of service-learning. But what if the partners we target are not interested? How do we deal with asymmetrical interests in having a relationship? Are we in danger of pestering our community partners with "unwanted attention"?
- Is it right or even possible to evaluate students on the basis of their being transformed or not by their service-learning experience?
- Doesn't any good teaching "transform" people? Doesn't any good relationship transform its participants? Is teaching per se a form of service?

Conclusion

The service-learning module in my Islam: Faith and Practice course was an effective tool for achieving the educational goals I set for the course. With organizational refinement, experience, and carefully planned media to access and publicize the oral histories we recorded, it could become a powerful model for educating our surrounding community to the diverse religious communities in our midst. Moreover, the course helps to redefine the parameters of "service" in service-learning itself.

Notes

1. Islam was not even my primary area of academic specialization. I had, in fact, borrowed the syllabus my former colleague at Colgate University, Arthur Buehler, an Islamicist, had composed and graciously shared with me. Thus, perhaps another reason I accepted Wheaton's invitation to transform my course into a service-learning course was my desire to do something to make my colleague's course my own. I needed to adapt Arthur's content to my pedagogical style. Experiential learning was a strategy I liked and found to be effective with Wheaton students.

2. I mention this because as a result of the workshops I did in service-learning, I learned to distinguish between generic experiential learning and service-learning. All service-learning is experiential, but not all experiential learning is service-learning. The sine qua non of service-learning seems to be that the experience involves a relationship between the student and other people (the "community partners"). Nevertheless, as both generic experiential learning and service-learning are forms of learning, writing a paper critically reflecting on the connections between what a student experiences and what she or he learns from the reading and writing assignments is a crucial component that both share, at least in the way I integrate both activities into my courses.

3. For developing this assignment, Psychology Department professor Gail Zucker recommended I use the chapter "Questionnaires and Interviews: Asking Questions Effectively" from *Research Methods in Social Relations* (C. Judd et al.; Holt, Rinehart & Winston, 1991). I asked students to do the following in class: "1. Write an example question aimed at discovering a fact, one aimed at an attitude or belief, and one aimed at behavior. 2. Imagine that you are designing a set of interview questions and (unethically) want to slant the results to make people appear to have unfavorable attitudes toward a particular foreign government or political organization. Write a few questions that you believe will introduce this bias — but be careful not to make their slant too obvious. 3. Construct three examples of open-ended questions. Write closed-ended versions of each. 4. You need to ask Muslims about their attitudes toward non-Muslims as part of an interview intended to gather information on how Muslim doctrines such as "peoples of the Book," *jihad*, etc., correspond to what Muslims really feel. Describe the question-construction and interviewing techniques that could help obtain valid information on this sensitive topic (especially if you or the teacher for whom you are gathering the information are yourselves not Muslim). 5. Describe types of research questions in religious studies in general, and of Islam in particular, that could best be approached by means of relatively unstructured interviewing techniques. Formulate two questions for each type of study."

4. This comment comes from a young woman from an Arab Christian background who grew up in Saudi Arabia before her family moved to the United States.

RELIGION 316B
ISLAM: FAITH AND PRACTICE

Instructor: Jonathan Brumberg-Kraus, x3694
Knapton 102
Office Hours: TBA

This course seeks to introduce the major religious and cultural dimensions of the Islamic world, both those that express its diversity and those that express its continuity. No previous work is presupposed. Emphasis will be given to the development of classical Islamic institutions and ideas as well as the diverse forms of Islamic religious and cultural life. The course has two major purposes: (1) to provide students with a better and deeper understanding of the importance of the Islamic past upon the Islamic world today and (2) to elucidate contemporary Muslims' own self-understanding of their system(s) of religious faith and practices. While it is not a history course, anyone taking the class should come away with a basic grasp of the larger historical framework within which Islamic civilization has developed. Moreover, students will learn from American Muslims themselves what it means to be a religious Muslim -- particularly in the modern American context -- by visiting the Islamic Center of New England in Sharon, MA, and by conducting interviews ("oral histories") of members of the local Muslim community.

N.B.: This course in Islam has a significant community service-learning component, through which we hope to (a) offer the Islamic Center a forum to educate others about Islam, especially to dispel prejudices about all Muslims being fundamentalist terrorists screaming for holy war, and (b) establish the personal relationships essential for mutual understanding and respect between Wheaton students and the Greater Boston Muslim community. I note here that I am proposing a somewhat different way of looking at service: The establishment of concrete opportunities for the development and encouragement of multicultural understanding is itself an important form of community service.

REQUIRED BOOKS
Frederick Denny, An Introduction to Islam
Kenneth Cragg and Marston Speight, eds., Islam From Within: Anthology of a Religion
Tayeb Saleh, The Wedding of Zein

STRONGLY RECOMMENDED
Ira Lapidus, A History of Islamic Society
Amina Wadud-Muhsin, Qur'an and Woman
Photocopied readings have been assembled in a reader that will be distributed at cost in the Knapton Basement Rm. 007. Readings are also available on reserve at Clark Library.

COURSE REQUIREMENTS

1. Class attendance (including film viewing) and full participation in class discussion.

An electronic discussion has been set up for this course to which students are required to subscribe. This online discussion group is intended to be a forum for students to continue discussions begun in class, to raise questions prior to in-class discussion, and for general communications, syllabus updates, etc., between class members and the professor. Students are expected to make at least 10 contributions to the online discussion (one contribution per weekly topic) in order to receive full credit for class participation.

2. 1-page response paper assignments (20%)

Ten one-page written responses to readings or videos due no later than the Sunday or Tuesday night before the class presentation. Send them by email to our Rel 316 electronic discussion. These will count toward your "quota" of online contributions for your class participation grade, too. You are exempt from this paper the week of your presentation.

3. Class presentation (10%)

Each of you will be responsible for leading a class discussion on the weekly reading(s) and/or on one of the films that we see. Thus, two to three students will lead discussions on each Wednesday from 9/22-12/1. You will need to choose your date to present by Wednesday, 9/15. To get full credit for your presentation you must:

    a. Meet with me before your presentation to discuss it!
    b. Read and comment on the other student response papers (as per guidelines I'll give you).
    c. Make a 5-10 minute presentation (as per guidelines I'll give you) that
        i. enumerates the main points of the book or movie
        ii. discusses and gives specific examples of the stylistic or cinematic means it uses to convey its main points
        iii. relates the book or movie to its proper place in the historical context of Islam
        iv. points out the important moral, theological, and/or philosophical issues raised by the reading or movie (pose at least 2 questions that you think your text or movie raises)
        v. generates a dynamic class discussion
You may choose to use handouts, visual aids, or whatever else you think might help make your points. Your grade will be based on how well you meet the criteria in "c." and the guidelines I give you. Your final paper will be on the same topic you choose for your presentation.

N.B.: You do not have to hand in a response paper on the film (or book) you present.

4. Memorize short passage from the <u>Qur'an</u> and Arabic calligraphy assignment (10%)

    i. Use the <u>Al-Fatiha</u> pronunciation free software program to memorize the 1st Surah of the <u>Qur'an,</u> or see this link for a transliteration and English translation. Radio Al-Islam Channel RA 100 has audio of <u>Al-Fatiha</u> and other Surahs of the <u>Qur'an</u> if you download the Realplayer software they suggest. For those interested, here is a Muslim discussion of rules for memorizing the <u>Qur'an.</u>
    ii. Read the Islamic and Arabic Arts and Architecture -- Calligraphy website for an overview, as resource information on Arabic calligraphy.
    iii. Copy the letters of the Arabic alphabet and their names from a chart to be provided, i.e., Arab_Calligraphy_Art1.html or List/Arabic alphabet. The Babel online tutorial for writing Arabic might also be helpful, though it doesn't present the Arabic alphabet in order.
    iv. Copy by hand, as best as you can, the <u>basmalah</u> phrase (=the first verse of the <u>Fatiha</u>) in Arabic script. You may choose one of the scripts demonstrated on the above-mentioned website. You may also embellish it artistically, using the designs we've studied as models. Sakkal Design's IslamiClip Calligraphic website also has some nice examples of <u>basmalahs</u> in different types of Arabic scripts. Of course, I want you to copy them by hand, not electronically!
    v. Hand in your copy of the <u>basmalah.</u>
    vi. 1-3 page reflection paper on both your memorization and copying of the Arabic Qur'an passages.

DUE DATES
Oct 4-Oct 8: Make appointment to recite <u>Al-Fatiha</u> during office hours.
Oct 29: <u>Basmalah</u> calligraphy, reflection paper

5. A one-hour midterm examination (10%).

The exam covers the first seven weeks of the course in a term-identification and essay format. The midterm is a sample of the kind of preparation needed for the final examination. Both will focus on comprehension and understanding of the material of the course other than sheer memorization of material. Study sheets will be handed out the prior week.

6. One essay (6-8 pages, typed, double-spaced) is to be based on the topic of your class presentation.(15%).

All essays are due Monday, December 6. You may submit an optional first draft to me, but I must receive it no later than Monday, Nov. 29. The purpose of this essay is to think about the source material at length, both in the light of one's own interests and ideas and in respect to the secondary readings, lectures, or any other information that helps one elucidate a particular text or idea in the reading(s) under discussion. Attention will be given to form as well as content. Use a manual of style and be consistent. You must use at least two other bibliographical sources besides those assigned on the syllabus. One of your additional sources should be the <u>Encyclopedia of Islam,</u> which is in the Permanent Reference section of the Library. While subject entries are according to their Arabic (or Persian, or other indigenous) terms, there are indices that give the English equivalents and the volume and page number where they can be found.

7. All students will participate in an oral history project, involving:

> **a.** assigned preparatory readings in oral history, focusing on use of interviews for "thick" cultural description; arranging, preparing, and conducting the interview; asking questions; writing up transcripts; ethical and legal ramifications of oral history; and examples of oral histories of Muslims or Arabs living in America.
> **b.** guest lecturers from Anthropology or History Departments (on doing oral history/field studies) or outside speaker
> **c.** practice assignment interviewing a friend or family member
> **d.** interview of member of the Islamic Center of New England
> **e.** transcription of the interview
> **f.** 3-4 page reflection paper relating their experience to concepts or procedures covered in prior class readings, lectures, or discussions.

Students have the option of working in teams of 2 (or 3 if the class is larger) where labor could be divided --one student performing and recording the interview, the other transcribing it -- if some students feel more comfortable with a behind-the-scenes role. Still, while steps (d) and (e) may be divided, all students will be responsible for (a)-(c) and (f).

The project requires 2 to 3 Sunday morning visits to the Islamic Center of NE in Sharon on dates TBA.

The completed project will be 25% of the course grade. It is due no later than the last day of class, M Dec 13.

8. A take-home final examination will be given during exam period. It will be 15% of the course grade.

"The History and Religion of Ancient Israel":
An Introductory Course to the Hebrew Bible

by Bradley D. Dudley

There are a number of unique challenges one must face when employing service-learning in religion classes generally and in text-based religion classes specifically. Among these, and certainly not the least, is the need to ensure scholarly academic work as opposed to what is often understood as the work of benevolent Christian organizations. It is in some ways related to the well-seasoned issue of whether the text is descriptive or normative. Regardless of one's position on this subject, service-learning can provide some useful learning tools that engage biblical texts both at a values level and also at a comprehension level. That is, one's shared experience with issues that span the millennia, even if seeking to be value neutral, aids in comprehending why texts address subjects such as social justice, oppression, hunger, homelessness, or societal moral health.

The currently charged issue of critical methodologies can also be addressed by service-learning. There has been a great deal of discussion during the last two decades regarding the future of historical-critical methods focusing on questions surrounding who, what, when, and where. These are vital, necessary, and demanding questions, but current interest seems to be shifting and asking a different set of questions with a more postmodern agenda. One could argue that the rise in interest in narrative criticism flanks the postmodern perspective and asks more personal questions such as, Who am I in light of this story? or, in more alarming terms, Which of my own interests can I read into this text? In fact, in the last two decades, there has been a rise in all modes of experiential education, and service-learning in particular has grown up in the era of "narrology." I am not arguing to replace historical criticism with narrative criticism; instead, I am suggesting that service-learning may provide the means by which students can ask the experiential questions of the age while also continuing to ask the more empirical questions that are at stake in historical-critical investigations. In the process of addressing both issues, we may well discover the text in a fuller way. What follows is an example of how service-learning functions in an introductory class on the Hebrew Bible.

Background Considerations

The course in question is taught at Pepperdine University and is one of three religion courses students take as part of the general-education requirement. Thus, the classes are composed of majors from all disciplines and a number of students whose major is yet to be declared. My section of this course requires service-learning of all students.

At Pepperdine, I serve as the service-learning coordinator as well as teaching in the Religion Division. When I was first invited to teach the introductory course on the Hebrew Bible, I thought I would not use service-learning in the class. As a biblical scholar, I needed convincing that service-learning would, in fact, positively affect my learning objectives in a text-based class, and even though I am responsible for service-learning at our university, I did not want to teach the class as a service-learning class unless I could ensure a quality design. After much deliberation, I ultimately determined that carefully selected service opportunities, especially involving the issues that surround the formation and life of any society (e.g., poverty, homelessness, hunger, oppression), would provide a unique opportunity to investigate the stories of the Hebrew Bible and the developing society of the Israelites. This design, I was convinced, would also challenge my students to think critically about both success and failure in ancient societies as well as in modern societies that continue to grapple with these complex issues.

Learning Objectives

I established two primary learning objectives to be advanced through both traditional assignments and service-learning experiences. First, I wanted the students to grow in their understanding of the content and structure of the Hebrew Bible, with an interest in its historical context and its literary qualities. Second, I sought to encourage them to think critically regarding the formation of Israel's society and its response to social issues of oppression, poverty, hunger, and homelessness. In addition, I placed a special emphasis on the various philosophies at work in our contemporary social setting with reference to these issues.

I knew, based on the profile of Pepperdine students, that most of them, while being aware of contemporary social problems, would have very little experiential knowledge of the true human effects of homelessness or hunger. By allowing them an opportunity to experience something of the scope and reality of these phenomena, I felt it could not only raise their social awareness but also provide them with an opportunity to understand many of the ethical demands of the Levitical law and the societal critiques of the prophets. Furthermore, while I recognized that the Hebrew Bible is larger than these issues alone, I knew that we would continually encounter them throughout our study of the Law, the Prophets, and the Writings and that they could thus provide a focal point for our work as well as a common language that spanned both time and culture. Our discussions and investigations both in and out of class could then take on a sense of greater relevance, moving our discussion from the abstract to the concrete.

The Blend of Service-Learning and Course Content

I sought to blend the scheduled readings in the Hebrew Bible and other resources with class discussions and lectures that drew upon three experiences of service. The first service event required the entire class's participation in a common effort. By performing the first service task together, we established a kind of baseline for our discussions. I chose an organization called Food Share, a food warehouse that supplies food to more than 200 small and large programs in Ventura County, California. Recognizing that 20 percent of all food produced in this country never reaches a consumer, Food Share solicits, stores, and distributes surplus food to agencies involved in feeding the hungry. Besides the donations that are made by businesses and corporations, some food is gleaned from farmers' fields, orchards, and vineyards.

Food Share's philosophy and practice of gleaning are adopted directly from the Hebrew Bible. Hence, if possible, I wanted my students to work in the fields gleaning, since we would later encounter this provision in the Law and its subsequent practice in the Writings. But because this particular experience is dependent on harvest schedules and farmers' generosity, I also needed a backup plan, which Food Share was able to provide. The plan involved sorting, cleaning, and packaging foodstuffs in its warehouse. Either way, this initial service event was designed to provide an intentional hands-off opportunity, where students did not openly interact with the hungry but took part in a consciousness-raising group experience during which a large amount of harvested or warehoused food could be seen and handled.

Students are always shocked by the size of the Food Share warehouse and the amount of food stored there — and thus, by implication, by the size of the hunger problem. Such an experience has more of an impact than does simply a rehearsal of the cold statistic that 20 million to 30 million Americans are hungry, or even that Food Share is able to provide 293,000 meals to 34,000 people per month. However, common student reactions to this project also included their feeling that because their service was impersonal, it did not have an effect on hunger, and hence they did not really do anything.

The second service opportunity was intentionally different in character. Students participated in groups of 10 in the Pepperdine Volunteer Center program Into the Streets. This program partners with inner-city Faith In Christ Ministries to provide meals to homeless individuals living in and around Los Angeles's McArthur Park. The program took students from the Malibu campus to the inner city for an intentionally hands-on experience involving a typical operation of feeding the homeless. Students prepared food at a church, transported it to the park, and served anyone who wanted to eat. Students had ample opportunity — and were encouraged — to interact with homeless individuals.

Common student reactions included surprise at how small the operation was, a sense of horror at the number of children who were hungry, puzzlement at the diversity among the homeless (especially the college-educated homeless), personal discovery regarding the students' own stereotypes, and sometimes sadness at the tragedy of running out of food. Since this experience was distributed throughout the semester and since one week in the inner city can be very different from the next, our weekly in-class discussions worked toward integrating each week's experiences with the experience of other students in previous weeks. I also encouraged students to compare their feelings of being personally involved with people as opposed to doing warehouse work. Quickly they realized the selfish side of service: Sometimes service can be about "how it makes me feel" as opposed to the actual effect of service.

The third and final service-learning experience was for each student to choose one of the above programs and return for another day of service. Ninety (90) percent of the students chose to return to the hands-on program in the inner city. In fact, it was not uncommon for students to return to serve additional times even after meeting their course requirements. I even had students ask to write extra reflection papers for no grade because they wanted a form of processing the events of a weekend.

Pedagogical Procedures

To reinforce the connections between the course content and the service experiences, I planned opportunities for reflection in both formal and informal settings. Formal reflection for each service event took place via a one- to two-page critical reflection paper due the class period immediately following the service experience. The formal act of submitting a paper provided students with both the discipline and the means to think through and process their feelings, expectations, fears, and questions. These short papers I always returned in the next class period so I could give the students reactions to their ideas. Additionally, during the class period following each service event, students reflected on their service orally with their peers. Because a maximum of 10 students could participate weekly, this allowed all of the class members in turn to think through and process their experiences. This also allowed each week's discussion to come into relation with those of the preceding weeks and allowed all of these jointly to interface with class readings. Because, moreover, the service activities required travel in groups, natural conversations while en route to and from the service site provided informal "preflection" and reflection time.

At the end of the course, I required a final paper that brought together course readings, the three service experiences, and independent research, and focused on the structure of society generally and oppression, poverty, hunger, and homelessness specifically. Students had to draw on each of the larger divisions of the Hebrew Bible (Law, Prophets, Writings) to discuss their service experience and societal struggles/solutions, thus allowing them to assemble the sometimes disparate segments of the Hebrew Bible with their service experience. The following quotations, excerpted from student papers, illustrate their appraisals of the connections they made.

> As I began taking this Religion 101 course . . . like many, I was under the assumption that because Pepperdine is affiliated with the Church of Christ, the students would be slathered in evangelism by way of the required religion courses. It turns out I was drastically wrong. . . . The Bible and its contents were vigorously discussed on a more literary basis rather than theological basis. The students were left alone to absorb the material, and expected to draw their own conclusions. . . . The cleverness of the integration of service-learning and a religion course is excellent. The two go hand in hand — which is stronger than any preacher or professor's lecture. The student is allowed to draw from the knowledge learned in class and expected to enter a situation that illustrates perfectly what the biblical readings imply. Unknowingly, by becoming exposed to severe poverty and those with loathsome living conditions, I developed a higher comprehension of the principles that underlie the text in the Old Testament.

> This semester was all about service-learning. At first glance I did not think that a class on the Hebrew Scriptures would have anything to do with today, let alone the same problems. Through doing the service projects and reading the Bible, I am now able to see the correlation. Our world has so much in common with that of Judah and Israel. . . . I learned so much this semester by relating my service work to the Bible.

> These three months have been like no other, felt like no other, passed like no other — a time of evolutional growth in the context of my own self-development and my awareness of the intricate workings of the world. . . . First, I must mention, that through the vehicle of this Rel. 101 class, a more sharpened degree of reality has been bestowed upon me. I had forgotten. I am terribly ashamed to admit it. I had forgotten the pain, the anguish, the

suffering that . . . the majority of the world has to endure day after day. This class, both through the close analysis of the Old Testament and the service-learning, has definitely made a profound impact on me. Through the course of this essay, I will attempt to interrelate my own personal experiences with the Hebrew Bible and, in doing so, address the world society as a whole.

Logistics, Management, and Administration

Among the common challenges to successful service-learning experiences are agency relationships and communications, and student transportation and tracking. I have been able to address each of these issues through a common venue. The Pepperdine Volunteer Center offers a suite of 15 ongoing programs that provide a variety of service opportunities to students. Each of these programs has a dedicated student coordinator who communicates with the agency and joins in program activities with other participating students. By selecting the Into the Streets program, I was assured of having ongoing communication with the agency via the student coordinator, as well as an available on-campus student contact. This choice also facilitated the transportation situation (which can otherwise be problematic at times), because the program coordinator arranges weekly transportation.[1] Further, the Volunteer Center logs can provide confirmation of any given student's participation, if this should be needed.

Additionally, the Pepperdine Volunteer Center schedules one special event each month. In the fall, the inaugural event is Step Forward Day, on which a thousand students, staff, and faculty work at 70 different sites. I scheduled my class's Food Share project to coincide with this event. Having made all necessary arrangements with the site, I communicated my needs and plans to the Volunteer Center's special events coordinator, who arranged for the needed transportation.

Assessment

Assessment has taken place on a number of levels. In some ways, the ongoing assessments and adjustments made across iterations of the course have been the most vital, yet also the most unscientific. Student reflections have been a primary source for them, and the statements quoted above give an indication of the students' general understanding by the end of the class. Additionally, the students' reading journals, while designed to track the students' development as readers, also provide evidence of the successful integration of reading and experience.

Regarding more standardized data, two questions on the university's standard student evaluations provide some insight about the service experiences, though no questions ask specifically about service-learning. One question asks students to rank, on a scale of 1 to 5 (1 being the least positive), the statement "The overall class experience has contributed to the development of my sense of personal values and moral integrity." Of 28 students responding from my fall 1999 class, 11 students ranked it as a 5, and seven others ranked it as a 4. Only one student rated it as a 1. A second question asks students, to appraise their learning experience: "The course has increased my knowledge or understanding of the subject." On this same scale, 15 students ranked their experience as a 5, and eight others ranked it as a 4. The lowest rating — a 2 — came from the same student who gave the first question a 1.[2] The evaluation form also provides an opportunity for students to write evaluative comments. Fourteen (14) students cited their service-learning experience as a key factor in their learning process.

Finally, I also administered a pre- and a posttest to the students in my Religion 101 class. Of the enrolled students, 30 completed both the pre- and posttest. The questions were primarily concerned with career expectations/preparations, civic values, and learning; and they called for the students to rank their support for statements on a six-point scale (1 being most negative).

For the statement "I am motivated by courses that contain hands-on applications of theories to real life situations," 18 students ranked themselves high (5 or 6) on the pretest. On the posttest, 11 student responses remained unchanged over the course of the semester, but the net change among the 19 other students was a 10-point increase. More striking still was the increase on a related question, "I learn course content best when connections to real life situations are made." Again, most pretest rankings were high (5 or 6), and on the posttest 16 responses were unchanged; however, among the other 14 students, this time rankings increased by an aggregate 19 points.

A related statement, "There is no relation between my real life experiences and what I learn in school," registered a dramatic decline in agreement, with 10 responses unchanged but the remaining 20 responses showing an aggregate decrease of 11 points. Interestingly, on the posttest, no students ranked themselves as strongly agreeing (5 or 6) with this question.

Questions that asked about students' civic values and understandings also showed dramatic change. For example, support for the statement "It is not necessary for me to volunteer my time" showed a net aggregate decline of 14 points. And for the statement "In the United States, people basically have equal opportunity to do what they want in life," support declined 17 points.

These statistics illustrate the growth in the students' critical thinking and understanding regarding very complex issues that transcend time and culture. The students resisted offering simplistic solutions to these issues and assumed increasingly responsible roles in and ideals for their own society.

Summary

The integration of service and learning into the curriculum of this introductory course on the Hebrew Bible has transformed not only student attitudes about a required general-education class but also, for many, their perception of both the world and their own civic responsibility. The vehicle of this transformation has been the combination of traditional course content and a personal investment in service.

Notes

1. One unique design feature of the Pepperdine service-learning and volunteer programs is the partnering of these experiences, especially with freshman classes. This partnering serves to enrich the volunteers' experience by their overhearing of and participation in informal service-learning reflections, and it reinforces the service concept for the service-learning students by the presence of other students who are volunteering without any course connection.

2. Unless the student was quietly displeased with all aspects of the course, perhaps this A-level student, who ranked all features of the course as either 1 or 2, mistakenly inverted the scoring order.

Location and Time: AC 244
Tuesday and Friday 8:00-9:30

Professor: Brad Dudley
bdudley@pepperdine.edu
TCC 230
Office: x4833

Office Hours: Tuesday and Friday 9:30-10:30 (other by appointment)

Course Description: This introductory study will survey the history and literature of the Old Testament. We will seek to discover how these diverse documents and literary genres function within the larger sphere of Israel's narrative, identity, and social development for the period covered by the Old Testament. To facilitate this discovery, we will employ various critical approaches.

Objectives: 1) Students will grow in their understanding of the content and structure of the Hebrew Bible with an interest in its historical context and its literary qualities.

2) Students will think critically regarding the formation of Israel's society in regard to the social issues of oppression, poverty, hunger, and homelessness, with an interest in exploring the impact of various philosophies at work within our contemporary social setting.

Textbook: The HarperCollins Study Bible (New Revised Standard Version)

Readings: A reading schedule is included in this syllabus. Other necessary readings that arise out of class interests and discussion will be placed on reserve and assigned specific due dates. You will be responsible for these readings in class discussions, on quizzes, and on tests.

Journal: You should keep a journal in which you reflect on your readings. The first entry in your journal needs to be written prior to the second class meeting. In this entry, you should "preflect" on what you hope to gain from this course and what goals you have for the coming semester. **Late journals will not be accepted.**

Requirements:

• Class Attendance and Participation. I allow 3 absences (2 tardies = 1 absence). For every absence beyond this limit, 5 points will be deducted from your final average.
• Completion of Assigned Readings and Journal. You should be prepared for periodic reading quizzes. If you miss them, you will have no opportunity to make them up. **10%**

- Two Exams. Exams will be composed of any combination of the following: multiple choice, matching, short answer, short essay. **20% each**
- Final Exam. The final will cover material after the second exam and one or two comprehensive questions. **20%**
- Service-learning. On Step Forward Day, **September 11,** the entire class will help with the Food Share Project. Food Share goes into fields to glean remaining crops and then distributes them to those in need. Additionally, you will need to participate in the Volunteer Center program "Into the Streets." Each student is required to sign up and attend this program **twice** during this semester (Sundays 12:30-5:00). **This service must be complete no later than November 15th.** "Into the Streets" serves warm meals to the homeless. You can contact the Volunteer Center at x4143. You will write a 1-2 page typed double-spaced critical reflection of your experience following each of your three service experiences. This is due on the Tuesday following your service. This reflection resembles a journal entry in that it is informal, describes what you saw, how you felt, what kind of thoughts you began with and how they have grown, your questions, etc. As you note connections with your service and the course readings, note them in your reflections. **15%**
- Short Paper (5-6 pages). This paper will incorporate your reflection on both your readings and service as they relate to the structure of society generally and oppression, poverty, hunger, and homelessness specifically. You will want to draw on each of the larger divisions of the Hebrew Bible (Law, Prophets, Writings) to discuss your service experience and societal struggles/solutions. This paper is about what you have experienced **and** learned. **Late papers will be penalized a half of a letter grade for each day late.** Your paper should follow the style guidelines found in Turabian, Manual for Writers of Term Papers, Theses, and Dissertations. **15%**

Ethics: Cheating or plagiarism on a test, paper, or other assignment will result in automatic failure of that assignment and possible failure in the course. Students suspected of cheating will be referred to the Academic Ethics Committee and face penalties up to expulsion from the University. It's not worth it!

Course Objectives

1) Students will grow in their understanding of the content and structure of the Hebrew Bible with an interest in its historical context and its literary qualities.

2) Students will think critically regarding the formation of Israel's society in regard to the social issues of oppression, poverty, hunger and homelessness with an interest in exploring the impact of various philosophies at work within our contemporary social setting.

Class Elements: Function and Rationale

Readings (Traditional)
1) Sections of the Hebrew Bible
2) Other Selected Readings and Introductions
3) Unscheduled but serendipitous readings about community organizations with which they will become involved.

Class Lectures and Discussions (Traditional)
Traditional class lectures provide guidance, structure, and explanation of the course content.

Tests (Traditional)
Tests are designed to measure to what extent students are learning the issues, content, and structure of the primary texts themselves.

Reading Journal (Traditional)
The journal affords an opportunity to preflect on and set learning goals for the course and to reflect on the many readings. It also provides a record of the student's development as a reader.

Three Service Project (Service-Learning)

1) Class project with the organization Food Share.
> Food Share is a food warehouse that supplies food to more than 200 small and large programs in Ventura County, California.

Recognizing that 20% of all food produced in this country never reaches a consumer, Food Share solicits, stores, and distributes surplus food to agencies involved in feeding the hungry. Besides the donations that are made by businesses and corporations, some food is gleaned from farmers' fields, orchards, and vineyards. If available, we work in the fields gleaning, since we will later encounter this practice in the Hebrew Bible. If there are no available fields, we work in the warehouse. This initial event provides an intentional hands-off opportunity where we do not directly interact with the hungry, but it is a consciousness-raising experience where the large amount of food is seen. Students are shocked by the size of the warehouse and the amount of food, and therefore the size of the hunger problem. This is more powerful in experiential form than the cold statistic that tells us 20-30 million Americans are hungry. Food Share is able to provide 293,000 meals to 34,000 people per month.

Common reflections from students:
- A sense of being overwhelmed.
- "We don't feel like we really did anything."
- "We would have liked to have given food to real people."

2) Participation in groups of 10 in the Pepperdine Volunteer Center program "Into the Streets" that partners with Faith In Christ Ministries to provide meals to homeless individuals living in and around Los Angeles's McArthur Park.

This opportunity takes students to the inner city for an intentional hands-on experience of being involved in a typical operation of feeding the homeless. In this setting they prepare food at a church, transport it to the park, and serve anybody who wants to eat. Students have ample opportunity to interact with homeless individuals.

Common reflections from students:
- Surprise at how small the operation is.
- Surprise at the number of hungry children.

- Surprise at the diversity of homelessness — especially the college-educated homeless.
- Sense of discovery regarding their personal stereotypes.
- Horrified by the fact of running out of food.

I always ask students to compare their feelings of being personally involved with the people. I want them to realize the selfish side of service so they can be more concerned with the actual purpose of service than with how they feel about serving.

3) A choice of returning to either of the above organizations.

This semester, only three of 35 students returned to Food Share. According to the students, this is explained primarily because of the human element — they felt like they helped somebody. While this is a predictable and understandable result, one must question how much of this kind of service is dependent on how the servers feel about themselves, as opposed to gaining a vision for the need for service.

Three Short Reflection Papers, Each Following a Service Event (Service-Learning)

These papers, like journal entries, are intended to allow for processing and recording both the externals (*what I saw*) and the internal (*how I felt, what changed*). In most cases, these papers will not be "deep" reflection — they are preliminary and aimed more at beginning a genesis of thought regarding these subjects. As the semester progresses, I would like to see the beginning of the tie-in to the Hebrew Bible that the larger paper will demand.

Final Paper (Blending of Traditional and Service-Learning)

The final paper is where the academics and the experience interface with the students' lives, goals, and majors. The paper incorporates both the readings and service as they relate to the structure of society generally and oppression, poverty, hunger, and homelessness specifically. Students are required to draw on each of the larger divisions of the Hebrew Bible (Law, Prophets, Writings) to discuss their service experience and the larger societal struggles/solutions.

"Fieldwork in the Jewish Community"

by Terry Smith Hatkoff

Fieldwork in the Jewish Community is a Jewish studies course offered at California State University, Northridge (CSUN). CSUN is one of the 23 campuses of the California State University, which is a comprehensive public university system. The Northridge campus is located in the greater Los Angeles area, and its current enrollment is 27,000 students. It is an ethnically diverse campus, with the vast majority of students commuters. A central component of CSUN's mission is to recognize teaching, research, and public service as its major responsibilities. The greater Los Angeles area has a Jewish population of 500,000, half of whom live in the San Fernando, Simi, and Conejo Valleys adjacent to CSUN. With Fieldwork in the Jewish Community, both the university and Jewish communal leaders have recognized a need to provide CSUN students — with no regard to religious affiliation — the opportunity to perform community service in a program that offers them academic growth through structured reflection and supervision.

The Jewish studies faculty formed an informal partnership with the Jewish Federation, Valley Alliance (the chief communal organization of the Jewish community in the area), and together submitted a grant proposal to develop and fund the present class. We received support, and the class was first offered, on an experimental basis, in the fall of 1996. It was approved as a permanent offering the following year. In addition to being an option in the minor in Jewish studies, the course can also be taken for upper-division general-education (breadth) credit in the area of applied arts and sciences (integrative, lifelong learning). It is a restricted class; enrollment is subject to professor approval. Only 12 students are accepted into this class each semester, and after an initial interview. Acceptance is based on the student's maturity, overall academic performance, and at least junior class standing. The service-learning component is the center of the class.

My involvement in service-learning grew out of my many years of teaching sociology at CSUN. I often supervised students in internship experiences. Sociology majors are required to take an internship class that allows them to apply their specialized knowledge in a work environment. One particular intern opened my eyes to the academic value of civic engagement. I supervised this intern, who worked as a youth director at a local synagogue. At that point, I saw the benefits for the student, who was directly involved in working in the Jewish community: It taught her about Jewish communal institutions, Jewish culture, and the value of providing service to others. In addition, my experience as her faculty supervisor provided me with unexpected rewards. It enabled me to guide her in a way not usually possible in my other classes: I saw firsthand her development as a contributing member of her community and the enormous joy she found in strengthening her religious and ethnic identity. Witnessing this student's personal growth — even facilitating it — gave me deep satisfaction. It was at that point that I first proposed the present class to the Jewish studies program coordinator. The partnership described above ensued.

The class that I constructed has learning objectives in three main areas: civic engagement, practical experience, and academic study. (I later realized that this corresponds with virtually all definitions of service-learning.) Qualified students are given the opportunity to work in the various nonprofit agencies funded by the Jewish community. Students either deal directly with the public or work internally with agency professionals. All students receive hands-on experience developing skills relevant to their interests or potential careers. In this way, they are able to enhance their resumes and begin to prepare for their futures. The students relate the assigned academic material, which deals with the American Jewish community, to their work settings. I also guide them in developing appropriate work ethics and basic principles of collegiality in the workplace. All three of my educational emphases are important and intertwined; all three are necessary for success.

Students choose this class for a variety of reasons. Some of the students are Jewish studies minors, while others have been enrolled in another of my classes and have heard me talk about this class. Each spring semester, the Jewish studies program begins to advertise the class by distributing fliers around campus and by placing an ad in the campus newspaper. In this way, we attract a variety of students from such diverse departments as business, child development, sociology, psychology, journalism, nutrition, biology, and family environmental sciences. While a majority of the students enrolled in the class are Jewish, there are always one or two who are not Jewish, and many of the Jewish students have not previously been involved in the Jewish community. The diversity of majors as well as religious and ethnic backgrounds enriches the class discussions. We hear a multitude of reflections and perspectives on the same reading material, the same guest speakers, and similar work environments.

The cooperation of the professional staff at the Valley Alliance office of the Jewish Federation has been invaluable. They introduced me to community partners and paved the way for me to place students in appropriate agencies. Because most of the Jewish communal service agencies are under the auspices of the Jewish Federation, my job was made easier. I am happy to say that all of the community partners I have contacted have been pleased to participate in the program and accept students. The large and active Jewish community in Los Angeles supports a wide range of communal agencies offering a number of different types of service. After-school and preschool day-care programs for children are included in local Jewish Community Center branches. Students desiring to work with children also can be placed at My Children's Jewish Discovery Museum, a local synagogue preschool, and Vista Del Mar foster facility, as well as formal religious educational programs at a synagogue and in informal youth work. Students who are interested in mental health can be placed in the Family Violence Project of the Jewish Family Service, Valley Storefront Senior Day Care, or Beit T'shuvah (a halfway house for recovering addicts and alcoholics). Students with an interest in politics and community relations may be assigned to Bet Tzedek (Jewish legal services), the Jewish Labor Committee (facilitating employee-labor relations), or the American Jewish Committee, as well as the Valley Alliance office of the Jewish Federation. Other agencies include Jewish Vocational Services, Project Chicken Soup (service to AIDS patients), and the campus Hillel-Jewish Student Center. While some of these placements require a strong Jewish background, others require no prior experience in the Jewish community.

I devote considerable energy to establishing a smooth and productive relationship between the students and the agencies. During my initial interview with each student, I identify his or her personal or career interests as well as strengths and passions. I then try to link each student with an appropriate Jewish communal agency. I am careful to explain to the community partners, and specifically to the field supervisors, what is expected of them. It is important for them to understand that while they are getting "free labor," they also have responsibilities to these students. These responsibilities include providing students with a meaningful experience (for example, by letting them sit in on staff meetings or showing them how the agency works) and mentoring. I explain that each student is expected to make a creative contribution and not merely engage in menial tasks. In the event that there is a problem, I encourage the field supervisor to call me so that it can be remedied as soon as possible.

During the semester, students spend eight hours a week for 15 weeks (120 hours during the semester) working at their agency. This is quite a commitment for CSUN students, who typically carry a 12-unit course load and work part-time. The grant that we received has enabled us, through the Jewish Federation, to offer each student a small stipend ($450) at the successful completion of the course. Each student signs a contract with his or her field supervisor. It explicitly identifies the student's as well as the field supervisor's responsibilities. The students are also given specific guidelines for service-learning — guidelines created to assist in making the service experience as productive as possible. They include general advice about being punctual and responsible, respecting the privacy of clients, respecting coworkers, and being flexible, plus a definition of sexual harassment. In addition, students can communicate with me by voice mail in case of an emergency.

Students are required to submit signed time sheets and weekly journals that include detailed accounts of their hours and reflection on their experiences. These journals are required to include, but not be limited to, first impressions, what happened during the service experience, what the students did, what the effect of this experience was, how they felt about their involvement and the people they worked with, and what was learned. Such reflections are intended to help guide the service-learning experience. If the situation allows for it, students are also encouraged to include a critical incident report (e.g., an event that took place in which a decision was made, a conflict occurred, a change was made, or a problem was resolved). Students know that I am the only one reading their journal entries, so they are free to identify their impressions and feelings as well as their tasks. Often in the process of articulating their experiences, they discover something new about the agency or about themselves. They have reported that writing these journal entries is the most difficult part of the class, more difficult than anticipated.

I meet with the students bimonthly in a seminar format. During this time, they share their reflections. This oral exchange has proven to be a very useful teaching aid. Students learn from one another, not only about how various Jewish agencies function but also about how to function within a Jewish communal agency. While some students are frustrated with how understaffed their agency is, most grow to see that this is a common problem in nonprofit work. For example, students observe agency directors engaging in menial work outside of their job description. This gives them insight into the real challenges of such careers. I remind the students that they themselves are the recipients of grant money (for their stipends), and I teach them the importance of writing thank you notes to the granting agency and acknowledging the efforts of their field supervisor. Class discussions also involve examining the needs of the community from a personal perspective. Through reflection, I can give students constant feedback and can monitor the quality of their service. This is an essential part of the class.

Another component of the class is discussion of class readings and visits by guest speakers. The readings focus on the local Jewish community, Jewish communal service, and nonprofit organizations. These provide a framework for the students' experiences. During the semester, I also bring in speakers from the Jewish community, such as the fundraising director of the Valley Alliance, the director of Jewish Free Loans, and rabbis from the Orthodox, Conservative, and Reform movements, to give students additional insight into the Los Angeles Jewish community. Finally, I bring in a career counselor from the University Career Center to help students incorporate this service-learning class into their resume.

Each student must write an evaluation research paper. The purpose of evaluation research is to assess the impact of a program in light of its mission. Jewish communal agencies have been established to produce some intended result — strengthening the Jewish identity of children or young adults, providing care for senior citizens, providing free legal services to those in need. Evaluation research is a process of determining whether the intended result was produced efficiently. In order to do this assignment, students must meet with various agency employees in addition to their field supervisor, be familiar with the mission statement of their agency, and, if possible, examine that agency's budget and funding sources. This process often serves to clarify their experience with the agency. While their personal service offers insight, they have to go beyond their own experience to complete this paper. All students give an oral presentation on their evaluation at the end of the semester. This serves further to educate their peers regarding the structure of each of the nonprofit communal service agencies.

Field supervisors are asked to evaluate the students both in the middle of the semester and at its conclusion. I provide an evaluation form that asks the field supervisors to evaluate the students' quality of work, creativity, ability to work with coworkers and/or clients, level of contribution to the agency, and attitude. There is also opportunity for additional comments. Supervisors are encouraged to call me if they have any special concerns at any time during the semester. Their evaluations, along with students' journals, evaluation papers, and class participation, are key to my assignment of final grades.

At the end of the semester, students fill out class evaluation forms. At this time, they evaluate both the academic and the service-learning components of the class. Of particular interest is whether the service-learning experience might be useful for future career goals, how they felt about their service, whether they would recommend their site to future students, and whether they were offered an opportunity to continue with their agency as a paid employee or a volunteer. In addition, students are required to send thank you letters to their field supervisor. Both of these activities provide an opportunity for students to assess their experience. One student, Marc, wrote in his thank you letter:

> I have learned so much I can't begin to tell you. The most important thing of all, at least on a personal level, I have decided to change my career goal. Instead of becoming a music professor, I am now pursuing a career teaching music to kids in kindergarten through the sixth grade, and I am determined that it be in the Jewish community.

Another student, Maria, wrote in her evaluation, "I believe it is very important to learn more about a religion other than your own." In another evaluation, Jon wrote, "The course exposed me to new things, for example, how to help a family member if she needed social assistance." A young woman wrote, "By keeping a journal, I felt that there was a connection between Dr. Hatkoff and myself without speaking." I have also received positive feedback from the community partners. Field supervisors have written such comments as "Jennifer is a self-starter and very motivated. She's a wonderful addition to our staff"; "Marc has been an invaluable addition to our staff"; "Karen performed extraordinarily well on our campaign"; "Elias has contributed on a very high level. He quickly became a partner in every enterprise, always willing to go the extra mile."

It is interesting for the students to see that while these communal agencies are funded by the Jewish community and most focus on providing social welfare assistance (economic, career training, counseling, legal aid, child care, etc.), the religious background of the needy is often not considered. While most of the professional staff and volunteer providers are Jews, many of the people served are not Jewish. This has surprised many students. The student working at Bet Tzedek, legal aid services, as well as the student working at the Family Violence Project both noted that the majority of potential clients were not, in fact, Jewish. The students were impressed to learn that the Jewish community did not serve just its own group, but rather the wider Los Angeles community. This helped to dispel some stereotypes that the students had and to expose them to other minority groups.

The success of this class is reflected in the wide support and interest it has generated. As I stated at the beginning of this chapter, this class began with a grant from the Jewish community. Subsequently, we have received an additional grant from a private family foundation to continue the class. Local newspapers have written feature stories about the project. It is a model for other service-learning classes on California State University campuses in that I am sharing my experience through the CSU Office of the Chancellor Community Service-Learning Office and the CSUN Office of Service-Learning. My three main goals — to provide opportunities for civic engagement, practical experience, and academic study — are clearly being met by this service-learning course.

California State University, Northridge
Dr. Terry Hatkoff
Jewish Studies 394 -- Fall 2000

FIELDWORK IN THE JEWISH COMMUNITY

E-mail: terry.hatkoff@csun.edu
Pager: 872-3770 (voicemail)

This class is a three-unit academic internship/service-learning experience and an upper-division GE class. Over the fall semester, students will have hands-on experience in a Jewish Community Agency while they are performing a service for others. I have three main objectives this semester: (1) increase student awareness of the Los Angeles Jewish Community and the diverse population that its agencies serve; (2) offer career development; and (3) increase student involvement in and commitment to community service. Students are expected to spend 6-8 hours a week for 15 weeks in the field (100 hours total). I will arrange students' placements in an agency with students' approval. Each student must keep a detailed weekly journal of his/her fieldwork experience. Writing in the journal will help with reflection on the experience. Students will share their experiences with the class. Students are responsible for submitting a weekly timesheet signed by their field supervisor.

Bimonthly class meetings (every other Wednesday) begin on Sept. 6, from 3:00 to 5:00 p.m. Students will be expected to complete class readings by assigned dates. The readings listed below may be supplemented with additional readings over the course of the semester.

Each student is expected to write an evaluation research paper at the conclusion of his/her service-learning work experience. This will include a discussion of who is served by this agency and how the agency serves the community, how policies are made, where funding is obtained, as well as an evaluation of how well the mission/goals of the agency are being met. The detailed requirements for this paper will be discussed in class. Each student will also be expected to give an oral presentation of the paper to the class.

Student's grades will be determined by:
>   Class attendance and participation
>   Field supervisor's evaluations at midsemester and at the end of the semester
>   Weekly journals
>   Student class presentation
>   Evaluation research paper

Students must complete all of their fieldwork hours and submit all journal entries and the evaluation research paper in order to pass the class. Grading will be +/-.

READINGS: Jewish Studies Reader available at Northridge Copy Center, 9130B Reseda Blvd.

Print and Electronic Resource Guide

Print Resources: Religion and Theology

Addams, J. (1910, 1981). *Twenty Years at Hull House.* New York: Macmillan.
Though meant to be an autobiography, most of the book is about Hull
House and the benefits of working with the poor. At times, Addams is
difficult to follow, but her ideals and her actions are truly inspiring;
this is a deeply optimistic book about hope and courage.

Boss, J. (1994). "The Effect of Community Service Work on the Moral
Development of College Ethics Students." *Journal of Moral Education* 23(2): 183-
198.
A study designed to test the effect of community service work on college ethics students. The study indicates that community service work
along with discussion of relevant moral issues is an effective means
of moving students into the postconventional stage of principled
moral reasoning.

Cates, D.F. (1997). *Choosing to Feel: Virtue, Friendship, and Compassion for Friends.*
Notre Dame, IN: University of Notre Dame Press.
Cates draws on an Aristotelian-Thomistic ethical foundation to develop an original theory of compassion as she explores how persons are
able, and why they would want, to deliberately orient themselves
toward the shared suffering of another person's pain.

Colby, A., and W. Damon, (1994). *Some Do Care: Contemporary Lives of Moral
Commitment.* New York: Free Press.
A look at the lives of 23 American moral leaders shows how these
hometown heroes acquired their moral goals and sustained them in
the face of grave risk and sacrifice, working for everything from civil
rights to the poor.

Coles, R. (1993). *The Call of Service.* New York: Houghton Mifflin.
A modern classic by Pulitzer Prize winner Coles, who draws on his
decades of experience with and studies of people who live out a calling or vocation of service.

Daloz, L.A., et al. (1996). *Common Fire: Leading Lives of Commitment in a Complex World*. Boston: Beacon.

A compelling narrative report of a study by the authors, in which they conducted interviews over a period of several years with more than 100 people who had sustained long-term commitments to work on behalf of the common good, even in the face of global complexity, diversity, and ambiguity.

Day, D. (1952, 1997). *The Long Loneliness*. San Francisco: Harper San Francisco.

The autobiography of the cofounder of the Catholic Worker movement that has become a classic work, important both as the narration of a personal spiritual journey and as a critical look at 20th-century American values.

Fowler, J.W. (1995). *Stages of Faith: The Psychology of Human Development and the Quest for Meaning*. San Francisco: Harper San Francisco.

Fowler's interviews with more than 600 persons who provide in-depth and intimate conversations about the various ways human beings give their lives meaning and purpose. It is this that Fowler calls *faith*, which is neither religious nor to be equated with belief; rather, it is simply the way of living and making sense of life.

Freire, P. (1970, 1995). *Pedagogy of the Oppressed*. Translated by M.B. Ramos. New York: Seabury Press.

A classic work on the inextricable connection between education and social change, in which Freire develops his perspective known as *critical pedagogy*.

hooks, b. (1994). *Teaching to Transgress*. New York: Routledge.

hooks shares her philosophy of teaching as a way to rethink democratic values and participation. The book explores her beliefs on the spiritual role of teachers, racism and sexism in the classroom, and the role of education toward personal freedom and liberation.

Horton, M., and P. Freire. (1990). *We Make the Road by Walking: Conversations on Education and Social Change/Myles Horton and Paulo Freire*. Edited by B. Bell, J. Gaventa, and J. Peters. Philadelphia: Temple University Press.

An inspirational work by two well-known social critics that discusses Horton's and Freire's philosophies and insights about how pedagogy must inform social change.

Johnson, C. (2000). "Spiritual and Ethical Values." In *Identifying Successes in Model Service-Learning Courses Across Iowa*. Edited by P. Steinke, P. Fitch, et al., pp. 55-71. Des Moines: Iowa College Foundation.

> A narrative and character-ethics analysis of the effects of service-learning on college students' spiritual and ethical lives. This chapter is part of a larger study of the effects of service-learning on students enrolled in 12 different courses, which also examined personal development, civic engagement, cognitive outcomes, and community impact.

Kraft, K. (1989). *The Wheel of Engaged Buddhism: A New Map of the Path*. New York: Weatherhill.

> In this short introduction to engaged Buddhism, Kraft highlights the activities and challenges of socially conscious Buddhists. His handbook revolves around a *mandala* of engagement that includes symbols for cultivating awareness, embracing family, participating in politics, and environmental care. He provides meaningful stories of Buddhists struggling to live lives of meaningful activism.

MacIntyre, A. (1984). *On Virtue: A Study in Moral Theology*. Notre Dame, IN: University of Notre Dame Press.

> The renowned exploration of and argument for the relevance of an Aristotelian-Thomistic ethics in a postmodern age, especially helpful in terms of its treatment of the concept of *practices* that shape moral character.

Palmer, P. J. (1990). *The Active Life: A Spirituality of Work, Creativity, and Caring*. San Francisco: Jossey-Bass.

> Palmer draws on several different faith perspectives, texts, and stories to explore the vocation of active, healthful engagement with the world. Theory is powerfully illustrated by stories told in an informal and conversational style.

Rhoads, R.A. (1997). *Community Service and Higher Learning: Explorations of the Caring Self*. New York: State University of New York Press.

> Through case studies and personal interviews, Rhoads presents a number of challenging and inspiring examples of community service and caring. He develops a moral imperative that we must reestablish an ethic of caring in the midst of a society that appears comfortable in demonstrating little mercy. Rhoads interplays his own personal story of poverty with the story and experiences of his students.

Shor, I., and P. Freire. (1987). *A Pedagogy for Liberation: Dialogues on Transforming Education*. New York: Bergin & Garvey.

> Freire and Shor speak of education as a *dialogue in action* by which teachers and students can become active participants in the learning process. The authors argue for the need to transform the classroom and illustrate the possibilities of liberating the classroom from its traditional constraints through their own experiences. They focus on the vital role of teachers to empower students to think critically about themselves and their society.

Tronto, J. (1994). *Moral Boundaries: A Political Argument for an Ethics of Care*. New York: Routledge.

> Tronto argues that *care* cannot be a useful moral or political construct unless it is liberated from its traditional and ideological connection as a "women's morality." She demonstrates that such an association is historically inaccurate and politically unwise; it degrades caring to a strategy by the privileged classes to maintain its power. In point of fact, care is one of the central activities of all human life.

Print Resources: Service-Learning

Albert, G. (1994). *Service Learning Reader: Reflections and Perspectives on Service*. Raleigh, NC: National Society for Experiential Education.

Cha, S., and M. Rothman. (1994). *Service Matters: A Sourcebook for Community Service in Higher Education*. Providence, RI: Campus Compact.

Exley, R.J., S. Johnson, and D. Johnson. (1996). *Expanding Boundaries: Serving and Learning*. Washington, DC: Corporation for National Service.

Eyler, J., and D. Giles, Jr. (1999). *Where's the Learning in Service-Learning?* San Francisco: Jossey-Bass.

Eyler, J., D. Giles, Jr., and A. Schmiede. (1996). *A Practitioner's Guide to Reflection in Service-Learning: Student Voices and Reflections*. Nashville, TN: Vanderbilt University.

Giles, D., Jr., and J. Eyler. (1994). "The Impact of a College Community Service Laboratory on Students' Personal, Social, and Cognitive Outcomes." *Journal of Adolescence* 7: 325-339.

Heffernan, K. (2001). *Fundamentals of Service-Learning Course Construction.* Providence, RI: Campus Compact.

————, and J. Saltmarsh, eds. *Introduction to Service-Learning Toolkit: Readings and Resources for Faculty.* Providence, RI: Campus Compact.

Hesser G. (1995). "Faculty Assessment of Student Learning: Outcomes Attributed to Service-Learning and Evidence of Changes in Faculty Attitudes About Experiential Education." *Michigan Journal of Community Service Learning* 2(1): 33-42.

Jacoby, B., ed. (1996). *Service-Learning in Higher Education: Concepts and Practices.* San Francisco: Jossey-Bass.

Kendall, J., and Associates, eds. (1990). *Combining Service and Learning: A Resource Book for Community and Public Service.* 3 vols. Raleigh, NC: National Society for Internships and Experiential Education.

Kolb, D.A. (1984). *Experiential Learning: Experience as the Source of Learning and Development.* Englewood Cliffs, NJ: Prentice-Hall.

Kraft, R.J., and M. Swadener, eds. (1994). *Building Community: Service-Learning in the Academic Disciplines.* Denver, CO: Campus Compact.

Stanton, T. (1994). "The Experience of Faculty Participants in an Instructional Development Seminar on Service-Learning." *Michigan Journal of Community Service Learning* 1(1): 7-20.

————, et al., eds. (1999). *Service-Learning: A Movement's Pioneers Reflect on Its Origins, Practice, and Future.* San Francisco: Jossey-Bass.

Electronic Resources: Service-Learning

American Association for Higher Education
One of the leading organizations in the service-learning movement, AAHE publishes this monograph series and has other information.
http://www.aahe.org

Campus Compact

The parent organization in the service-learning movement, Campus Compact sponsors a number of funded programs and awards. It is currently promoting a vision of the *engaged campus* as a next step in the movement.

http://www.compact.org

Campus Outreach Opportunity League

COOL is a national nonprofit organization that helps college students start, strengthen, and expand their community service.

http://www.cool2serve.org

Communications for a Sustainable Future

The site contains a wealth of information about service-learning programs at colleges and universities throughout the United States, as well as current research in the field, publications, and other information. This site also can be used to access an important service-learning listserver.

http://csf.colorado.edu/sl

Corporation for National Service

This federal agency supports service-learning in higher education through its Learn and Serve America: Higher Education grant program.

http://www.cns.gov

International Partnership for Service-Learning

This organization has originated, designed, and implemented intercultural/international service experiences since 1982.

http://www.ipsl.org

Michigan Journal of Community Service Learning

The *Michigan Journal of Community Service Learning* is a peer-reviewed journal consisting of articles written by faculty and service-learning educators on research, theory, pedagogy, and issues pertinent to the service-learning community.

http://www.umich.edu/~mjcsl/

National Society for Experiential Education

NSEE comprises primarily practitioners. Many of its programs, however, feature service-learning, and this site contains information on those programs. (Previously called the National Society for Internships and Experiental Education)

http://www.nsee.org

Contributors to This Volume

Volume Editors

Richard Devine is professor of moral theology at St. John's University in New York City. He received his doctorate in theology from the University of Fribourg in Switzerland. The second edition of his textbook on medical ethics, *Good Care: Painful Choices,* was published by Paulist Press in 2000. He also is the NGO representative to the United Nations for the Congregation of the Mission, a world-wide religious community of priests and brothers.

Joseph A. Favazza is associate professor of religious studies and director of interdisciplinary humanities at Rhodes College, Memphis, Tennessee. He and Michael McLain coordinate the Rhodes service-learning initiative. He recently spent five months in Romania as a Fulbright Senior Scholar and is the author of "The Pedagogy of Service Learning: Perspectives and Proposals" in *Religious Studies News* (September 1999).

F. Michael McLain is the R.A. Webb professor of religious studies at Rhodes College, Memphis, Tennessee. He and Joseph A. Favazza coordinate the Rhodes service-learning initiative. He founded the Associated Colleges of the South Service-Learning Maymester in Honduras and has led service-learning trips to South Africa.

Other Contributors

Peter M. Antoci is adjunct professor of religious studies and associate director at the Shriver Center, University of Maryland, Baltimore.

Raj Ayyar currently teaches world religions and humanities courses at Seminole Community College in Sanford, Florida, and has spent 19 years teaching in the Florida community college system. He has been actively involved with academic service-learning since 1991.

M. Elizabeth Blissman recently completed her Ph.D. at the University of Denver and Iliff School of Theology. She is currently director of the Center for Service and Learning and a lecturer in the Environmental Studies Program at Oberlin College in Oberlin, Ohio.

Kim Bobo is executive director of the National Interfaith Committee for Worker Justice.

Elizabeth M. Bounds is associate professor of Christian ethics at Candler School of Theology and the Graduate Division of Religion at Emory University, Atlanta, Georgia. Most recently, she coedited *Welfare Policy: Feminist Critiques* (Pilgrim Press, 2000).

Jonathan Brumberg-Kraus is associate professor of religion at Wheaton College, Norton, Massachusetts. He is currently writing a book, "Memorable Meals: Symposia in Luke's Gospel, the Rabbinic Seder, and the Greco-Roman Literary Tradition."

Bradley D. Dudley is director of service-learning and an adjunct professor of religion at Pepperdine University, Malibu, California.

Fred Glennon is professor of religious studies and the Kevin G. O'Connell distinguished teaching professor in the humanities at Le Moyne College, Syracuse, New York, and, with Joseph A. Favazza, is the author of "Service Learning and Religious Studies: Propaganda or Pedagogy?" in *Religious Studies News* (November 2000).

Terry Smith Hatkoff is assistant professor of Jewish studies and sociology at California State University, Northridge.

Chris Johnson was assistant professor of religion and director of service-learning at Buena Vista University in Storm Lake, Iowa, and has since become director of the Center for Vocational Reflection at Gustavus Adolphus College in St. Peter, Minnesota.

John Leahy is associate professor of religious studies and director of the academic minor in community-based service-learning at DePaul University in Chicago.

Robert Masson is an associate professor in the Department of Theology at Marquette University, Milwaukee, Wisconsin.

Thomas G. McGowan is associate professor of sociology and chair of the Department of Anthropology and Sociology at Rhodes College, Memphis, Tennessee.

Keith Morton is associate professor of American studies in English and director of the Feinstein Institute for Public Service at Providence College, Providence, Rhode Island.

Barbara A.B. Patterson is a lecturer in the Religion Department of Emory University, Atlanta, Georgia. She also directs the Theory Practice Learning Program, a faculty development program in the pedagogies of experiential education, service-learning, and community-based teaching, learning, and research.

Tina Pippin is associate professor of religious studies and chair of the Religious Studies Department at Agnes Scott College, Atlanta/Decatur, Georgia.

Walter H. Schuman is associate professor of religion at Ashland University, Ashland, Ohio.

Sandra K. Smith Speck is director of service-learning at the Center for Values and Services and associate professor of strategic and organizational studies-marketing at Loyola College in Maryland, Baltimore, Maryland.

Charles R. Strain is associate vice-president for academic affairs and professor of religious studies at DePaul University in Chicago. His most recent publication is "Teaching and Practice: Experiential Education and the Transformation of Liberation Theology" in the *Journal of Religion and Society* (2000).

Series Editor

Edward Zlotkowski is senior associate, AAHE Service-Learning Projects, senior faculty fellow, Campus Compact, and a professor of English at Bentley College. Founding director of the Bentley Service-Learning Project, he has published and spoken on a wide variety of service-learning topics. Among his publications is *Successful Service-Learning Programs: New Models of Excellence in Higher Education* (Anker, 1998).